Christianity and European Culture

St. Michael's Abbey
19292 El Toro Road
Silverado, CA 92676

Christianity and European Culture

Selections from the Work of Christopher Dawson

Edited by Gerald J. Russello

The Catholic University of America Press

Washington, D.C.

Library of Congress Cataloging-in-Publication Data
Dawson, Christopher, 1889–1970.
    Christianity and European culture : selections from the work
of Christopher Dawson / edited by Gerald J. Russello.
        p.   cm.
    Includes bibliographical references.
    1. Christianity—Europe.   2. Christianity and culture—
Europe.   3. Europe—church history.   1. Russello, Gerald J.,
1971-   .   II. Title.
BR735.D38   1998
261'.094—dc21
97-38951
ISBN 0-8132-0914-5 (pbk. : alk. paper)

Matri patrique meo

Contents

Introduction

This edition of selected works of the historian Christopher Dawson (1889–1970) brings together his thoughts on two general themes. The first is Dawson's contention that the modern era presents a challenge to traditional ways of living in the West that is totally new and inhospitable, yet one that at the same time offers a rare opportunity for evangelization and the development of an authentic Christian culture. The second theme presented by these selections is Dawson's answer to this contemporary challenge and his suggested method of exploiting the present opportunity.

Dawson noted the paradox that a great expansion of the Christian faith throughout the world has taken place during the very centuries when Europe itself was losing its connection with its spiritual foundations. This dissociation of religious faith from other aspects of life has only increased since his death. Through his works Dawson sought to reconnect Europe's material wealth and economic power with the fundamental values that had made that wealth and power possible.

He proposed to meet the challenges he saw for Christianity in the modern world by engaging in a deep study of the Christian past. This course of study, however, was not intended to recall a way of life that, however admirable, has disappeared. Rather, Dawson sought to refresh the theological and historical resources of Christian belief in order to build the foundations of a new Christian culture. Dawson did not think that the present age had the spiritual depth required for such a task, and he turned especially to the early centuries of Christianity for guidance. Dawson's vision of the basis of Christian society was (and is) an ambitious one. In "The Recovery of Spiritual Unity," an essay included in this collection, he described the task in this way:

[I]f we are to make the ordinary man aware of the spiritual unity out of which all the separate activities of our civilization have arisen, it is necessary in the first place to look at Western civilization as a whole and to treat it with the same objective appreciation and respect which the humanists of the past devoted to the civilization of antiquity.

Dawson advocated the study of Christendom as a cultural entity united by a common faith and common moral standards. He would focus on Europe, but would include the other, non-Western Christian societies, such as North Africa and the several cultures served by the Orthodox Churches. Indeed, Dawson's treatment of the cross-cultural nature of Christianity is a model of engagement with other cultures, in sharp contrast to the more partisan contemporary forms of cultural studies. Dawson also stressed the importance of studying the Christian cultures both before and after the Middle Ages, an emphasis the philosopher Russell Hittinger has called Dawson's most significant contribution to Catholic historiography.[1]

Dawson's point, in essence, is a simple one. Europe—indeed, any cultural unit—cannot be understood as a whole by studying only its parts; to study a culture through its parts alone renders its most important aspects unintelligible. Dawson saw much of Europe's modern difficulty as arising either from a loss of historical memory, as in his own Britain, or from the totalitarian attempts of the Nazis and Communists to borrow Christianity's salvific message and transform it into a stage along the road of Aryan domination or the classless society. These ideologies share an extremely narrow view of European history, which either exaggerated differences between the European peoples or elevated some aspects of culture over others. Nationalist and racial-

---

1. Russell Hittinger, "The Metahistorical Vision of Christopher Dawson," in *The Dynamic Character of Christian Culture,* ed. Peter J. Cataldo (Lanham, Md.: University Press of America, 1984), 17.

ist history deny the unitive nature of Christianity, which creates a supranational spiritual community from disparate nationalities. If anything, the fragmentation of European identity has accelerated since Dawson first wrote. In addition to a revived nationalism in many parts of Europe, scholars have increasingly chosen to view history through the narrow prisms of race, class, or gender, to the exclusion of other motivating forces in Western and world history. For Dawson, the prime motivating force was spiritual.

Dawson believed that it is only when we acknowledge the historic role of the Christian Church as the agent of and inspiration for the community of nations called Europe that we can confront the problems that face it, now that the influence of Christianity has diminished. With great advances in material wealth has come a loss of the religious and moral values that alone give life to a civilization. In Europe, those values were provided by Christianity, a faith that exists as a separate entity from its constituent cultures even as it informs them. Dawson saw in the Christian faith the sole antidote to the secularism that originated with the West and has now spread throughout the world. While Dawson knew that the secular—the things of this world—were good because they are part of God's creation, he saw the ideology of secularism—the belief that the things of this world were made for this world alone—as a threat. He believed that severing a society from its defining faith will have tragic moral, social, and political consequences. Because Christianity maintains within itself the seeds of its own renewal, it can remain independent of secular culture and can draw on its own internal resources when challenged. Therefore, the Christian faith retains its capacity to resist the forces that wish to make religion an appendage of the state, or to eliminate it altogether as a social and cultural force.

Dawson's vision of our age was therefore both hopeful and anxious. In an early essay, "Progress and Decay in Ancient and Modern Civilizations," he wrote that the horrors of the present day had convinced the average person "how fragile a thing our civilization is, and how insecure are the foundations on which the elaborate edifice of the modern world order rests." This was written in 1924, with the memory of the First World War still fresh in his mind. The Great War vividly revealed to Dawson that the future would hold no sure utopias for the world.

So Dawson searched the past, seeking the elements for a new cultural program that would replace the old order swept away first at Verdun and on the Marne, then finally in Normandy and at Hiroshima. He published his first book, *The Age of the Gods*, in 1928, after almost a decade and a half of intense personal study. It was the first installment in what was to be a five-volume history of culture. Two other volumes were completed—the magisterial *Progress and Religion* in 1929 and *The Making of Europe* three years later—before the chaos of the 1930s and 1940s disrupted his schedule. Dawson went on to discuss in periodicals much of the subject he had planned for the remaining volumes and began to apply his knowledge of European history to contemporary affairs. The three completed volumes were received to great acclaim and earned praise from historians as well as anthropologists and sociologists, who marvelled not only at Dawson's immense erudition, but also (as anthropologist Gordon Childe said in a review) at the "wider vision" that Dawson brought to his scholarship.

These early works reveal the central core of Dawson's thought, which he would express in various forms throughout his writings: religious cult is at the heart of every culture, and the society that disregards its spiritual foundations will collapse, no matter the level of its material well-being. *The Age of the Gods* first presents this argument, and Dawson was to expand and elaborate upon it in subsequent works. He saw that a culture was not limited by its geographic location or material resources: to genetic, geographic, and economic factors Dawson added "a fourth element—thought or the psychological factor—which is peculiar to the human species" and which cannot be explained by the other components. Indeed, Dawson noted the paradox of a "lower" material culture being the vehicle of a higher and richer spiritual culture, as in the case of the early

Christians in the Roman Empire. This fourth factor organizes the remaining three; each society contains a core of belief that forms its identity.

Dawson often likened society to a living organism; like a living creature, it grows slowly and is influenced by outside forces it cannot completely control. The analogy was purposeful, because it underscored the difference between Dawson's view of human culture and that of modern theorists of Progress. They see a reified Humanity advancing according to a predetermined course that leaves no room for extrarational factors such as spiritual insight or individual action. Dawson recognized that societies, like living things, grow but can also decay; that is, both progress and degeneration are possibilities for any human society. As he wrote in 1939, "Civilization is not the result of a natural process of evolution, it is essentially due to the mastering of nature by the human mind. It is an artificial order, governed by man's intelligence and will." The crucial question for the modern world is whether that artificial order will be a purely material one or whether it will integrate a spiritual element.

To combat "scientific" theories that left no place for the individual human mind, Dawson made clear the reliance every civilization places on those who most fully represent its ideals and can shape the entire culture through their actions. This individualism can serve as a third theme running through the essays collected here. The unfolding of a Hegelian World-Spirit according to a rational plan does nothing to explain cultural achievements, nor do theories of survival of the fittest or the end of history account for the spiritual resources of a civilization. Dawson maintained that "history is at once aristocratic and revolutionary. It allows the whole world situation to be suddenly transformed by the action of a single individual." The seeming irrationality of history—as being dependent upon separate individual acts—is fatal to a secular understanding of history. To the Christian, however, this understanding of historical development permits interpretation in the light of divine will and spiritual forces that may be hidden from the actual actors themselves.

In Christian life, it is the saints who undertake this dynamic activity, although more broadly each individual Christian shares responsibility in forming a culture. In *Religion and the Modern State* (1935), Dawson explained that

the supreme example of this vital religious action is to be seen in the saints, in whom alone the potentialities of Christianity are fully realized. And their action is not limited, as we sometimes suppose, to the sphere of their supernatural virtues, it flows out into the world and shows itself in social activity and intellectual culture. Whenever there has been a great outburst of spiritual activity it has been followed by a fresh development of Catholic thought and culture.

By the time this passage was written, Dawson had come to realize that the new age would be one not only of saints but also of the common man, to a greater extent than ever before. The Western democracies were spreading their influence throughout the world, and the ordinary citizen was able to influence the larger society in ways not imaginable even during the last century. Dawson became convinced that the connection between cultural and religious development he discerned was more important for the coming democratic age than it had been for previous eras. Dawson sought to communicate his message to a larger audience, and his books and essays are written for a general literate public. This strategy may in part explain his lack of academic influence, in light of the increased specialization and professionalization among his fellow historians. His use of nontraditional historical evidence—at least by the standards of his time—may be another reason for his relative neglect

Dawson saw hope of Christian renewal in the actions of ordinary Christians, who must withstand by their individual action the onslaught of secularism. "[I]t seems as though the future of religion would depend far more than in the past on the thought and initiative of the ordinary man ... the only thing that can stand against such forces [secularism] is the spiritual vitality of the Christian community." Historic change comes about only as the "cumulative result of a number of [individual] spiritual decisions." The end of Communism in Eastern Europe, especially in Poland, proved Dawson's insight. The resistance of individual Christians, united in their local churches, wore down the forces of oppression. The religious foundations of the resistance movements in Eastern Europe surely would have echoed in Dawson's mind the activities of persecuted Christians from every period of the Church's history.

The following essays, therefore, are of more than antiquarian interest. They represent an innovative attempt to revive the idea of Christian culture in an age when religious approaches are less respected than they used to be. Dawson of course did not wish to alter traditional answers for their own sake, or merely to keep up with the times. He did believe, however, that traditional formulae needed to resonate with modern intellectual forms. The aftereffects of Vatican II proved unwarranted the confidence some Catholic educators had in a traditional pedagogy unsuited to the new challenges faced by the Church. The plan for a comprehensive, multidisciplinary examination of Christian culture, encompassing not only history, philosophy, and theology, but also art and architecture, literature, and poetry, was a bold suggestion in the 1950s and early 1960s. When Dawson proposed it, his suggestion received some commentary but little practical application either in the United States or in Britain. Now, however, when the average Catholic undergraduate lacks so much basic knowledge of the Christian past as to make traditional educational methods inapplicable, and when popular culture offers so little in the way of spiritual sustenance, Dawson's proposal takes on new relevance.

While Dawson did not doubt the value of the philosophical method, he questioned its almost undisputed dominance in his day as the sole way to understand Christian culture. The strengths of Neoscholastic philosophy—its analytical self-sufficiency and its freedom from the historical relativism some thought they discerned in Dawson's work—were to be its down-

fall. Its collapse in the 1950s and 1960s as the unifying force of
Catholic education left a vacuum in Catholic intellectual life.
Dawson astutely perceived that every people needs an historical
faith that can account for its existence and can interpret that
existence within a larger pattern. Philosophy alone could not
provide a substitute for this historical understanding. Christianity was and is far larger than any philosophical school. In comparison with the new strength of such ideologies as nationalism,
which provided an alternative historical vision, the older philosophy seemed dry and unusable.

The fall of Communism, meanwhile, has left purely secular
theories suspect in the eyes of its former subjects and supporters. Communism was—with the significant exception of American liberalism—one of the last stages of the overreliance upon
the powers of material factors and human reason that had dominated European thought since the eighteenth century. As Dawson describes in *Progress and Religion*, faith in a limitless progress began with the optimists of the eighteenth century, who
saw no limit if the dictates of reason were followed. This faith
soon devolved into the dreary social theories of the nineteenth
and early twentieth centuries, like that espoused by Bertrand
Russell, who described the life of man as "brief and powerless."
Such is the legacy of the idea of progress when severed from
spiritual concerns.

Dawson's critique applied as well to Britain, the United States,
and other non-Communist nations. Indeed, while Britain at least
has kept the arrangements of the older understanding, such as
the monarchy and an established church, the United States was
founded on modern principles and has been devoted to the modern conception of progress from its beginnings. This has led,
albeit at a slower place, to a similar process of secularization
and centralization, but one in the end little different from that
of regimes openly hostile to religious faith. All modern states
are totalitarian, Dawson thought, in their effort to bring every
aspect of human life under their control. Such regimes in their
extreme stages are fundamentally opposed to Christianity, as

they deny the eternal and spiritual element of man that is beyond politics.

Now the Western world faces another of its occasional periods of cultural discontinuity, as an old order passes away and a new one emerges. Just as the humanism of the Renaissance overthrew the medieval synthesis and was in turn replaced by the secularized liberalism of the nineteenth and early twentieth centuries, that world has been in its dying stages since the late 1930s. Whereas the Victorians had at least a tenuous connection to their religious past, this new world has lost even those vestiges of faith. In "Christianity and the New Age," Dawson concludes:

[T]he goal of the Enlightenment and the Revolution had been reached, and Europe at last possessed a completely secularised culture ... [the churches] had been pushed aside into a backwater where they were free to stagnate in peace and to brood over the memory of dead controversies which had moved the mind of Europe three centuries before.

The consequences of this denial of spiritual reality have become clear. Europe is faced with a number of serious problems, both physical and cultural. Economic agreements cannot substitute for cultural unity, nor can the ignorance of a millennium of common history be overcome by political arrangements. As Dawson recognized so long ago, Europe is possible only with Christianity, for it is a spiritual unity rather than a political one.

The need for a revivified Christian culture is acute; it is attested by the growth of interest in alternatives to authentic tradition, such as the "New Age" and occult movements. Dawson believed all people have a natural religious impulse, and if the influence of Christianity were to diminish, substitute belief systems would take its place. These new movements represent a retreat from the West's traditional heritage rather than an advance. Far from being a liberation of humanity from superstition, such movements cloak their adherents in a shroud of sentimentalism and pseudo-theology. In a passage evocative of contemporary problems, Dawson described the modern trends as a "revolt against the moral process of Western culture and the dethronement of the individual conscience from its dominant position at the heart of the cultural process." The medieval Christian insight concerning the central importance of the rationality and freedom of the individual personality, a hallmark of Western thought, is in danger of being overwhelmed by a return to idolatry and a vague supernaturalism. This new religiosity is as false to the Western tradition as were the earlier efforts to construct entirely materialistic social systems. Both deny the Christian integration of the spiritual and the material.

II

Nineteen-ninety five marked the twenty-fifth anniversary of the death of Christopher Dawson. Dawson was born in 1889 at Hay Castle in the Wye River Valley, where he spent much of his early childhood. His mother was Welsh and his father English. This confluence of two cultures was to be an early impetus for Dawson's interest in cultural interaction. In 1896 the family moved to the Yorkshire Dales and Hartlington Hall, built by his father on land that had been in the Dawson family for generations. Educated at Winchester and Trinity College, Oxford (where his tutor was Sir Ernest Barker, the great scholar of ancient political philosophy), Dawson never received the doctorate, preferring instead to engage in an extended period of intensive private study. Perhaps the last of the amateur historians, Dawson wrote in crisp prose uncluttered with excessive footnotes or jargon, and he relied largely upon his own private library to conduct his research.

Much of Dawson's interest in becoming an historian stemmed from living in places with strong historical connections; Hay Castle, for example, was built in the twelfth century and is mentioned in Celtic myth. In an autobiographical memoir he stated, "It was then [in my youth] I acquired my love of history, my interest in the difference of cultures and my sense of the importance of religion in human life." Before going up to Oxford,

Dawson read the works of Edward Gibbon and of Saint Augustine, both of whom, in different ways, influenced him deeply. At nineteen, Dawson traveled to Rome and retraced Gibbon's steps to the very place where the historian had decided to compose *Decline and Fall of the Roman Empire*. It was there as well that Dawson conceived of writing a history of culture that would take into account the spiritual factors he thought missing from Gibbon. Although in later years his admiration for Gibbon lessened, Dawson still considered his prose the model for an historian and sought to achieve in his own work the "perfect fusion" of history and literature he found in *Decline and Fall*.

In 1914, with his boyhood friend E. I. Watkin (also a convert to Catholicism) as sponsor, Dawson was received into the Catholic Church. His reasons for conversion were distinctly intellectual, although his friendship with Watkin and the Roman Catholic faith of his fiance and future wife Valery were strong personal influences. As he recounts in a short essay entitled "Why I Became A Catholic,"[2] Dawson moved from Anglo-Catholicism through a period of agnosticism toward established churches and finally to the Roman Church by a steady progression of reading, travel in Catholic Europe, and conversations with Catholic friends. There seems to have been no earth-shattering revelation or emotional conversion experience. The example of the Catholic saints impressed him greatly, not only for their own merits but also from his realization that any "theory of life" that took no account of these exemplars of Christ lacked explanatory power. In addition, the saints represented for Dawson "the perfect manifestation of the supernatural life that exists in every individual Christian." E. J. Oliver has written that Dawson combined in his faith an outward form of ritual that denoted membership in a universal spiritual society and an inner life in which he shared in the "deeper mystical life of [the] Saints."[3] This

2. *Chesterton Review* 9, no. 2 (May 1983): 110. The essay was originally published in the *Catholic Times* in 1926.

3. E. J. Oliver, "The Religion of Christopher Dawson," *Chesterton Review* 9, no. 2 (May 1983): 161, 163.

combination reflected his deep reading of Saint Paul and Saint
Augustine and their emphasis on the dual nature of human life.

Throughout his career, Dawson published in both sociological
journals and popular newspapers, and he attracted the attention
of such admirers as T. S. Eliot; indeed, Eliot was to call him
the most powerful intellectual influence in Britain. During the
1930s, Dawson contributed a number of articles for Eliot's journal The Criterion. His fame in America grew while he served
as the first holder of the Charles Chauncey Stillman Chair in
Roman Catholic Studies at Harvard University from 1958 to
1962, which was in fact his first full-time academic position.
His work during the 1920s and 1930s established his reputation
as an historian, and Dawson went on to publish a number of
other important volumes. His two sets of Gifford lectures, the
first delivered in 1946–47, the second in 1948–49, were published, respectively, as *Religion and Culture* (1948) and *Religion
and the Rise of Western Culture* (1950). They gained him a
sizeable audience. His other books include *Mediaeval Religion*
(1934) and *The Spirit of the Oxford Movement* (1933).

Although an historian, Dawson adopted the analytical method
of the then-emerging disciplines of anthropology and sociol-
ogy. He even demonstrated an understanding of the principles
of Freudian psychology, although he disagreed with its reduction-
ist view of the human person. As James Ambrose Raftis has
shown, this method in its full form worked most effectively
when Dawson studied European pre-history, where a body of
research by specialists in other fields existed.[4] He was less successful in transplanting the new method to areas such as medieval studies, where the necessary sociological and anthropologi-
cal work had not yet been done. Whatever the field, however,
Dawson retained some elements of his integrated approach, the
most important of which was his insistence on a broad definition of culture. At various times he defined the word as "a way

4. James Ambrose Raftis, "The Development of Christopher Dawson's
Thought," *Chesterton Review* 9, no. 2 (May 1983): 115.

of life with a tradition behind it, which has embodied itself in institutions and which involves moral standards and principles," or the principle of moral unity, or a society's "whole complex of institutions and customs and beliefs." Such flexible terminology enabled Dawson to incorporate a broad range of cultural practices from all levels of society into his analysis. In contrast to culture, Dawson reserved the term "civilization" for the more advanced world-cultures, such as China and India as well as Europe. His method also exposed him to a broader range of materials than traditional history was accustomed to employing. Dawson integrated texts with art and other physical embodiments of culture in a way that would not reach the wider historical community for decades. His modern methodology, called "daring" by Dermot Quinn, however, competed with a strong anti-modern sentiment.[5]

As James Hitchcock has noted, the early and middle decades of this century witnessed a remarkable flowering of Catholic intellectual and literary life throughout Europe and America.[6] The leading lights of this renaissance were almost all found among the laity (in many cases converts), and in Europe included Jacques and Raissa Maritain, François Mauriac, Jean Danielou, Etienne Gilson, Evelyn Waugh, and Sigrid Undset. America had its share of influential Catholic writers as well, Allen Tate, Flannery O'Connor, and Walker Percy being the most prominent. Generally, these writers and thinkers attempted to address the problems facing traditional Christianity in the modern era and to reaffirm the validity of their faith. Dawson, however, was the most significant British Catholic historian of this revival.

In addition to this wider European Catholic society, Dawson was heir to two separate but interrelated traditions of British thought: those of British Catholicism and a broader heritage of

5. Dermot Quinn, "Christopher Dawson and the Catholic Idea of History," in *Eternity in Time: Christopher Dawson and the Catholic Idea of History*, ed. Stratford Caldecott and John Morrill (Edinburgh: T&T Clark, 1997), p. 69.

6. James Hitchcock, "Postmortem on a Rebirth: The Catholic Intellectual Renaissance," *American Scholar* 49, no. 2 (1980): 211.

British religious and romantic antimodernism.[7] Of the former, the Italian critic Giuseppe Tomasi di Lampedusa has written that centuries of oppression had sharpened the intellects as well as the faith of British Catholics. Dawson was part of a larger group of Catholic writers, artists, and scholars who sought both to raise the intellectual and spiritual appeal of Catholicism in Britain during the pre-war years and to counter the fierce anti-Anglican posture of the British Catholic establishment. Clustered loosely around the short-lived journal Order, they included the publisher Tom Burns, David Jones, and Christopher Dawson himself.[8] The latter tradition of British antimodernism, comprising a number of disparate figures over the last two centuries, not all of them Catholics, sought to preserve elements of traditional British life from industrialism and a secular worldview.

Dawson addressed two different audiences in his work. On the one hand there were the large non-Catholic and agnostic populations of Britain, which had little patience for triumphalist Catholic history. To them Dawson advanced a basic historical argument: a Christian culture had existed in Europe for over one thousand years, does exist at present and is relevant to contemporary events and the future of Europe. This was more than a mere rhetorical point; Dawson was countering the Victorian historians of the "Whig" school who alleged that Christianity was only a deviation from the normal course of European development, rather than its source and fulfillment. The supreme example of this school was Gibbon. In *The Making of Europe* and elsewhere, Dawson traced the path of Western thought and demonstrated that the Christian faith had resonance even into the twentieth century. It was this kind of Christian history that won Dawson the respect of non-Catholics like Dean Inge (who found Dawson the only Catholic who didn't annoy him) and even agnostics like Aldous Huxley and Arnold Toynbee. They were impressed with his mastery of modern

---

7. I am indebted to Adam Schwartz for this distinction.

8. See Aidan Nichols, O.P., "Christopher Dawson's Catholic Setting," in *Eternity in Time: Christopher Dawson and the Catholic Idea of History*, p. 25, for a more detailed discussion.

scholarship as well as the lack of partisanship, but not of passion, in his writings.

Catholics, both in Britain and abroad, composed Dawson's second audience. To them, Dawson stressed the broader sweep of Catholic life, and he de-emphasized the importance of the Middle Ages. Dawson himself saw the medieval period as a classical age, like Augustan Rome or Periclean Athens, when the ideals of a culture become represented in physical institutions. In that respect, the medieval period was worthy of study and admiration. To conceive of it, however, as the "high point" of Christian civilization makes Christian culture of historical interest only—for the modern world will not return to the thirteenth century—and also denies the continuing creative power of the Spirit in human life. Dawson saw history essentially as a creative process and held that progress is possible only when there is a capacity to incorporate the past into the present and to allow for spiritual growth. The Middle Ages held appeal for Dawson not so much for its supposed static perfection, but because of its conscious attempts to integrate religious principles into everyday life.

III

The centerpiece of the present collection is Dawson's *The Historic Reality of Christian Culture*. Written in 1960, a result of the lectures Dawson gave at institutions throughout the United States, this slim volume is a précis of Dawson's thoughts on the state of Christian culture. Subtitled *A Way to the Renewal of Christian Life*, Dawson discusses in eight short, pointed chapters the definition of a Christian culture, its likelihood in the present world, and its adaptability to non-Western cultures. While not denying the specific historical relationships and cultural products Christianity has produced over the ages, Dawson is reluctant to discover any permanent link between the validity of the Christian faith and a particular Christian culture. That was the problem of the Church in the nineteenth-century, when it was seen as too closely tied to the old order to serve as a catalyst for social progress.

The caution Dawson demonstrates in distancing advocacy of
a return to Christian learning and faith from any specific political or cultural arrangements was well founded. Dawson was
aware that his audience was composed of a large number of non-
Catholics who did not idealize the Middle Ages as did their
Catholic counterparts. Dawson stressed instead the idea that no
feature of human life stands outside the Kingship of Christ.
As Christianity recognizes a supra-temporal element to human
history, so all the historical forms of Christian culture and the
different Christian peoples share this contact with the eternal
and experience it as a present reality. This emphasis paralleled
his personal development. At the outbreak of the Second World
War, Dawson became involved in an ecumenical organization
called the Sword of the Spirit. It had been organized to resist
totalitarianism and to place Christian values at the center of a
new European civilization. Dawson believed that Catholics must
play a central role as instruments of Christian unity and in
reimagining Christian culture. If Catholics choose to remain
passive, as Dawson wrote for the Catholic Herald in 1947, "they
prove false to their own temporal mission, since they leave the
world and the society of which they form a part to perish."

Dawson's emphasis on the transcendental nature of Christian
culture should be distinguished from the abstract theories of
civilization developed by Condorcet or Herbert Spencer. These
secular theories posit the application of a set of perfect cultural
forms upon human society, developed by "pure reason." This
new society would be identical for all times and places. Dawson
understood the cultural process in a more dynamic fashion. Religious influences continually inspire cultural transformations, so
much so that Dawson found the primary feature of Western
culture to be the "continuous succession and alteration of free
spiritual movements." The process of secularization and sacralization (to use the terminology of Dawson scholar Glenn W.
Olsen)[9] is a continuous one, which cannot without qualification

9. Glenn W. Olsen, "Cultural Dynamics: Secularization and Sacralization," in
Christianity and Western Civilization (San Francisco: Ignatius, 1995): 97.

be praised or condemned. Rather than lamenting a lost world of medieval unity—that in any event existed more often in theory than in fact—we should recognize that it is precisely because the West has lacked a stable cosmic order, such as those found in ancient China or Byzantium, that it was able to preserve its religious resources and interior life even as it was battered by political pressure and the science of progress. The tension produced by the conflict between Church and State in the West has laid the groundwork for the independence of the individual person from the claims of the totalitarian state.

In Dawson's mind, the conflict between the new liberalism and Christianity is finished; the criticisms of Matthew Arnold and others of the weaknesses they discovered in Victorian Christianity are of no help in facing the excessive secularism of the present. The challenge for Christians now is to reach into their own tradition and to develop new spiritual resources to rescue the modern world from the precarious position in which it has placed itself. A Christian culture is not a perfect culture, but only one that accepts Christian values as true and frames its institutions to give expression to those values. For the last fifty years and more the West has tried to live as if these ideals do not exist and has tried to construct a civilization from valueless compromises or neutral processes. Dawson (like his contemporary Eliot) understood, however, that if the West would not have Christian faith, it would have Hitler or Stalin, and that to reject its heritage is equal to cultural suicide. Humanity's natural religious impulse cannot be stifled.

The contemporary value of Dawson's work lies in this recognition and explication of the continuing mission of the Church to use the present world situation of increased communication and ease of travel to bring about a new evangelization and to fill the great spiritual need that exists alongside of great wealth and technological advances. During his own lifetime, Dawson supported the developing social teachings of the modern Popes. They realized that the locus of the Church's concern should shift from the traditional European tension between Church and State to the more important and global relationship between religion and culture. As Father Joseph Koterski, S.J., has written, the efforts of the papacy, as represented in a document like Dignitatis humanae, are "an effort to ready the Church for the struggles of the next century and the new millennium, with a better vision than any current political regime or national culture shows."[10] As early as 1942, Dawson discerned this shift in papal emphasis, and himself announced a commitment to religious freedom as an essential step in the process of Christian unity.

In many of Dawson's books, there is a clear tension between the Christian virtue of hope and anxiety over the present world situation. Dawson expresses more doubt about the chances for a Christian civilization than T. S. Eliot, but prefers to see in the contemporary state of affairs a challenge similar to that faced by the early Christians. They faced what they thought was the end of the world with hope and joy. They were able to surmount the decaying Roman Empire and create a new civilization for the world while keeping their eyes fixed on the promise of eternal life. It is the paradox of Christianity that those disdainful of temporal affairs created a new world, while the pagans whose vision was fixed on this life disappeared.

One additional feature of this book should be mentioned. The last two chapters of Historic Reality take up the question of the relation between Christianity and the non-Western world, an aspect of what in recent years has been called "multiculturalism." The essay "Christianity and Western Culture" is another opportunity for Dawson to expound his program of Catholic education, a program he went on to elaborate in more depth in The Crisis of Western Education (1961). For our purposes, the importance of this essay lay in its judicious approach to the subject. Dawson rejects a partisan equation of Christianity with Western culture, yet does not surrender his contention that the culture of Europe has something unique to offer the world.

---

10. Joseph Koterski, S.J., "Religion as the Root of Culture," in *Christianity and Western Civilization* (Ignatius, 1995): 15, 18.

"Is the Church Too Western?" was written in the midst of the anticolonial movements and the assertion of national identity in the developing countries in the Third World and the older nations of Asia. This chapter addresses some aspects of the question now known as "inculturation:" the introduction of Western Christianity into non-Western cultures. Dawson long had an interest in these non-Western and non-Christian cultures, to which he devoted several essays over the years. Relations between Asia and the West, for example, constitute a large portion of his *Movement of World Revolution* (1959). He was consistently interested in non-Western cultures and relationships with Western Christianity, admiring in particular the culture of Islamic Spain, which he discusses in *The Making of Europe*.

Dawson makes three points in his essay that together supply a needed corrective to the historical myopia that plagues so much of the writing in this area. First, we must distinguish between the modern industrial society in Europe and the older Christian tradition. Both are of course "Western" in some sense, but both do not stand in the same relation to the sources of European culture. The latter is the authentic continuation of the culture of Jerusalem, Rome, and Athens, the former is a departure from that culture that can survive only so long as remnants of the latter remain to support it. Second, Dawson reminds us that the Church Herself is not indigenous to the West. She was born in the Near East, nourished by the early Greek Fathers, and received Her most eloquent early defenders from Roman North Africa. Her most distinctive characteristics—for example, the religious orders—have variants in all the major world religions and were themselves adapted from the monastic traditions of Egypt.

Finally, Dawson contends that the provenance of a particular practice is irrelevant so long as that practice aids the Church in Her universal mission; if so, the Church will adapt and change it as needed. Some practices will be discarded; some modified; but the measure is their effectiveness in spreading the Gospel. Inculturation is a two-way process. Even as the Church transforms the culture, She is enriched by that culture's history and traditions. As Pope Paul VI has said, inculturation is "an incubation of the Christian mystery in the genius of a people." The Church is not restrained by the limitations of human society, and so neither should the choice of vehicles to express and elaborate Her teachings.

IV

The remaining essays supplement the themes discussed above. Ranging in time of composition from the 1930s to the 1950s, the essays illustrate Dawson's deep knowledge of European history and convey his belief that the Christian tradition has had and continues to have a central place in forming a "community of peoples" into Europe. The structure Dawson devises in "Europe and the Seven Stages of Western Culture" may usefully be compared with the six ages of the Church Dawson describes in *Historic Reality*. Even the tradition of Greece and Rome, another constituent part of the European tradition, was interpreted by and through Christianity, as Dawson's excellent analysis of "The Classical Tradition and Christianity" makes clear. Dawson sought to discern the eddies and cross-currents in European history, which show the distinctive nature and mission of each generation of Christians. They must respond to the problems of their own day with appropriate institutions and cultural forms. This course does not argue for meaningless fluidity, so that the Christian message is lost in a constant flux. Rather, Dawson stresses the ability of Christianity to consecrate any activity to the service of God, and its acceptance of the things of this world as good. First published in 1932, "The Modern Dilemma" underscores Dawson's concern with the integration of the spiritual and secular in the present world of expanding technology and an explosion in information. He calls for a new balance between the transcendental and the historical aspects of Christianity to address the spiritual needs of the modern age. Yet he cautions against an easy partnership between the church and government: each must be independent of the other if both are to serve their proper functions. To place religion at the service of the state would empty it of spiritual content and make it a tool of totalitarianism. To make the state serve religious faith would compromise individual freedom.

"The Secularization of Western Culture" and "The Planning of Culture," from Dawson's 1942 work, *The Judgment of the Nations*, confronts the idea of the "planned society," which was seen as the way of the future in the years leading to the Second World War. Dawson does so by highlighting the novelty of the modern world's situation: the complete separation of religion and culture, at all levels of society and throughout much of the world. For Western culture at least, this state is unusual, because it represents the first time a culture has attempted to live without acknowledging in its social and political structures the existence of a spiritual sphere that, although independent of the world, nevertheless informs it and exists beside it. In several short paragraphs, Dawson traces what contemporary political theorists have called the "crisis of liberalism": the removal from the public sphere of higher moral or religious values in the name of pluralism. Yet, as recent theorists like Michael Sandel have shown, liberalism has resulted not in the removal of tyranny, but merely in the desiccation of public life. Writing from the depths of the war, Dawson understood that liberal culture, although claiming to preserve religious values through "rights" that preserved freedom, could not resist the increase in sophisticated forms of social control that are now possessed not only by governments but by those in control of enormous economic power.

In "The Kingdom of God and History" and "The Christian View of History," Dawson offers extended reflections on the nature of history. Saint Augustine is at the center of Dawson's historical approach, and he stresses again the dual nature of the Church: on the one hand, the Church transcends the contingent facts of this world, yet it remains, in contrast to the great mystical faiths of the East, deeply connected to historical events. This is due, of course, to the centrality of the Incarnation to the

Christian faith, which centers salvation history in a specific time and place, and indeed in a specific Person. All subsequent history is shaped by this event, which reveals the hidden divine purpose. "For the Christian view of history is a vision of history sub specie aeternitatis, an interpretation of time in terms of eternity and of human events in the light of divine revelation. And thus Christian history is inevitably apocalyptic, and the apocalypse is the Christian substitute for the secular philosophies of history."

The final essay, "The Recovery of Spiritual Unity," returns us to a central theme of *Historic Reality:* Dawson's belief that every culture is shaped as much by spiritual and moral factors as by political or economic ones. In his day, Dawson sought to integrate secular and spiritual insights to arrest the increasing nationalism that resulted in two world wars. Today, his project is no less relevant, as we face what Samuel Huntington (who discusses Dawson in his book) has called the clash of civilizations.[11] An understanding of Western culture as a living entity with a moral basis in a particular religious tradition is vital for an open and honest dialogue with other world cultures. Dawson wrote in his *Religion and Culture* (1948) that "it is only when the religions of different cultures come into touch with one another . . . that real contact is made" between the cultures.

Rooted in this fashion by historical events that point to a superhistorical end, the Christian Church is able to develop its own history—interpenetrated, it is true, with secular history, yet still separate from it. The City of God and the City of Man exist side by side, and the members of each are known only in the light of eternity. Dawson then offers in these essays a concise history of Christian historiography and concludes with a profound analysis of the differences between the modern and Christian historical senses.

Dawson's prose in the essays collected here is always provoking, often stirring, and sometimes disturbing. He reminds us

---

11. Samuel Huntington, *The Clash of Civilizations and the Remaking of World Order* (New York: Simon & Schuster, 1996).

that the common state of the Church is one of persecution, and that the Christian's victory prize is the Cross and not the state-house or corporate boardroom. In his writings, Dawson did indeed achieve that union of history and literature that he so admired in Gibbon. But he performed an even greater task, that union of reason with faith that is the mark of a Christian scholar.

V: A NOTE ON THE TEXT

All the selections have been left just as Dawson wrote them. I have not edited the selections. Although some of the passages may be "outdated," in rereading these essays I was struck by how fresh Dawson's writings remain and how appropriate to our own day. More often than not, editing would impede the flow of the argument and not be of any great help to the reader. For example, Dawson discusses in several places the real danger posed by communism. This is no longer the concern it once was, yet to delete those references from the text would diminish Dawson's larger point concerning the fate of any society that excises its spiritual elements, a fate that faces the democratic West as much as it did the communist nations. I have added a few notes to help explain obscure references, but I have left all of Dawson's original citations.

The Historic Reality of Christian Culture was first published by Routledge & Keegan Paul Ltd. in 1960; a paperback edition was issued by Harper & Row in 1965. "The Study of Christian Culture" appeared in *Medieval Essays* (Image Books, 1959), first published by Sheed & Ward in 1953. "The Modern Dilemma" appeared in *The Modern Dilemma*, Essays in Order No. 8 (Sheed & Ward, 1932). "The Recovery of Spiritual Unity" (first published as "How to Understand Our Past") and "Europe and the Seven Stages of Western Culture" appeared in *Understanding Europe* (Image Books, 1960), first published by Sheed & Ward in 1952. "The Classical Tradition and Christianity" appeared in *The Making of Europe* (Sheed & Ward, 1932). "The Secularization of Western Culture" and "The Planning of Culture" appeared in *The Judgement of the Nations* (Sheed & Ward, 1943).

"The Kingdom of God and History" first appeared in a sympo-
sium of the same title, published by Allen & Unwin in 1938;
"The Christian View of History" first appeared in Blackfriars 32
(July-August 1951); both were republished in *The Dynamics of
World History*, John J. Mulloy, ed. (Sheed & Ward, 1957).

Acknowledgments

First and foremost, I would like to thank Christina Scott, daughter of Christopher Dawson and executor of his literary estate, for taking a chance on an amateur scholar and for allowing me to undertake this project. Her excellent biography of her father, *A Historian and His World*, has been extremely helpful, and her suggestions and advice for this project were invaluable. Annette Kirk was of great help in discussing the project with me while I stayed at her home during the summer of 1995, and in sharing the interest she and her late husband, Dr. Russell Kirk, had in Christopher Dawson. David McGonagle and Susan Needham of The Catholic University of America Press have been patient and understanding in helping me to prepare this volume.

I would also like to thank John Connelly, of Regis High School in New York City, for introducing me to Dawson; his advice on this and other projects has always been to the point and a spur to further reflection. I am grateful to the following for their suggestions and comments on earlier drafts of this Introduction: Mitchell Muncy, Gregory Doolan, William Fahey, Adam Schwartz, and my wife, Alexandra. Their patience in listening ad nauseam to my thoughts on this project is greatly appreciated. Any mistakes or omissions are, of course, mine alone. Finally, thanks are due to the editors of *Crisis* and *Commonweal*, who allowed me to explore some themes of Dawson's work in the pages of their journals.

PART ONE

The Historic Reality of Christian Culture
A Way to the Renewal of Human Life

I

The Outlook for Christian Culture

THERE IS ALWAYS a danger in speaking of so wide and deep a question as that of Christian culture that we may be speaking at cross-purposes. It is therefore just as well to start by defining our terms. When I speak of culture I am not thinking of the cultivation of the individual mind, which was the usual sense of the word in the past, but of a common social way of life—a way of life with a tradition behind it, which has embodied itself in institutions and which involves moral standards and principles. Every historic society has such a culture from the lowest tribe of savages to the most complex forms of civilized life. And every society can lose its culture either completely or partially, if it is exposed to violent or farreaching changes.

What then do we mean by a Christian culture? In fact the word Christian is commonly used in two different senses. There is a sense in which it is identified with certain forms of moral behavior which are regarded as typically or essentially Christian, so that a Christian society may mean an altruistic and pacific society, and an unchristian society or form of behavior is taken to mean one that is aggressive and acquisitive.

3

Whether this use of the word is justifiable or not, it is certainly different from the traditional use of the word. Thus if we judge by the utterances of statesmen and the programs of governments and political parties, there has never been an age in which society has concerned itself more with the welfare and conditions of life of the common people than our own. Yet though this concern is wholly consonant with Christian ideals and may even owe its ultimate inspiration to them, it does not suffice to make our society Christian in a real sense; and the tendency to put exclusive emphasis on this aspect of the question will be a serious cause of error, if it leads us to a confusion of Christianity with humanitarianism.

The only true criterion of a Christian culture is the degree in which the social way of life is based on the Christian faith. However barbarous a society may be, however backward in the modern humanitarian sense, if its members possess a genuine Christian faith they will possess a Christian culture—and the more genuine the faith, the more Christian the culture.

And so when we talk of Christian culture, we ought not to think of some ideal pattern of social perfection which can be used as a sort of model or blueprint by which existing societies can be judged. We should look first and above all at the historic reality of Christianity as a living force which has entered into the lives of men and societies and changed them in proportion to their will and their capacity. We see how it has been spread broadcast over the world by the grace of God and the accidents of historical necessity. Often it has fallen on stony ground and withered away, often it has been choked by the secular forces of a civilization, but where it has taken root, we see again and again the miracle of divine creativity and a new spiritual harvest springing from the old soil of human nature and past social tradition.

This flowering of new life is Christian culture in the highest sense of the word, but every believing Christian society already has in it a living seed of change which is bound to bear fruit in due time, even if its growth is hidden or hindered by the many other growths which are so deeply rooted in the soil of human nature that they can never be eradicated. We cannot measure spiritual achievement by cultural achievement, since the two processes lie on different planes; but though the former transcends the latter it may also find in it its means of expression and outward manifestation. But there is always a time lag in this process. The spiritual achievement of today finds its social expression in the cultural achievements of tomorrow, while today's culture is inspired by the spiritual achievement of yesterday or the day before.

If we take the case of the first introduction of the Christian faith in Europe, we see how complex and profound is the process that we are attempting to understand. When St. Paul sailed from Troy in obedience to a dream and came to Philippi in Macedonia, he did more to change the course of history and the future of European culture than the great battle which had decided the fate of the Roman Empire on the same spot more than ninety years before. Yet nothing that he did was notable or even visible from the standpoint of contemporary culture. He incurred the hostility of the mob, he was sent to prison and he made at least three converts: a business woman from Asia Minor, a slave girl who was a professional fortuneteller, and his jailer. These were the first European Christian—the forerunners of uncounted millions who have regarded the Christian faith as the standard of their European way of life.

All this took place, as it were, underneath the surface of culture. The only people who seem to have realized the importance of what was happening were the half-crazed slave girl and the hostile mob at Philippi and Salonica, the riffraff of the market place, who attacked St. Paul as a revolutionary, one who turned the world upside down and taught there was another king than Caesar—one Jesus.

Yet at the same time St. Paul himself was very much alive to the significance of culture. He was a Roman and a Jew and he was proud of both traditions; but he was always careful to adapt his teaching to the cultural background of his audience,

whether they were simple, peasant-minded Anatolians or skepti-
cal Athenians or supercilious Roman administrators. So that
when one turns from St. Paul's own utterances to the writings
of his learned contemporaries, one feels that one is going down
in the cultural scale, descending from a rich and vivid vision of
reality to a stale and superficial repetition of platitudes and
rhetorical commonplaces which belonged to a spiritual order
that had already lost its vitality.

At first sight the problem of modern culture is entirely different from that of the Roman world. The latter was living in the
tradition of the pagan past, and Christianity came to it as a new
revelation and the promise of new life. But today it is Christianity that seems to many a thing of the past, part of the vanishing
order of the old Europe, and the new powers that are shaping
the world are non-Christian or even anti-Christian.

It is no wonder that the conscience of Christians is uneasy.
On the one hand there are those who still retain an internal
bond with the Christian culture of the past, and a deep love
and reverence for it; and in that case they must feel that something in the nature of a national apostasy has occurred and that
they bear some share of the guilt. And on the other hand there
are those who have lost contact with that social tradition and
who know only the new secularized world. These are likely to
feel that the Christian culture of the past failed because it was
not really Christian and that it is for us and our successors to
discover or create for the first time a new way of life that will
be truly Christian.

I believe both these points of view are fundamentally true.
They represent the two aspects of the problem of Christian
culture in our time, and they are wrong only in so far as they
are one-sided. I do not think it is possible to deny the fact of
Christian culture, as an objective social reality. It is hardly too
much to say that it is Christian culture that has created Western
man and the Western way of life. But at the same time we must
admit that Western man has not been faithful to this Christian
tradition. He has abandoned it not once, but again and again.

For since Christianity depends on a living faith and not merely on social tradition, Christendom must be renewed in every fresh generation, and every generation is faced by the responsibility of making decisions, each of which may be an act of Christian faith or an act of apostasy.

No doubt it is very seldom that a society is clearly conscious of what is at stake. The issues are complicated by all kinds of social, economic and political influences, so that the actual decision usually takes the form of a compromise.

Now, as I have pointed out with reference to the origins of Christianity, the creative activity which is the essence of the Christian life takes place far below the visible surface of culture; and the same thing is true of the spiritual failures and apostasies which are the other side of the picture. But this does not mean that religion and culture are two separate worlds with no relation to each other. The assumption of such a separation has been the great error of the Western mind during the last two centuries. First we have divided human life into two parts—the life of the individual and the life of the state—and have confined religion entirely to the former. This error was typical of bourgeois liberalism and nowhere has it been more prevalent than in the English-speaking countries. But now men have gone further and reunited the divided world under the reign of impersonal material forces, so that the individual counts for nothing and religion is viewed as an illusion of the individual consciousness or a perversion of the individual craving for satisfaction.

This is the typical error of Marx and Engels and of the totalitarian mass state in all its forms.

But to the Christian the hidden principle of the life of culture and the fate of nations and civilizations must always be found in the heart of man and in the hand of God. There is no limit to the efficacy of faith and to the influence of these acts of spiritual decision which are ultimately the response of particular men to God's call, as revealed in particular historical and personal circumstances. Burke wrote very truly and finely that the so-called laws of history which attempt to subordinate the future to some kind of historical determinism are but the artificial combinations of the human mind. There always remains an irreducible element of mystery. "A common soldier, a child, a girl at the door of an inn have changed the face of the future and almost of Nature."

But to Christians the mystery of history is not completely dark, since it is a veil which only partially conceals the creative activity of spiritual forces and the operation of spiritual laws. It is a commonplace to say that the blood of martyrs is the seed of the Church, yet what we are asserting is simply that individual acts of spiritual decision ultimately bear social fruit. We admit this in the case of the Church and we have admitted it so long that it has become a platitude. But we do not for the most part realize that it is equally true in the case of culture and history.

For the great cultural changes and the historic revolutions that decide the fate of nations or the character of an age are the cumulative result of a number of spiritual decisions—the faith and insight, or the refusal and blindness, of individuals. No one can put his finger on the ultimate spiritual act which tilts the balance and makes the external order of society assume a new form. In this sense we may adapt Burke's saying and assert that the prayer of some unknown Christian or some unrecognized and unadmitted act of spiritual surrender may change the face of the world.

No doubt any great change of culture, like the conversion of the Roman world or the secularization of Western Christendom, is a process that extends over centuries and involves an immense variety of different factors which may belong to different planes of spiritual reality. The secularization of Western Christendom, for example, involved first the loss of Christian unity, which was itself due not to secularism but to the violence of religious passion and the conflict of rival doctrines. Secondly it involved the abdication by Christians of their responsibilities with regard to certain fields of social activity, so that we may say that nineteenth-century England was still a Christian society, but a Christian society that had diverted its energies to the pursuit of wealth. And finally it involved a loss of belief, which was to a certain extent involuntary and inevitable, since the stability of faith had already been undermined by the two processes which I have mentioned.

To state the problem in a simplified form, if one century has destroyed the unity of Christendom by religious divisions, and a second century has confined the Christian way of life to the sphere of individual conduct and allowed the outer world of society and politics to go its own way, then a third century will find that the average man will accept the external social world as the objective standard of reality and regard the inner world of faith and religion as subjective, unreal and illusory.

Thus the process of secularization arises not from the loss of faith but from the loss of social interest in the world of faith. It begins the moment men feel that religion is irrelevant to the common way of life and that society as such has nothing to do with the truths of faith. It is important to distinguish this secular separation between religion and society from the traditional opposition between the Church and the World—or between the present world and the world to come—which has always been so deeply rooted in the Christian tradition. It is often difficult thus to differentiate, since what is described as the "otherworldly" type of religion is in some cases directly connected with the divorce between religion and culture of which I have spoken. In other cases the opposition springs from the Christian dualism which finds expression not only in St. Augustine, or in the later mystics, but in all ages of the life of the Church from the New Testament to the twentieth century. Indeed it is this vital tension between two worlds and two planes of reality which makes the Christian way of life so difficult but which is also the source of its strength. To live for eternal truths, to possess the first fruits of eternal life, while facing every practical responsibility and meeting the demands of the present moment and place on their own ground—that is the spirit by which a Christian culture lives and is known. For Christian culture involves a ceaseless effort to widen the frontiers of the Kingdom of God—not only horizontally by increasing the number of Christians but vertically by penetrating deeper into human life and bringing every human activity into closer relations with its spiritual center.

The return from a secular civilization to a Christian way of life no doubt involves a reversal of many historical forces that transcend the limits not only of our personal experience but even of our particular society. But in spite of the modern totalitarian tendency to control the development of culture by the external methods of legislation and international organization and the control of parties and political police, it is still the individual mind that is the creative force which determines the ultimate fate of cultures. And the first step in the transformation of culture is a change in the pattern of culture within the mind, for this is the seed out of which there spring new forms of life which ultimately change the social way of life and thus create a new culture. I do not, of course, mean to assert that new ideas are more important than new moral action and new spiritual initiative. Knowledge and will and action are inseparable in life, and the soul is the principle of all life. But I do believe that it has been on the plane of ideas that the process of the secularization of culture began, and that it is only by a change of ideas that this process can be reversed. It has always been the weakness of the Anglo-Saxon tradition to underestimate the influence of ideas on life and of contemplation on action, and the result of this error has been that many Christians in England and America never realized the existence of culture until the culture of the age had ceased to be Christian.

That was the situation a hundred years ago. It is true that there were several religious minority movements that were aware of the issues—on the one hand the Christian Socialists, such as F. D. Maurice;[1] on the other hand, there was the idealization of the ages of faith which characterized the Catholic

1. [John Frederick Denison Maurice (1805–72), Professor of English at King's College, London, and a leader of the Christian Socialist movement.—Ed.]

revival and the Oxford Movement. But for the most part Victorian England was dominated by that attitude of Protestant Philistinism which was the object of Matthew Arnold's denunciations. Now it is true, as Mr. T. S. Eliot has recently pointed out, that Arnold's view of culture is vitiated not only by its individualism but even more seriously by its implicit assumption that intellectual culture is itself a sort of sublimated religion which is a substitute for traditional Christianity. But, for all that, he still deserves to be read, for no one has shown more clearly and mercilessly the effects of the divorce between religion and culture on English society and the English way of life; and since our present predicament is the direct result of this cleavage, his work is a historical document of the first importance for the inner history of the English culture of the nineteenth century.

Moreover, Arnold's main criticism of the religion of his day is not invalidated by his misconceptions concerning the nature of religion and the nature of culture. The burden of his complaints is always that *religious people would not think*—that they made religion a matter of strong emotion and moral earnestness so that it generated heat and not light. And that at the same time they were complacent and uncritical in their attitude to their own bourgeois culture: so long as men went to church and read the Bible and abstained from gambling and drunkenness and open immorality, it did not matter that they were at the same time helping to turn England into a hideous and disorderly conglomeration of factories and slums in which the chapel and the gin palace provided the only satisfaction for man's spiritual and emotional needs.

The reaction against this degradation of Christian culture has carried us very far in the opposite direction. And the improvement of social conditions—one might almost say the civilizing of our industrial society—has coincided with the secularization of English culture.

This secularization has been the great scandal of modern Christendom. For the Christian cannot deny the crying evils of that nineteenth-century industrial society from which the ordinary man has been delivered by the social reforms of the last fifty or one hundred years: while at the same time he is forced to reject the purely secular idealism which has inspired the new culture. Nevertheless this has been a salutary experience for Christians. It has made us examine our conscience to see how great has been our responsibility for this decline of Christian culture and for the conversion of our society to a new kind of paganism.

But we ought not to concentrate our attention on the failures of nineteenth-century Christianity. Today we are faced with a new situation and an entirely different range of problems. The modern world is in a state of violent confusion and change, and it is not the traditional Christian culture of the past but the secularized culture of the present which is being tried and found wanting. The material security and the confidence in the future which have long been characteristic of Western civilization have suddenly disappeared. Nobody knows where the world is going. The course of history has suddenly been changed from a broad, placid river into a destructive cataract.

Christianity is not left unaffected by this change, for it threatens all the values and traditions which the liberal secularism of the last age still respected and preserved. Yet this catastrophic element in life which had been temporarily exiled from the nineteenth-century world is one that is very familiar to Christians. Indeed, in the past it formed an integral part of the original Christian experience and the changes of the last forty years have confronted us with a situation which is not essentially different from that the primitive Church faced under the Roman Empire. The eschatological aspect of Christian doctrine, which was so alien to the Edwardian age, has once more become relevant and significant. For even though we may not believe in the imminent end of the world, it is hardly possible to doubt that *a* world is ending. We are once more in the presence of cosmic forces that are destroying or transforming human life, and therefore we have a new opportunity to see life in religious terms and not merely in terms of humanism and social welfare and political reform. Arnold's ideal of culture as a "general harmonious expansion of those gifts of thought and feeling which make the peculiar dignity, wealth and happiness of human nature" obviously belonged to an age and a class which could reckon on social security. For that age the four last things—Death and Judgment and Heaven and Hell—had become remote and unreal. But today they are real enough even for the unbeliever who knows nothing of the Christian hope of eternal life. The Christian way of life has indeed become the only way that is capable of surmounting the tremendous dangers and evils that have become a part of the common experience of modern man. No doubt, as the Gospel says, men will go on eating and drinking and buying and selling and planting and building, until the heaven rains fire and brimstone and destroys them all. But they do this with only one part of their minds; there is another part of their minds which remains uneasily conscious of the threat that hangs over them; and in proportion as they realize this, they feel that something should be done and they seek a way of salvation, however vaguely and uncertainly.

In a sense this has always been so, and men have always been partially conscious of their spiritual need. But there has been during the last generation a fundamental change in the nature of their anxiety. During the last few centuries the appeal of Christianity has been largely personal. It has been an appeal to the individual conscience and especially to the isolated and introverted types. It is the experience which finds a classical expression in Bunyan's *Pilgrim's Progress*, which is all the more classical because it was also popular. But today the appeal is greatest to those who have the strongest sense of social responsibility, and it is no longer merely a question of individual salvation but of the salvation of the world—the deliverance of man in his whole social nature from the evils that express themselves in political and social forms, in anonymous mass crimes and criminal instincts which nevertheless are not less opposed to the Christian spirit than are the sins of the individual. This is the reason why the chief rivals to Christianity at the present time are not different religions but political ideologies like Communism, which offers man a social way of salvation by external revolution, by faith in a social creed and by communion with a party which is a kind of secular church.

Nor is it surprising that these secular counter-religions should tend to produce the very evils from which men are seeking to be delivered. For this is just what the early Church experienced with the pagan counter-religions which tried to satisfy the spiritual needs of the ancient world in opposition to the Christian way of salvation.

And the anti-Christian character of the forces which are making an attempt to conquer the world is also another sign of the relevance of Christianity to the problems of the present age. Religion is ceasing to be a side issue—it is no longer regarded as belonging to a private world remote from the real world of business and politics and science. It is once more felt to be a vital issue even by its enemies who are determined to destroy it.

Consequently, in spite of the increasing secularization of culture both in the West and in the world at large, I feel that the outlook for Christian culture is brighter than it has been for a considerable time—perhaps even two hundred and fifty years. For if what I have been saying about spiritual changes and their cultural fruits is true and if the changes of the last forty years have the effect of weakening the barrier between religion and social life which was so strong a century ago, then the new situation opens the way for a new Christian movement of advance.

This is no excuse for facile optimism. For even if the change has begun, it must go a long way before it can affect the structure of social life and bear fruit in a living Christian culture: and meanwhile things must grow worse as secular culture undergoes the inevitable process of corruption to which it is exposed by its nature. From all that we can see, and from the experience of the past, it is practically certain that the period of transition will be a time of suffering and trial for the Church. Above all we have little or no knowledge of how Christians are to meet the new organized forces with which they are confronted. However much these forces may have misused the new techniques that science has put into their hands, these techniques cannot be ignored and they are bound to become an integral part of the civilization of the future, whether it is Christian or anti-Christian. So long as it is only a question of material techniques—of the machine order and all that it implies—Christians are ready enough to accept the situation, perhaps almost too ready. But what of the social and psychological techniques on which the totalitarian state relies and which may almost be said to have created it? All these methods of mass conditioning, social control by centralized planning, the control of opinion by propaganda and official ideologies, the control of behavior by methods of social repression are not restricted to defending society from the evil-doer but are directed against any type of minority opinion or activity. Most of these things have been rejected and condemned by Western opinion, whether Christian or secular, yet many of them are already invading and transforming Western society, and they are likely to become more and more a part of the modern world. Seen from this point of view, the Nazis and the Communists are not the only totalitarians, they are only parties which have attempted to exploit the totalitarian elements in modern civilization in a simplified and drastic way in order to obtain quick results.

The whole tendency of modern life is toward scientific planning and organization, central control, standardization and specialization. If this tendency was left to work itself out to its extreme conclusion, one might expect to see the state transformed into an immense social machine, all the individual components of which are strictly limited to the performance of a definite and specialized function, where there could be no freedom because the machine could only work smoothly so long as every wheel and cog performed its task with unvarying regularity. Now the nearer modern society comes to this state of total organization, the more difficult it is to find any place for spiritual freedom and personal responsibility. Education itself becomes an essential part of the machine, for the mind has to be as completely measured and controlled by the techniques of the scientific expert as the task which it is being trained to perform.

Therefore the whole society has to move together as a single unit. Either it may be a Christian unit which is governed by spiritual standards and directed toward spiritual ends, or it is wholly secular—a power machine, or a machine for the production of wealth or population.

As I have said, this is an extreme conclusion, and at the present time even the most totalitarian forms of society are not and cannot be as totalitarian as this. Nevertheless the modern world is moving steadily in this direction, and the margin between the old forms of liberal or social democracy and this new Leviathan is growing narrower every year. Hence we can hardly doubt that when ultimately a conflict takes place between the new state and the Christian chruch, it will be far more severe in character than anything that has been known before.

Here again the trend of events is following the same pattern as in the early days of Christianity. Nothing was clearer to the Christians of that age than the imminence of a tremendous trial, in which the mystery of iniquity that was already at work in the world would come out into the open and claim to stand in the place of God Himself. It was with the constant awareness of this coming catastrophe that the new Christian way of life took form, and it was this that made the Christian belief in a new life and in the coming of a new world, not an expression of other-worldly pietism, but an active preparation for vast and immediate historical changes. There is no need to idealize their behavior. At times the actual outburst of persecution was followed by wholesale apostasies, as in the time of Decius in the year 250. Yet in spite of such failures, throughout the long periods of persecution and semipersecution a gradual change was taking place beneath the surface until finally, after the last and fiercest persecution of all, the world suddenly awoke to find that the Empire itself had become Christian.

We today are living in a world that is far less stable than that of the early Roman Empire. There is no doubt that the world is on the move again and that the pace is faster and more furious than anything that man has known before. But there is nothing in this situation which should cause Christians to despair. On the contrary it is the kind of situation for which their faith has always prepared them and which provides the opportunity for the fulfillment of their mission.

It is true that we do not know where the world is going. We cannot say it must go toward a Christian culture any more than toward destruction by atomic warfare. All we know is that the world is being changed from top to bottom and that the Christian faith remains the way of salvation: that is to say, a way to the renewal of human life by the spirit of God which has no limits and which cannot be prevented by human power or material catastrophe. Christianity proved victorious over the pagan world in the past, because Christians were always looking forward while the secular world was looking back. This note of hope and expectation is one of the characteristic notes of Christianity: it runs through the New Testament from beginning to end. One of the most striking expressions of this is to be seen in St. Paul's last letter to his first European converts—the Philippians—written during his captivity and trial, yet making even his trial a ground of encouragement, since it was providing a means to spread the knowledge of the faith in the Roman prætorium and the palace of Caesar. And after describing all his gains and all his losses, he concludes:

"Not that I have already reached fulfillment. I do not claim to have attained. But this one thing I do. Forgetting all that is completed and reaching out to the things that lie before, I press on to the goal for the prize of the high calling of God in Christ Jesus."

This attitude of detachment and confidence in the future which St. Paul expresses in such an intensely personal, vivid way is also the social attitude of the Church as a whole, and it is this which gives Christianity such a great power of spiritual renewal.

Nevertheless, though Christianity is prepared to accept every external change, though it is not bound to the past in the same way as a particular form of society tends to be, it has its own internal tradition which it maintains with the most scrupulous fidelity and which it can never surrender. Looked at from the secular standpoint, the primitive Church might have seemed to lack everything that the educated Roman regarded as culture. Yet in reality it was the representative of a cultural tradition older than that of Greece and Rome. To the Christian, the people of God was a real historical society with its own history and literature and its perennial philosophy of divine wisdom. And when eventually the world became Christian, this specifically religious culture-tradition came to the surface and was accepted by the new world as the source of the new Christian art and literature and liturgy.

The same tradition exists today, for though the Church no longer inspires and dominates the external culture of the modern world, it still remains the guardian of all the riches of its own inner life and is the bearer of a sacred tradition. If society were once again to become Christian, after a generation or two or after ten or twenty generations, this sacred tradition would once more flow out into the world and fertilize the culture of societies yet unborn. Thus the movement toward Christian culture is at one and the same time a voyage into the unknown, in the course of which new worlds of human experience will be discovered, and a return to our own fatherland—to the sacred tradition of the Christian past which flows underneath the streets and cinemas and skyscrapers of the new Babylon as the tradition of the patriarchs and prophets flowed beneath the palaces and amphitheaters of Imperial Rome.

2

What is a Christian Civilization?

THE QUESTION which I have taken as the title for the present chapter is one of the vital questions of our times. It is very necessary that we should ask it, yet the fact that we are doing so is a symptom of the state of doubt and uncertainty in which modern man exists. For in the past it was no problem to the ordinary man. Everyone thought—however mistakenly— that he knew what Christian civilization was; no one doubted that it was possible; and most people would have said that it was the only form of civilization possible for Western man.

This was true of the whole Christian world down to the eighteenth century, and the fact that I can use this expression— the Christian world—and assume that the reader will know what I mean is sufficient in itself to prove the point. No doubt after the eighteenth century this was no longer the case on the European continent, and there the concept of Christian civilization had already become a controversial one. But this change did not occur to anything like the same degree in England and America. The Anglo-Saxon missionary movement of the nineteenth century, for example, as represented by men like David

Livingstone,[1] seems to have taken for granted that the expansion of Christianity was inseparable from the expansion of Western civilization. In the eyes of such men Western civilization was still a Christian civilization as compared with pagan barbarism and the non-Christian civilizations of the ancient peoples.

It is easy enough for us today to realize their mistake and to see its tragic consequences. But the danger today is that we should go to the opposite extreme by denying the social or cultural significance of Christianity. A man like Livingstone could not have done his work without the Christian background in which he had been bred. He was the offspring of a Christian society and a Christian society involves a Christian culture. For however widely one separates the Word and the World, Christian faith and secular activity, Church and State, religion and business, one cannot separate faith from life or the life of the individual believer from the life of the community of which the individual is a member. Wherever there are Christians, there must be a Christian society, and if a Christian society endures long enough to develop social traditions and institutions, there will be a Christian culture and ultimately a Christian civilization.

But perhaps I have gone too far in assuming general agreement in the use of terms which are by no means so clear as they appear at first sight. For words like "civilization," "culture," and "Christian" are all of them likely to become highly charged with emotional and moral associations. I mean that the word "Christian" is used or was used in the recent past in the sense of morally excellent; "civilization" usually involved a judgment of value and implies a very high type of social and intellectual development; while "culture" is used in two quite different senses but usually implies a rather sophisticated type of higher education.

But for the purposes of the present discussion I shall attempt to use these words in a purely descriptive way, without implying

1. [David Livingstone (1813–73), Scottish missionary and explorer.—Ed.]

moral judgments—that is to say, judgments of value. I use the word "culture" as the social anthropologists do, to describe any social way of life which possesses a permanent institutional or organized form, so that one can speak of the culture of a tribe of illiterate cannibals. And I use the word "civilization," of any culture that is sufficiently complex to have developed cities and states. Similarly, when I speak of individuals or societies as Christian, I mean that they profess the Christian faith or some form of Christian faith, and not that they are men or peoples who behave as we believe Christians ought to behave.

Let us start at the beginning and inquire what culture—any culture, even the lowest—involves. No culture is so low as to be devoid of some principle of moral order. Indeed, I think we may go further than that and say that a culture is essentially a moral order and this is just what makes it a culture. Even those sociologists who are most inclined to minimize or deny the spiritual element in culture and to view it in a purely behavioristic fashion, like the late Professor W. G. Sumner, are ready to admit that a culture is essentially a system or pattern of "folkways" or "mores" and their use of this Latin term points to a fundamental agreement in the conception of culture. For the word "mores" means morals as well as manners, and though we today make a sharp distinction between ethics and customs, the distinction is a very recent one. The Romans themselves, who were exceptionally aware of ethical problems and possessed a genuine moral philosophy, still had only one word for the two concepts, so that while to the Roman *"boni mores"* had come to mean what we call "good morals," it was also used indifferently to describe good manners. Even today we cannot ignore the close relationship and parallelism between moral education and training in good manners, so that children do not distinguish very clearly between the guilt of a moral offense and the shame of a breach of good manners.

Now when we come to primitive societies, we cannot expect to find any clear distinction such as we take for granted between ethics and customs. But this does not mean that ethics are less important; on the contrary, they cover a much wider field and extend further in both directions, inward to religion as well as outward to society. For in all primitive cultures, ethics are related to a whole series of concepts which are now distinguished from one another, but which formerly constituted different provinces of one moral kingdom, and embraced law and religious rites as well as morals and social customs. Take the case of law: the distinction between the moral and the legal codes is relatively modern, not only in simple cultures but even in the great historic civilizations of the ancient world. For the great legal codes were all-inclusive and possessed a sacred character which conferred the same ultimate sanctions on the precepts which we should regard as secular, public or political as on those which seem to us moral or religious or ceremonial.

This unification of standards is familiar to us historically in the case of the Hebrew Torah: here the unity of religion, ethics, law, rites and ceremonies is peculiarly clear and we see how this sacred law is also regarded as the foundation of the national culture and the very essence of the people's being. But there is a similar relation between religion, law, morals and rites, in the great world cultures of China and India and Islam no less than in the more primitive cultures.

In China, for example, we see how the Confucian ethics have been the moral foundations of Chinese culture for more than two thousand years, so that it is impossible to understand any aspect of Chinese history without them. They were linked on the one hand with Chinese religion and ritual, and on the other with the Chinese political and social order. And they were also inseparably connected with Chinese education and the Chinese tradition of learning. Seen in this light, Chinese culture is an indivisible whole—a web of social and moral relations woven without seam from top to bottom.

We are now in a better position to understand what Christian civilization means. For in the past Christianity has played the same part in Western civilization as Confucianism did in China or Islam in the Middle East. It was the principle of moral unity which gave the Western peoples their spiritual values, their moral standards, and their conception of a divine law from which all human laws ultimately derive their validity and their sanction. Without Christianity there would no doubt have been some kind of civilization in the West, but it would have been quite a different civilization from that which we know: for it was only as Christendom—the society of Christian peoples— that the tribes and peoples and nations of the West acquired a common consciousness and a sense of cultural and spiritual unity. This is not just the theory of a Christian apologist. It is admitted just as much by historians who have no sympathy with Christianity. Edward Gibbon, for example, was notoriously hostile to the whole Christian tradition. Yet he never denied that the Church was the maker of Europe and he concludes his highly critical survey of Christian origins by showing how religious influences and "the growing authority of the Popes cemented the union of the Christian republic; and gradually produced the similar manners and the common jurisprudence which has distinguished from the rest of mankind the independent and even hostile nations of modern Europe."[2]

But when Gibbon speaks of "manners" we must understand it in the extended sense which I have been discussing. For what distinguished the new Christian peoples of Europe from their pagan ancestors was their acceptance of a new set of moral standards and ideals. No doubt their adhesion to these new standards was very imperfect in practice, but the same thing was probably true of their old standards, for there is always a considerable gap between the moral standards of a society and the moral practice of individuals, and the higher the standards, the wider the gap; so that we should naturally expect the contrast between moral principles and social behavior to be much wider in the case of Christianity than in a pagan society. Nevertheless, this does not mean that moral and spiritual values are socially negligible. They influence culture in all sorts of ways—

2. *Decline and Fall,* ch. XXXVII, ii, "The Conversion of the Barbarians."

through institutions and symbols and literature and art, as well as through personal behavior. Take for example the case of the transformation of the barbarian king or war leader by the sacramental rite of consecration as practiced throughout Europe in the Middle Ages. This obviously did not convert the ordinary feudal monarch into a St. Louis or a King Alfred, but it did establish an ideal norm by which rulers were judged and which moralized the institution itself. And the same is true of the institution of knighthood, and still more true of essentially Christian institutions, like priesthood and episcopacy and monasticism. A Christian civilization is certainly not a perfect civilization, but it is a civilization that accepts the Christian way of life as normal and frames its institutions as the organs of a Christian order. Such a civilization actually existed for a thousand years more or less. It was a living and growing organism—a great *tree of culture* which bore rich fruit in its season. As I say, it was by no means a perfect civilization. In its origins, it was a civilization of converted barbarians and it retained certain barbaric elements which reasserted themselves again and again in the course of its history.

Now our modern Western civilization in Europe and America is the direct successor and heir of this Christian civilization. Without the latter, it would never have existed. Nevertheless, our modern civilization is not a Christian one. It is the result of two hundred years of progressive secularization during which the distinctively Christian institutions and social standards have been gradually eliminated. This process was a complex one. On the continent of Europe, especially in France, it was a violent and catastrophic change, which involved political revolutions and religious persecutions. In England on the other hand it was extremely gradual and piecemeal and even today some of the typical institutions of the old Christian order, like the State establishment of the national Church and the solemn religious consecration of the monarch, still survive. The case of America, or rather of the United States, differs from each of these types. It was the first country in the Christian world to inaugurate the complete separation of the State from the Church. But this did not at first involve the secularization of culture. Throughout the greater part of the nineteenth century it was the churches rather than the State that were responsible for education and culture, especially in the newly settled territories of the Middle and Far West. The complete secularization of public education is a relatively recent factor; so that its impact on American culture has only recently been fully realized.

Thus in all Western lands the outcome of the last two hundred years' development has led to similar results. The traditional Christian civilization has now become a part of history and can only be understood by a considerable effort of study and imagination, while the whole Western world is coming to share a common secular technological civilization which it has transmitted and is in the course of transmitting to the rest of the world—to the old civilizations of Asia and to the new peoples of Africa and Oceania. Yet this secularized civilization both in Europe and America still bears marks of its Christian origins and contains living Christian traditions and institutions, though these are, so to speak, scattered and no longer integrated into the organic structure of the civilization.

Opinions differ as to the relative importance of these elements, according to the personal experience of the individual. As far back as the end of the eighteenth century there were localities and social strata in which the Christian religion was no longer practiced, while there are other regions where it is still accepted today as the basis of social life and education. And it is this broken pattern of Christian culture which is the source of most of our practical difficulties in finding clear answers and satisfactory solutions to the problem that we are discussing. On the one hand we have the point of view presented by Mr. T. S. Eliot in his thoughtful and provocative studies in Christian culture.

In the first of them, *The Idea of a Christian Society*, he writes:

A society has not ceased to be Christian until it has become positively something else. It is my contention that we have today a culture which is mainly negative, but which in so far as it is positive, is still Christian. I do not think that it can remain negative, because a negative culture has ceased to be efficient in a world where economic as well as spiritual forces are proving the efficiency of cultures which, even when pagan, are positive; and I believe the choice before us is between the formation of a new Christian culture and the acceptance of a pagan one. Both involve radical changes; but I believe that the majority of us, if we could be faced immediately with all the changes which will only be accomplished in several generations, would prefer Christianity.[3]

Now though I naturally agree with Mr. Eliot about the choice we should make, I think he underestimates the degree to which modern civilization has acquired a positively secularized character and I am doubtful whether the majority of modern men are unwilling to accept this state of things. Christian civilization was inaugurated by the acceptance of the Cross as the Standard—*In hoc signo, vinces.* But modern civilization has adopted a different standard and it is the sign of the dollar rather than the cross that now marshals the forces of Western civilization. I do not think that the majority of men are unwilling to accept this new standard. The dollar is a very good thing in its way and there are many good Christians who are quite ready to make it the standard of our civilization. It is true that they do not fully realize what the total secularization of our civilization would mean. They are ready to accept a secular state and secular education, but they still hope to maintain Christian ethical standards and they do not understand how deeply and in how many ways the spirit of a civilization influences the moral values of its individual members.

No doubt in the past it has proved possible for churches and other minority groups to maintain their ethical standards against those of the dominant culture. But they paid a high price for this. In the case of the early Christians it meant a fight to

3. *The Idea of a Christian Society* (New York: Harcourt, Brace and Co., 1939), p. 13.

the death between the Church and the pagan world, in which Christianity triumphed only after long centuries of persecution. In the case of the Jews in Europe, it has meant the life of the ghetto and the cramping and impoverishment of their culture; and in the case of the minority groups in the modern Christian world, like the Mennonites and the Quakers, it produced a somewhat parallel phenomenon in the form of sectarianism which sets the group apart from the wider national culture.

Now if it were possible to preserve the Christian standards in the life of the family and the religious group, it might well be worth paying the price, even if it meant a certain loss of social advantages. But in the highly organized life of the modern secular state it is becoming increasingly difficult for such separate groups to exist and to maintain their own way of life in a sort of religious underworld or subculture. For the modern state, whether it is democratic as in the United States, or communistic as in the U.S.S.R., or Fascist as in pre-war Italy and Germany, or nationalistic as in the new states of Asia and Africa, is no longer content to confine itself to certain limited functions like the liberal state of the nineteenth century. In fact all modern states are totalitarian in so far as they seek to embrace the spheres of economics and culture, as well as politics in the strict sense of the word. They are concerned not merely with the maintenance of public order and the defense of the people against its external enemies. They have taken on responsibility for all the different forms of communal activity which were formerly left to the individual or to independent social organizations such as the churches, and they watch over the welfare of their citizens from the cradle to the grave.

Thus the modern democratic state even in America is something quite different from the form of state envisaged by the men who formed the American Constitution. Generally speaking one can say that they were the enemies of state intervention and aimed at creating a system which would leave the community and the individual free to lead their own lives and frame their own cultural institutions. But the modern democratic state partakes of the nature of the Church. It is the educator and spiritual guide of its citizens and any influence which withdraws the citizen and especially the citizen's children from this universal guidance is felt to be undesirable, if not positively disloyal.

It is clear that such a situation is full of dangers for a Christian society. In the United States, at least, the danger is not acute at present. So long as an overwhelming majority of members of the American Congress are at least nominal church members, there is little possibility of the State adopting an actively anti-Christian policy. But the prospect for the future is more disquieting. For the more completely secularized public education becomes, and the more the State acquires an educational monopoly, as it is bound to do, considering the growing cost of education, the more the Christian element in our culture will diminish and the more complete will be the victory of secularization as the working religion, or rather counter-religion, of the American people. Even today the public school is widely regarded not as a purely educational institution in the nineteenth century sense—that is, as an elementary introduction to the literary and scientific traditions of culture—but as a moral training in citizenship, an initiation and indoctrination in the American way of life; and since the public school is essentially secular this means that only the secular aspects of American culture are recognized as valid. It is only a short step from here to the point at which the Christian way of life is condemned and outlawed as a deviation from the standard patterns of social behavior.

The Christians, like the Jews before them, have held that the fear of God is the beginning of wisdom, so that without the knowledge of God there can be no true education. Our modern secular civilization has decided otherwise. As the former head of UNESCO, Dr. Julian Huxley, has recently said, "Today God is becoming the erroneous hypothesis in all aspects of reality, including man's spiritual life."[4] Hence it seems clear that the

4. *New Bottles for New Wine* (New York: Harper & Brothers, 1958), p. 272.

present state of the post-Christian world, a world which is no longer Christian but which retains a vague sympathy for or sentimental attachment to Christian moral ideals, is essentially a temporary one. Unless there is a revival or restoration of Christian culture—of the social life of the Christian community—modern civilization will become secularist in a more positive and aggressive way than it is today. And in a Godless civilization of this kind, it will be far more difficult for the individual Christian to exist and practice his religion than it has ever been before, even in ages of persecution. In the past, as for instance under the Roman Empire, the family formed an independent society which was almost immune from the state, so that it could become the primary cell of an unrecognized Christian society or culture. But today the very existence of the family as a social unit is threatened by the all-persuasive influence of the state and the secular mass culture. Yet without the Christian family there can be no Christian community life and indeed no church in the traditional sense of the word: only a few scattered individuals who maintain an isolated prophetic witness, like Elias in the wilderness.

But, it will be asked, is not the idea of a return to Christian civilization irreconcilable with the conditions of the modern world which are accepted today by Christians as well as secularists? Certainly there can be no question of a return to the old regime of the alliance of Church and State or the ecclesiastical domination of society. But this does not mean that we can afford to reject the ideal of a Christian civilization or the need for a return to spiritual unity. The kingdom of God is a universal kingdom: there is no aspect of human life that stands outside it or which is not in some way tributary to it. It is the nature of Christianity to be a world-transforming movement. It transforms humanity itself and in the course of this process it changes societies and civilizations. As St. Pius X wrote half a century ago, "To restore all things in Christ has always been the Church's motto, to restore in Christ not only what directly depends on the divine mission of the Church to lead souls to

God but also, as we have explained, that which flows naturally from this divine mission, i.e.: Christian civilization in each and all the elements that compose it."

This same doctrine runs through the whole series of the social Encyclicals from the time of Leo XIII to the present time and I do not suppose that anyone will question that this is the normal accepted teaching of the Catholic Church. But, of course, it may be objected that this does not hold good for Protestants and that this is one of the main points on which Catholics and Protestants differ. This is certainly true of some Protestants and in our days the rejection of the idea of Christian civilization has become one of the hallmarks of the school of existentialist neo-Kierkegaardian Christianity which has had such an influence on the religious intelligentsia, if one may use the expression. But so far as my reading goes, it has never been characteristic of Protestantism in general. One of the most influential of the English Protestant thinkers of the last century, F. D. Maurice, made the positive affirmation of the universal kingship of Christ over every aspect of human culture and every form of human life the center of his whole teaching; and one of his modern disciples, Canon Alec Vidler, in his Hale lectures here in the United States some years ago, maintained that though Maurice may seem an isolated and almost fugitive thinker, his views are being endorsed by many of the most representative Biblical and dogmatic theologians of our day.

No doubt it is equally possible to find names on the opposite side; and in the United States especially there is an old established tradition of religious individualism and minority movements which is naturally uninterested in the problem of civilization in its religious aspects. This tradition, if I understand it right, is due to the meeting of two different influences—the Calvinist doctrine of the elect minority on the one hand, and the revivalist insistence on a particular type of intense religious experience on the other. But it certainly does not hold good of the Calvinist tradition in its pure form. For no Protestant was more insistent than Calvin on the importance of Christian standards in the life of the community and on the religious duties of the Christian State, and the same is true of the Puritans in New England. Indeed the reaction against the Puritans alike in seventeenth century England and in modern America was due to a resistance to the Puritan attempt to impose too rigid a standard of Calvinist ethics and culture on society. But here the attack came not from theologians who disbelieved in the possibility of a Christian civilization, but from humanists, or secularists who wished to emancipate culture from ecclesiastical control.

And the objections are still strong today. The average man's objection to Christian civilization is not an objection to medieval culture, which incorporated every act of social life in a sacred order of sacramental symbols and liturgical observances—such a culture is too remote from our experience to stir our emotions one way or the other: it is the dread of moral rigorism, of alcoholic prohibition or the censorship of books and films or of the fundamentalist banning of the teaching of biological evolution.

But what the advocates of a Christian civilization wish is not this narrowing of the cultural horizons, but just the reverse: the recovery of that spiritual dimension of social life the lack of which has cramped and darkened the culture of the modern world. We have acquired new resources of power and knowledge of which the old Christian civilization had hardly dreamed. Yet at the same time, we have lost that spiritual vision man formerly possessed—the sense of an eternal world on which the transitory temporal world of human affairs was dependent. This vision is not only a Christian insight: for it is intrinsic to the great civilizations of the ancient East and to the pagan world as well, so that it is not Christian civilization alone that is at stake. Here I think John Baillie, in his little book on *What is Christian Civilization?*, makes a useful and necessary distinction when he objects to the use of the word "pagan" to describe the dominant spirit of a secularist society.

The word pagan [he says] is often unthinkingly used as if it meant a man who was devoid of all religious sentiment and worshipped no gods. But all real pagans are full of religious sentiment and their fundamental error rather lies in worshipping too many gods. The alternative today is not between being Christian or being pagan, but between being Christian and being nothing in particular, not between belonging to the Church and belonging to some social spiritual community that claims an equally wholehearted allegiance, but between belonging to the Church and belonging nowhere, giving no wholehearted allegiance to anything. Such is the tragedy that has overtaken so much of our common life that it belongs nowhere, has no spiritual home, no ultimate standards of reference and little definite conception of the direction in which it desires to move.[5]

I think this is surely true as a diagnosis of our present civilization. But society cannot remain stationary in this kind of spiritual no man's land. It will inevitably become a prey to the unclean spirits that seek to make their dwelling in the empty human soul. For a secular civilization that has no end beyond its own satisfaction is a monstrosity—a cancerous growth which will ultimately destroy itself. The only power that can liberate man from this kingdom of darkness is the Christian faith. For in the modern Western world there are no alternative solutions, no choice of possible other religions. It is a choice between Christianity or nothing. And Christianity is still a live option. The scattered elements of Christian tradition and Christian culture still exist in the modern world, though they may be temporarily forgotten or neglected. Thus the revival of Christian civilization does not involve the creation of a totally new civilization, but rather the cultural reawakening or reactivization of the Christian minority. Our civilization has become secularized largely because the Christian element has adopted a passive attitude and allowed the leadership of culture to pass to the non-Christian minority. And this cultural passivity has not been due to any profound existentialist concern with the human pre-

5. John Baillie, *What is a Christian Civilization?* (New York: Oxford University Press, 1945), p. 39.

dicament and divine judgment, but on the contrary to a tendency toward social conformity and too ready an acceptance of the values of a secularized society. It is the intellectual and social inertia of Christians that is the real obstacle to a restoration of Christian culture. For if it is true that more than half the population of this country are church members, Christians can hardly say that they are powerless to influence society. It is the will, not the power, that is lacking.

3

The Six Ages of the Church

IN SPITE OF the unity and continuity of the Christian tradition, each of the successive ages of the Church's history possesses its own distinctive character, and in each of them we can
study a different facet of Christian life and culture. I reckon
that there are six of these ages, each lasting for three or four
centuries and each following a somewhat similar course. Each
of them begin, and end, in crisis; and all of them, except perhaps
the first, pass through three phases of growth and decay. First
there is a period of intense spiritual activity when the Church
is faced with a new historical situation and begins a new apostolate. Secondly there is a period of achievement when the Church
seems to have conquered the world and is able to create a new
Christian culture and new forms of life and art and thought.
Thirdly there is a period of retreat when the Church is attacked
by new enemies from within or without, and the achievements
of the second phase are lost or depreciated.

At first sight these successive movements of achievement and
retreat are a somewhat perplexing phenomenon since they seem
to suggest that the history of Christianity is subject to some

sociological law which limits its spiritual freedom and prevents the complete fulfillment of its universal mission. It is however a commonplace of Christian teaching that the life of the Church on earth is a continual warfare and that it cannot rely on any prospect of temporal and terrestial success. From this point of view the successive ages of the Church are successive campaigns in this unending war, and as soon as one enemy has been conquered a new one appears to take its place.

This pattern of Christian history is found most clearly in *the First Age of the Church*, when from the first moment of its existence it became involved in a life-and-death struggle with the Roman Empire and with the civilization of the pagan world. And when after three centuries of conflict the Church was victorious and the Empire became Christian, the Church almost immediately had to face a new enemy in the form of a Christian heresy supported by the new Christian Empire. At the same time the first age of the Church is unique inasmuch as it was not following an existing tradition of faith and order as all the rest have done, but creating something absolutely new. Hence its initial phase, the Apostolic Age, stands in a sense outside the course of Church history as the archetype of spiritual creativity. For in that movement the creative activity of the Church was inseparable from the actual creation of the Church itself, so that Pentecost was at once the birthday of the Church and the beginning of the Church's apostolate. Moreover the new-born Church was faced almost at once with a second change of a more revolutionary character than she ever had to meet subsequently—that is to say, the extension of the apostolate from a Jewish to a Gentile environment and the incorporation in the new society of the great body of new converts drawn from the anonymous mass society of the great cosmopolitan centers of the Mediterranean world from Antioch to Rome itself. We have a contemporary account of this change in the New Testament and this gives us an invaluable and unique insight into the beginnings of the Church of the Gentiles. But we possess no comparable account of the change from the Judaeo-

Christian point of view, nor are we much better informed with regard to the origins of the vernacular Syriac Christianity which was to have so great an importance for the future of the Church in the East.

But the main achievement of the first age of the Church was the successful penetration of the dominant urban Roman-Hellenistic culture and for this there is no lack of materials. Although the Church remained outside the pale of civic society, without legal rights and subjected to intermittent persecutions, it nevertheless became the greatest creative force in the culture of the Roman world in the second and third centuries. It created a new Christian literature, both Greek and Latin. It laid the foundations of a new Christian art, and above all, it created a new society which existed alongside of the established order of society and to some extent replaced it. There is perhaps no other example of a similar development of which we possess such a full historical record, and apart from its religious significance, it is also of great sociological interest, since the primitive Church was not a mere sectarian cult-organization but a real society with a strong sense of citizenship and a highly developed hierarchical order.

The cultural achievement of this first age reached its full development in the first half of the third century—the age of Clement and Origen in the East, of Tertullian and Cyprian in the West. But the third phase of cultural retreat and disintegration, which normally marks the later years of every age, hardly exists in this case; it was overshadowed by the vast catastrophe of the last great persecution which threatened to destroy the existence of the Church but actually ended in the Church's triumph.

The Second Age of the Church begins with the most spectacular of all the external victories which Christendom has known—the conversion of Constantine and the foundation of the new Christian capital of the Christian Empire. This marks the beginning of Christendom in the sense of a political society or group of societies which find their principle of unity in the public profession of the Christian faith, and also of the Byzantine culture as the translation into Christian terms of the Hellenistic culture of the late Roman Empire. Both of them were to endure, for good or ill, for more than a thousand years, since the alliance of Church and State in a Christian Commonwealth which was inaugurated by Constantine and Theodosius remained a fundamental factor in Christian culture right down to the modern period.

But from the point of view of Church history, the three centuries or three hundred and thirty years between the Peace of the Church and the Moslem conquest of Jerusalem and Antioch and Alexandria have an internal unity and coherence. It has always been known as the Age of the Fathers *par excellence,* and both the Eastern and the Western Church have looked back to it as the classical age of Christian thought and the fountainhead of theological wisdom. The Fathers were not systematic theologians in the same sense as St. Thomas Aquinas and the great theologians of later periods. But they formed the mind of the Church and determined the norms of theological thought that were followed by the theologians of the Christian world in later centuries. In this way the three great Cappadocian Fathers, St. Basil, St. Gregory of Nazianzus and St. Gregory of Nyssa, remain the classical exponents of Eastern Orthodox theology, as St. John Chrysostom was the classical exponent of Scripture; while in the West St. Augustine was the seminal and creative mind that moulded the theological thought of the West, and St. Jerome laid the foundations of the Western tradition of Biblical and historical scholarship.

Now if we apply to this second age the threefold divisions which I described at the beginning of this chapter, we have first the period of creative achievement which covers the age of the greatest of the Fathers in East and West alike, from St. Athanasius to St. Augustine, St. Jerome and St. John Chrysostom. This first century also saw the rise and development of Christian monasticism which had such an immense historical and spiritual influence on Christian culture and which represents the most distinctive contribution of the Oriental as opposed to the Hellenic element in Christianity. For though monasticism spread with extraordinary rapidity from one end of the Christian world to the other—from Persia and Mesopotamia to Gaul and the British Isles—it retained the imprint of its Egyptian origin. The solitary ascetics of the Nitrian desert and the cenobitical monasticism of St. Pachomius remained the two archetypes of the monastic life, whether in the center of the Byzantine world or in the barbarian societies of Wales and Ireland.

At the same time this first century also saw the flowering of Christian art and architecture and liturgical poetry, which reached their full development during the second phase of this period as the Eastern Empire became fully mature. The Age of Justinian was a great age of Christian culture in the sense that every aspect of social and artistic life was subject to Christian influence. St. Sophia and the basilicas of Ravenna still give us some idea of the greatness of Byzantine culture and the closeness of its association with the liturgy and with the life of the Church. Yet already the spiritual vitality of the age was beginning to flag and it was evident that the vast opportunity that had been offered to the Church of the previous period for the conversion of the Eastern world to Christianity had been lost.

During the last phase of the period the progressive alienation of the subject nationalities of the East from the state Church of the Byzantine Empire showed itself by the formation of new national churches that rejected the orthodox dogmas as formulated in the third and fourth general councils and were in open schism with Constantinople and Rome.

Finally the Age of the Fathers ended in the loss of the Christian East and the establishment of the new world power of Islam which separated not only Syria and Egypt but the rest of North Africa and the greater part of Spain from the community of Christian peoples. Thus at the beginning of *the Third Age* in the seventh century the Church found herself beset by enemies on all sides, by the Moslem aggression in the South and by the pagan barbarism of the North. In the South she failed to regain what had been lost, but she won the North by a long and painful missionary effort and thus laid the foundation of a new Christian culture which has been somewhat ineptly termed "medieval."

In this age, more than ever before or since, the Church was the sole representative of the higher culture and possessed a monopoly of all forms of literary education, so that the relation between religion and culture was closer than in any other period. The transplantation of Catholicism from the civilized Mediterranean world in which it had been born to the coasts of the Atlantic and the North Sea had far-reaching effects on its social organization. It ceased to be a predominantly urban religion; the old link between bishop and city was broken, and the monastery became the real center of life and Christian culture. There was a remarkable, but short-lived, flowering of Christian culture in these new lands which produced a classical historical record in the case of Bede's great *Ecclesiastical History of the English People.*

In the course of the eight century this new Christian culture extended its influence to continental Europe by the work of the Irish and Anglo-Saxon missionaries, above all St. Boniface, who was the chief agent in bringing about the alliance of the Frankish monarchy, the Papacy and the Benedictine order which was the cornerstone not only of the Carolingian Empire but of the social order of Western Christendom in the Middle Ages. For the enduring importance of the Empire of Charles the Great is not to be found in its political achievements, which were ephemeral, but in its educational and liturgical work, which laid the foundations of that common Latin ecclesiastical culture which underlay the subsequent development of medieval civilization. On the other hand the attempt to create a new form of Christian state on these foundations, in the Anglo-Saxon kingdom and in the Carolingian Empire alike, failed owing to their lack of material resources and the absence of an educated class of lawyers and officials, such as still existed in the Byzantine world.

The collapse of the new Christian state under the pressure of the barbarian invasion was followed by a social relapse into a state of barbarism which threatened to overwhelm the Church itself. Nevertheless even in the darkest hour of this dark age the missionary apostolate of the Church continued, and the conversion of the Scandinavian peoples of the North and of the Czechs, the Poles and the Magyars, together with the Bulgarians and the Russians, in the East completed the task which had begun more than five centuries before, in the dark days of the barbarian invasions.

The *Fourth Age* of the Church began with a movement of spiritual reaction against the secularization of the Church and its absorption in the feudal society. It began as a movement of monastic reform in Lorraine and Burgundy and gradually extended its influence throughout Western Christendom. The turning point came in the middle of the eleventh century when the influence of the reformers reached Rome, and the Papacy put itself at the head of the movement to free the Church from its dependence on the feudal State and to restore the hierarchical order and the canonical discipline of Catholic tradition. Although this involved a tremendous and long-drawn-out conflict with the temporal power as represented by the Western Empire and the feudal principalities, it was not in principle a contest for political power. Its true aims are expressed in the final appeal which Gregory VII addressed to the Christian people from his exile in Salerno:

Since the day when the Church placed me on its apostolic throne my whole desire and the end of all my striving has been that the Holy Church, the Bride of God, our mistress and our Mother, should recover her honor and remain free and chaste and Catholic.

So long as this alliance between the Papacy and the monastic reformers continued—that is to say, for nearly two and a half centuries—the Church exercised a dynamic influence on almost every aspect of Western culture; and the spiritual reformers, like St. Hugh of Cluny, St. Gregory VII, St. Anselm and above all St.

Bernard, were also the central figures in the public life of Western Christendom. So too in the following period it was the influence of the Church that inspired the revival of Western learning and philosophy and the creation of the universities which were founded as international centers of higher study for Western Christendom as a whole.

Yet in spite of all this the movement of reform was never completely successful. The medieval Church was so deeply involved in the territorial economy of feudal society that it was not enough to free the Church from secular control so long as it retained its own temporal power and privileges. The reformers were indeed conscious of this dilemma and they found a personal solution in a strict adherence to the ascetic ideals of the monastic life, but this was not enough since even the most ascetic of the reformed orders, like the Cistercians, still remained wealthy and powerful in their corporate capacity. It was left to St. Francis, the Poor Man of Assisi, to take the further, final step by renouncing corporate property also and pledging his followers to total poverty. His ideal was not to found a new monastic order but to institute a new way of life, consisting in the simple and literal observance of the precepts of the Gospel, "the following of the poor life of Christ."

This marks the climax of the reforming movement, and the greatness of the medieval Papacy is nowhere more evident than in the way in which it accepted this drastic breach with the traditional order and made the new institution an organ for the evangelization of the masses and an instrument of its international mission. A century later this would not have been possible, for from the end of the thirteenth century the international unity of Western Christendom had begun to disintegrate and the alliance between Papacy and the party of religious reform was breaking down. During the last two centuries of the Fourth Age this disintegration shows itself in the defeat of the Papacy by the new national monarchies, like that of Philip IV of France, and in the rise of new revolutionary movements of reform, like the Wycliffites and the Hussites, and finally by the

Great Schism in the Papacy itself. The attempt to overcome the schism by the Conciliar movement only widened the gap between the Northern European reformers and Rome, and the age ends with the acute secularization of the Renaisance Papacy and the great religious revolution of Northern Europe which is known as the Reformation *par excellence.*

Thus *the Fifth Age of the Church* began in a time of crisis which threatened the unity and even the existence of Western Christendom. On the one hand there was the direct theological and ecclesiastical challenge of the Protestant Reformation which separated the greater part of Northern Europe from Catholicism, and on the other there was the cultural challenge of the new lay culture of the Italian Renaissance, which had replaced the theological and philosophical traditions of the medieval universities. Finally the external relations of Western Christendom had been transformed by the Turkish conquest of Southeastern Europe, and by the widening of the horizon of Western culture by the discovery of America and the opening of the Far East to European trade and navigation.

All these factors affected the character of Catholicism in the following age. The reaction against the Reformation produced the Tridentine reform of the Church and the revival of the religious life through the influence of new religious orders. The cultural issue was met by the development of a new form of Christian humanist culture and education, while the age of discovery was followed by a great outburst of missionary activity, which found its greatest representative in St. Francis Xavier, the apostle of the Far East. These new developments reached their maturity in the first half of the seventeenth century when the Catholic revival found expression in the new Baroque culture which dominated the artistic and intellectual life of Europe and represents the more or less successful fusion of the tradition of the humanist Renaissance and the spirit of the Catholic revival. In its religious aspect the most distinctive feature of this Baroque culture was the great development of Catholic mysticism which took place at this period and had a considerable influence on the art and literature of the age.

But the success of the Baroque culture was comparatively a short one. Its weakness, and that of the Catholic revival itself, was that it was too closely dependent on the success of the Catholic monarchies, especially the Hapsburg monarchies in Spain and Austria. When these declined, the Baroque culture declined with them, and when the third great Catholic monarchy was destroyed by the great political and social cataclysm of the French Revolution, the Church was the first victim of the change. As the armies of the French Republic advanced through Europe, the established order of the Catholic Church was swept away. The monasteries and universities were destroyed, church property was confiscated and the Pope himself was deported to France as a political prisoner. In the eyes of secular opinion, the Catholic Church had been abolished as a superannuated relic of the dead past.

Thus *the Sixth Age of the Church* began in an atmosphere of defeat and disaster. Everything had to be rebuilt from the foundations. The religious orders and the monasteries, the Catholic universities and colleges and, not least, the foreign missions had all been destroyed or reduced to poverty and impotence. Worst of all, the Church was still associated with the unpopular cause of the political reaction and the tradition of the *ancien régime.*

Yet in spite of all these disasters the Church did recover and a revival of Catholicism took place, so that the Church was in a far stronger position by 1850 than it had been a hundred years before when it still possessed its ancient wealth and privileges. This revival began in France during the Revolution, under the shadow of the guillotine, and the exiled French clergy contributed to the creation or restoration of Catholicism in England and America. Indeed the whole history of Catholicism in the United States belongs to this sixth age and is in many aspects typical of the new conditions of the period.

American Catholicism differs from that of the old world in that it is essentially urban, whereas in Europe it was still firmly rooted in the peasant population. Moreover from the beginning it has been entirely independent of the state and has not been restricted by the complex regime of concordats which was the dominant pattern of European Catholicism in the nineteenth century.

But at the present day it is the American rather than the European pattern which is becoming the normal condition of the Church everywhere except in those regions like Eastern Europe or China where it exists on sufferance or under persecution. I will say no more about the present age as it is dangerous to generalize about a period which is still unfinished. The present age of the Church still has centuries to run and who can say what even the present century will bring forth? On the one hand Christians are faced with an external threat more formidable than anything we have known since the time of Islam. On the other hand the intellectual and spiritual lassitude that marked the last two centuries has largely disappeared and we see on every side the awakening of a new apostolic spirit and a wider concern for the unity of the Church.

Each of these ages has only a limited duration; each ends in a crisis, a divine judgment in which a whole social world is destroyed. And insofar as these social worlds have been Christian ones, their downfall creates a problem for the Christian who sees so much that appeared to be part of the consecrated, God-given order swept away together with the evils and abuses of a corrupt society. This however is only a particular example of the problem of the relativity of culture with which all historians have to deal. But whereas the secular historian is in no way committed to the cultures of the past, the Catholic, and indeed every Christian, is bound to recognize the existence of a transcendent supra-temporal element at work in history. The Church exists in history, but it transcends history so that each of its temporal manifestations has a supernatural value and significance. To the Catholic all the successive ages of the Church and all the forms of Christian culture form part of one living whole in which we still participate as a contemporary reality.

One of the main reasons why I dissent from the current threefold division or periodization of Church history as ancient, medieval and modern is that it is apt to make us lose sight of the multiplicity and variety of the life of the Church, and of the inexhaustible fecundity with which, in the words of the liturgy of Easter Day, God continually calls new peoples into the divine society, multiplying the Church by the vocation of the Gentiles. I have spoken of the Six Ages of the Church— there may be sixty before the universal mission of the Church is completed. But each age has its own peculiar vocation which can never be replaced, and each, to paraphrase Ranke's famous saying, stands in a direct relation to God and answers to Him alone for its achievements and its failures. Each too bears its own irreplaceable witness to the faith of all.

4

Christian Culture as a
Culture of Hope

THE SCIENCE OF CULTURE—culture history, cultural morphology and the comparative study of cultures—is of very recent origin. It grew up in the nineteenth century with the development of the new social sciences, above all anthropology, and it had no place in the traditional curriculum of liberal education. But during the present century its development has been rapid, especially perhaps in Germany and in America, so that today it is no longer confined to scientific specialists but has been adopted, however superficially, by publicists and politicians and has a growing influence on modern social thought.

Nevertheless there still remains a certain contradiction and confusion between this new idea of culture and the old unitary conception which is deeply rooted in our educational traditions. To the average educated man culture is still regarded as an absolute. Civilization is one: men may be more cultured or less cultured, but in so far as they are cultured, they are all walking along the same high road which leads to the same goal. The

46

idea that there are a number of different roads leading, perhaps, in opposite directions, still remains a difficult idea to assimilate. Humanism, the Enlightenment and the modern conceptions of "the democratic way of life" and the "one world" all presuppose the same idea of a single universal ideal of civilization toward which all men and peoples must move.

Against this we have the anthropologist's and ethnologist's conception of a culture as an artificial creation which has been constructed by particular men in particular circumstances for particular ends. The cultures are as diverse as races and languages and states. A culture is built, like a state, by the labor of generations which elaborate a way of life suited to their needs and environment and consequently different from the way of life of other men in other circumstances. The Negro in the tropical rain forest makes his own terms with life which are different from those of the herdsman of the steppes, as these terms again are different from the ways of the hunters of the Arctic. All these simple cultures have their limits set by nature. They cannot go far, but they can endure indefinitely, until their environment is changed or some external force, like a conquering race, displaces or destroys them. The primitive existence of the Eskimos or the Bushmen is in a sense timeless and has remained outside history, so that it seems to take us back to a prehistoric world.

But with the higher cultures this is not so. They are essentially the children of time and of history, and the more they emancipate themselves from their primitive dependence on nature, the more closely do they become confined to the human restrictions and laws of the artificial social world that they create. We see this tendency already operating in barbarian cultures like those of Polynesia where social institutions are fortified and protected by an elaborate system of taboos which seem so inexplicable and irrational to the foreign observer. And yet the same principle is to be found in the more advanced cultures. In fact the more advanced they are, the more elaborate are the artificial rules of caste and status, of custom and law, of ceremonial and etiquette with which they surround themselves. It is the great paradox of civilization that every victory over nature, every increase of social control, also increases the burden of humanity. When man builds a fortress he also builds a prison, and the stronger it is, the greater its cost in human suffering.

When we look back at the civilizations of the past, we cannot fail to be impressed by their achievements. The Egyptian pyramids still stand today after nearly five thousand years as monuments of human power. But while we marvel we are appalled at the suffering and the waste of human labor that they represent. For at the heart of the pyramid there is nothing but the corpse of a despot.

So too in Mesopotamia, it was from the spectacle of those vast artificial mountains or ziggurats which towered over the cities of Babylonia that the inspired writer drew his image of the nemesis of human power and pride—the curse of Babel. For whenever a culture reaches its culmination of power and social control, as in the age of the pyramids or the Empires of Babylon and Rome, it breaks down under its own weight which has become too heavy for human nature to endure, and so the whole process has to begin again until a new Babylon has been built.

Now it may be said that this is true of the slave states and military empires of the past but that humanity has freed itself from this curse by the scientific control of nature and that democracy and socialism open the prospect of universal happiness to the oppressed and exploited who have hitherto carried the burden of civilization without receiving its benefits. St. Just said, "Happiness is a new idea in Europe," and for a century and a half Western culture has been sustained by this hope of the immediate coming of a social millennium. But during the last forty years the old devils which seemed to have been banished have returned with sevenfold force, so that at the present moment civilization is suffering from a sense of pessimism and frustration and loss of hope which finds poignant expression in such works as George Orwell's *1984.* It is not merely that the socialist paradise has turned into the totalitarian hell; even worse is the deception of scientific progress which promised the nineteenth century a new world and has given the twentieth century the atomic bomb.

There are some Christians who feel a certain satisfaction—a kind of *Schadenfreude*—at the sudden collapse of the liberal idealism of the nineteenth century and the loss of hope in the future of modern civilization. Christianity, they say, is a religion of crisis, a judgment which regards even the highest achievements of human culture as vitiated by man's fallen nature and doomed to destruction. This no doubt is the tradition of the Calvinist and the Jansenist and it finds a certain justification in the history of the past with its record of the frustration of achievement and the death of cultures. Nevertheless this is essentially a one-sided view. Christianity is certainly not to be identified with religious individualism or with the rejection of history and the condemnation of culture.

On the contrary there is no religion, and perhaps no philosophy, which is so deeply concerned with man as part of a community or which attaches a higher significance to history. For Christianity is essentially the religion of the Incarnation, of the divine intervention in history at a particular time and in a particular social context and of the extension and incorporation of this new spiritual creation in the life of humanity through the mediation of an historic institutional society.

Hence while Christianity rejects the modern optimistic illusion of an automatic process of material progress which leads inevitably to a social millennium, it does not deny the existence of progress in a deeper sense. On the contrary it teaches that throughout the ages the life of humanity is being leavened and permeated by a transcendent principle, and every culture or human way of life is capable of being influenced and remoulded by this divine influence. Thus Christianity has always been a culturally creative force. It came first into a world which was overcivilized, where the social soil was becoming exhausted and the burden of empire and law was becoming too heavy for human nature to bear. And it transformed and renewed this civilization, not by any program of social or political reform but by revealing the existence of a new spiritual dimension and bringing the light of hope to those who sat in darkness and in the shadow of death.

An English writer of the last century has described in a remarkable passage how this atmosphere of hope pervades the art of the catacombs and the cult of the martyrs with the promise of the dawn of a new Christian culture.

Penetrating the whole atmosphere, touching everything around with its peculiar sentiment, it seemed to make all this visible mortality, death itself, more beautiful than any fantastic dream of old mythology had hoped to make it; and that in a simple sincerity of feeling about a supposed actual fact. The thought, the word, *Pax —Pax Tecum!*—was put forth everywhere, with images of hope, snatched sometimes even from that jaded pagan world, which had really afforded men so little of it, from first to last, of succour, of regeneration, of escape from death—Hercules wrestling with Death for possession of Alcestis, Orpheus taming the wild beasts, the Shepherd with his sheep, the Shepherd carrying the sick lamb upon his shoulders. Only, after all, these imageries formed but the slightest contribution to the whole dominant effect of tranquil hope, there—of a kind of heroic cheerfulness and grateful expansion of the heart; again, as with the sense of some real deliverance; and which seemed actually to deepen, the longer one lingered through these strange and fearful passages. A figure, partly pagan, yet the most frequently repeated of all these visible parables—the figure of one just escaped as if from the sea, still in strengthless, surprised joy, clinging to the very verge of the shore—together with the inscription beneath it, seemed best to express the sentiment of the whole.

> I went down to the bottom of the mountains;
> The earth with her bars was about me forever;
> Yet has Thou brought up my life from corruption.[1]

The remaking of an old culture by the birth of a new hope was not the conscious aim of the Christians themselves. They tended, like St. Cyprian, to believe that the world was growing

1. Walter Pater, *Marius the Epicurean*, 1885, II, pp. 117–18 (first edition).

old, that the empire was irremediably pagan and that some world catastrophe was imminent. Nevertheless they lived in a spiritual atmosphere of hope, and this atmosphere gradually spread until the climate of the world was changed. The heartless, hopeless Rome which found its monstrous expression in the Colosseum and the gladiatorial games became the Rome of St. Leo and St. Gregory—a city which laid the foundations of a new world while its own world was falling in ruin around it.

We see the same process at work in northern Europe during the Dark Ages. The men who converted the warrior peoples of the North and laid the foundations of medieval culture had no conception of the new world that they were creating and no belief in the temporal future of civilization. But they were men of hope, as they were men of faith, and therefore their work endured for a thousand years and bore rich fruit in every field of cultural activity, as well as on its own religious level.

This is the paradox of Christendom which so impressed G. K. Chesterton[2] and which is the theme of his longest poem, *The Ballad of the White Horse*. It is the paradox that the pagan worship of nature is in the end a religion of death, while the Christian who is indifferent to the temporal results of his actions is the servant and guardian of life.

Chesterton's Christian optimism is out of fashion today, when the external perils of Western civilization are reflected in the moral discouragement and spiritual anxiety of Western man. Nor is this confined to the non-Christian world. It is impossible to deny that there have been tendencies in Western Christianity which are actually inimical to that spirit of hope which inspired the Christian culture of the past.

At the moment when the Renaissance announced a new faith in man and a new hope in the possibilities of human culture, the Reformers reacted in the opposite direction by the pessimism of their views on the total corruption of human nature

2. [Gilbert Keith Chesterton (1874–1936), English writer, social theorist, and Christian apologist. His *Ballad* had impressed Dawson greatly.—Ed.]

and the rigorism of their doctrines of predestination and election. Nor was this tendency confined to the Protestant world; it was also present in the Catholic world in the form of Jansenism, and though Jansenism was always a minority movement it would be difficult to exaggerate the extent to which it divided the Christian mind and depressed the Christian spirit. No doubt neither Calvin nor Saint-Cyran consciously denied the traditional Christian hope. But it is no less certain that the practical effect of their teaching was to erect a barrier between religion and life which contributed so largely to the progressive secularization of Western culture. Thus we see in the classical culture of the *grand siècle* how this Jansenist rigorism combined with the Renaissance prejudice against the "gothic" barbarism of medieval culture to make Boileau ban the traditional religious drama of the Christian past—a tradition which was still flourishing in Spain when Boileau wrote:

> De la Foy des Chrestiens les Mystères terribles
> D'ornaments Egayez ne sont pas susceptibles.
> L'Évangile à l'Esprit n'offre de tous costez,
> Que pénitence à faire, et tourmens méritez.

> The mysteries which Christians must believe
> Disdain such shifting pageants to receive.
> The Gospel offers nothing to our thoughts
> But penitence, or punishment for faults.

In Protestant Europe it was not only the religious drama that was outlawed but Christian art as well, and with it disappeared all the other expressions of Christian culture which united the Church with the life of the people. Religion became a specialized activity which was confined to church and chapel and limited to one day in the week. Thus the destruction of Christian culture was the work of the Christians themselves who allowed the new Babylon of modern materialist civilization to be built on the soil of Christendom.

But this failure or abdication on the part of Christians in the past is no reason for despair in the present. The loss of hope was indeed the source from which all these ills have flowed, for when men were deprived of spiritual hope, it was inevitable that they should turn eagerly to the new secular hope of a social millennium held out to them by the preachers of materialism.

But today, as we have seen, these hopes have proved delusive and the new Babylon is threatened by an even more catastrophic and suicidal end than any of the world empires of the past. Thus we find ourselves back in the same situation as that which the Christians encountered during the decline of the ancient world. Everything depends on whether the Christians of the new age are equal to their mission—whether they are able to communicate their hope to a world in which man finds himself alone and helpless before the monstrous forces which have been created by man to serve his own ends but which have now escaped from his control and threaten to destroy him.

5

The Institutional Forms
of Christian Culture

W<small>E CANNOT SEPARATE</small> culture from religion any more than we can separate our life from our faith. As a living faith must change the life of the believer, so a living religion must influence and transform the social way of life—that is to say, the culture. It is impossible to be a Christian in church and a secularist or a pagan outside. Even a Christian minority, which lives a hidden and persecuted life, like the early Christians in the ages of the catacombs, possesses its own patterns of life and thought, which are the seeds of a new culture.

Nevertheless it must be admitted that Christians are sometimes opposed to the very idea of Christian culture, since it seems to lead to an identification between a religious reality which is absolute and divine and a social reality which is limited and human. It was this point which inspired Kierkegaard's tremendous onslaught on "Christendom" as a colossal fraud—a betrayal of Christianity. He writes:

What we have before us is not Christianity but a prodigious illusion, and the people are not pagans but live in the blissful conceit that they are Christians.[1]

When one sees what it is to be a Christian in Denmark, how could it occur to anyone that this is what Jesus Christ talks about: cross and agony and suffering, crucifying the flesh, suffering for the doctrine, being salt, being sacrificed, etc.? No, in Protestantism, especially in Denmark, Christianity marches to a different melody, to the tune of "Merrily we roll along, roll along, roll along!"— Christianity is enjoyment of life, tranquilized, as neither the Jew nor the pagan was, by the assurance that the thing about eternity is settled, settled precisely in order that we might find pleasure in enjoying this life, as well as any pagan or Jew.[2]

God's thought in introducing Christianity was, if I may venture to say so, to pound the table hard in front of us men. . . . God succeeded in this, he really overawed men. But gradually the human race came to itself, and shrewd as it is, it saw that to do away with Christianity by force was not practicable—"so let us do it by cunning," they said. We are all Christians and so Christianity is *eo ipso* abolished.[3]

Man's knavish interest consists in creating millions and millions of Christians, the more the better, all men if possible; for thus the whole difficulty of being a Christian vanishes, being a Christian and being a man amounts to the same thing, and we find ourselves where paganism ended.

Christendom has mocked God and continues to mock Him— just as if to a man who is a lover of nuts, instead of bringing him one nut with a kernel, we were to bring him tons and millions of empty nut-shells.[4]

What Kierkegaard attacked with such passion, however, was not Christendom but the secularization of Christendom, and especially that particular form of secularization which he found

1. S. Kierkegaard, *Attack upon "Christendom,"* trans. by Walter Lowrie (Princeton: Princeton University Press, 1944), p. 97.
2. *Ibid.,* pp. 34–35.
3. *Ibid.,* pp. 166–67.
4. *Ibid.,* p. 156.

in the Danish State Church of the mid-nineteenth century. For he was living in a culture which was undergoing a rapid and complete process of secularization, and what infuriated him was the refusal of the clergy to admit the real state of affairs, so long as they could retain their official status and prerogatives.

But the fact that Christian culture had become moribund in Denmark in 1850 does not prove that it had never existed. There had been a time, as he himself admitted, when "Christendom" had meant something. Christianity was a historical reality which had actually come into the world and had transformed the societies with which it came into contact. Leaving aside for the moment the question of the relation between the religious ideal of Christianity and the social forms in which it embodied itself, there can be no doubt that Christianity in the past has been a creative cultural force of the first magnitude, and that it has actually created a Christian culture or a number of Christian cultures. The same, of course, is true of other religions. In fact every great civilization that exists in the world today has a great religious tradition associated with it, and it is impossible to understand the culture unless we understand the religion that lies behind it.

This is accepted by the orientalist and usually also by the student of more primitive cultures. No one pretends to understand Arab or Persian culture without knowing something about Islam and the beliefs and institutions that are common to the whole Moslem world. Only in the case of Europe has this elementary consideration been neglected. We have had countless studies of Western culture and histories of European society which leave out Christianity or treat it as of secondary importance.

To a great extent this state of things is due to that educational schism of which I have spoken elsewhere. Our approach to the study of our culture has been influenced for centuries by the image of an idealized classical culture which was treated as the absolute standard of Western culture, so that whatever conflicted with or diverged from this was ignored as barbarous.

But this is not the only factor. For in addition to the cultural idealism of the humanists there was also a religious idealism which had a very similar effect on men's judgments on the history of Western culture. For at the time that the humanists were exalting the ideal of a classical culture which had been forgotten for a thousand years, the reformers were preaching the return to an ideal type of Christianity which had also been lost for a thousand years.

The cumulative effect of these tendencies was to turn men's attention away from the historical reality of Christian culture and toward an ideal classical culture and an ideal primitive Christianity, so that in looking for something that was not there, they overlooked the things that were before their eyes—the historical forms of Western Christian culture as they had actually existed.

But by this time these historical forms have become remote and unfamiliar, so that it is necessary to study them anew in the same objective way in which we study the great oriental cultures of the past. Indeed in many respects the Christian culture of the past resembles the culture of Islam more than it resembles modern Western culture. Nor is this surprising, since the three great Western religions—Judaism, Christianity and Islam—are closely related to one another and share a number of common features. In all of them, in contrast to the modern world, the primary social bond was not political but religious, and consequently a man's relation to his religious community had many of the characteristics that we associate with political citizenship. The religious community was the absolute one, and all other communities—family, state and nation—were relative ones, parts of a greater whole.

In the second place all these cultures centered in a tradition of sacred learning: a divine Scripture, a sacred law, a sacred history and a sacred oral tradition. This sacred tradition was alone regarded as learning in the absolute sense. In some cases this sacred learning might represent the whole of learning and the only literary culture; in other cases there was also a tradition of secular learning, but this was secondary and supplementary.

In the third place in all these cultures the first social duty, and consequently the primary cultural activity, was the act of worship. In Islam this act was so closely connected with the recitation of the Koran that it produced little liturgical development, yet even so it holds a central place in Moslem culture.

In Christianity, on the other hand, the liturgy was the center of a rich tradition of religious poetry and music and artistic symbolism. In fact the art of Christendom in both its Byzantine and medieval phases was essentially a liturgical art which cannot be understood without some knowledge of the liturgy itself and its historical origin and development. And the same is true to a great extent of popular and vernacular culture. The popular religious drama, which had such an important influence on the rise of European drama as a whole, was either a liturgical drama in the strict sense, like the Passion plays and Nativity plays, or was directly related to the cult of the saints and the celebration of their feasts. For the cult of the saints, which had its basis in the liturgy, was the source of a vast popular mythology and provided a bridge between the higher ecclesiastical and literary culture and the peasant culture with its archaic traditions of folklore and magic.

In the same way the church itself—I mean the liturgical edifice—was at the same time the organ of both the higher and the lower culture, and consequently a great instrument of social integration. On the one hand it was the temple in which the liturgy was celebrated in the common language of educated Christendom, and, on the other, in the village and the pilgrimage place it was the center of the common people for whom it was at once school and theater and picture gallery.

It is at this point that the cultural division produced by the Reformation is seen most clearly. The church ceased to be the organ of popular culture in art and symbolism. It retained its educational importance to a great extent, but the change of the liturgy changed the nature of the religious culture. And thus while in Catholic Europe, as for example in Spain, the drama and painting and sculpture retained their religious character and were still the organs of a Christian culture common to the educated and the uneducated, in Protestant Europe the arts became secularized and the Bible only—the reading of the Bible and the preaching of the Bible—became the chief and almost the only vehicle of Christian culture.

In all these respects there is a remarkable agreement between the cultures of Byzantine Orthodoxy and Western Catholicism. The liturgies are different, the art is different, the music is different, but there is the same organic relation between them in the two cultures. The Byzantine attitude to the Holy Images is more rigid and in a sense more theological than the Western attitude to the images of the saints, but there is the same conception of religious art as a necessary organ of Christian culture and there is the same attitude to the cult of the saints as the mirrors of Christian perfection and the mediators between the spiritual and sensible worlds. Moreover both cultures share the same conception of spiritual hierarchy—that analogy between the ecclesiastical and the celestial hierarchies which is one of the keys to the traditional Christian conception of the universal order.

Finally there is one great religious institution which is common to the two cultures and which has perhaps had a greater and more direct influence on the formation of Christian culture than any other single factor: I mean the Monastic Order. It is in monasticism that religion and culture attain their most complete fusion. For the monastic rule is a sacred law which is applied to every detail of individual life and becomes the basis of a common way of life and a common society. So the latter was in principle a totally Christian society in which there was no longer any room for the conflict between religious and secular standards, a society without private property or family bonds or political and military obligations. At first sight it seems an impossible system, since its social order rests on the denial of the three main forces which have created society—sex and war and economic acquisitiveness. Nevertheless, in spite of manifold failures, it exerted a dynamic influence on every aspect of Christian culture. Its influence on the new Christian society of the barbarian North, where there was no tradition of city culture, was especially important. Here the coming of the monks meant not only a new religious way of life but a new civilization, so that the Western monasteries were islands of Christian culture in a sea of barbarism.

No institution in the history of Christian culture has been more intensively studied than this. But the best studies are those of particular orders and monasteries, and I do not think there is any work which deals adequately with Christian monasticism as a whole and particularly with the relation between the different forms of monasticism and the different forms of Christian culture. We can distinguish a number of successive types of monasticism, each of which is typical of a particular phase in the development of Christian culture.

First there is the original oriental type of monasticism, as it was organized by St. Pachomius in Egypt in the year 323, and which was rapidly diffused from one end of the Christian world to the other. This is the form of monasticism which was practically the creator of Celtic Christian culture and determined the ecclesiastical character of the Celtic Church.

Second there is Benedictine monasticism, which is the classical type of Western monasticism and was the foundation of Carolingian and early medieval culture and of Western education. From this common Benedictine tradition there developed first the Cluniac reform of the tenth century, and second the Cistercian order, which attained such a vast extension in the twelfth century and which was the first religious order in the modern sense of the word.

Third there are the Friars, above all the Franciscans and the Dominicans, who were the leading force in thirteenth-century culture and who played such a decisive part in the life of the medieval universities and in the development of scholastic philosophy.

Finally there are the Jesuits, the great Counter Reformation order, whose influence on the post-Renaissance and Baroque culture of Catholic Europe can hardly be exaggerated, above all in the sphere of education.

Thus the development of monasticism corresponds very closely with the development of Christian culture, so that the history of Christian culture is comprised in the one thousand four hundred and fifty years between the foundation of the first monastery by St. Pachomius at Tabennisi in 323 to the dissolution of the Society of Jesus in 1773.

Of course this criterion excludes the culture of Protestant Europe, and in fact it was the dissolution of the monasteries and the rejection of the monastic ideal which, more than any theological question or any question of ecclesiastical order, was the revolutionary change that separated Protestant Europe from the Christian culture of the past. Nevertheless, the same spiritual forces which produced monasticism remained active in the Protestant world.

This activity is to be seen in the formation of the sects, considered not as theological doctrines but as new ways of religious life. And accordingly, if we wish to find the sociological analogies of the religious orders in the Protestant world we must look to such organizations as the Anabaptists, the Puritan sects, the Pietists, the Quakers, the Methodists and the Plymouth Brothers (not to mention the more eccentric American developments, like the Shakers, which went so far as to insist on celibacy and the community of property).

In some of these sects, like the Dunkers and the Amana Society, we find a conscious attempt to create a totally separate Christian culture with its own economic and social order, its own forms of dress and behavior and even its own rudimentary forms of art. But none of them have any historical or religious importance except as specimens of eccentric development.

Excluding these extreme and abnormal types, this sectarian development has had considerable influence on the culture of Protestant Europe and America, as has been shown in detail by writers like Max Weber and Ernst Troeltsch. But in so far as sectarianism involves the separation of church and state and regards secular society as a neutral field common to the different sectarian groups, each of which is spiritually self-contained, it has been a factor which has made for the secularization of culture, or for that semi-secularized type of culture that was characteristic of Britain and the United States of America in the nineteenth century.

Nevertheless, as we cannot understand Western culture as a whole without a study of the great Christian culture which lies behind it, so also we cannot understand the culture of modern England and Wales and America unless we have studied the underworld of sectarian Christianity—a world which has been so neglected by the political and economic historian, but which none the less contributed so many vital elements to the complex pattern of nineteenth-century society.

This, however, is a digression; what I am primarily concerned with is the need for a more thorough and systematic study of the main tradition of Christian culture in its three great phases: the Age of the Fathers, the Middle Ages, and the Baroque period. For it is only by this large-scale study of a whole civilization, covering many centuries of continuous development, that we can understand the process of change by which a new religion enters an old society and is partially assimilated by it, so that the way of life of the society as well as of the individual is changed; and how out of this process a new culture arises which may be transmitted to other societies and may change them also.

Furthermore it is essential for us to study this particular religion-culture because it is the source of our own culture; and our judgment of other religions and other cultures must inevitably be seen through this medium. For the idea that the historian or the sociologist is in a privileged position, from which he can study any and every culture and religion in Olympian detachment, is really an absurdity and the source of countless errors and absurdities in thought and practice.

Finally there is a peculiar value in the study of Christian culture, because there is no culture that illustrates so completely the essential dualism of religion and culture and the element of conflict and spiritual tension which this dualism involves. There are societies, especially the more primitive and backward societies, in which this dualism seems absent, and in these cases religion becomes inseparable from custom and has little or no dynamic importance as a cause of social change. On the other hand there are religions that are nonsocial, which expressly disassociate themselves from any responsibility for social life and culture, and while these often possess considerable dynamic energy their appeal is a negative one, so that they are revolutionary and subversive forces.

But in Christianity the tendency to a world-renouncing asceticism coexists with a tendency toward social and cultural activity, and it is the tension of these two forces that has given Christianity its characteristic power to change society and to create new cultural forms.

This question of the influence of Christianity on social change has received a good deal more attention from the historians recently than it did in the past. In particular, a number of writers like Stepun and Berdyaev[5] have interpreted the Russian revolutionary movement in terms of the Russian religious traditions—both the tradition of the Orthodox Church and that of the sects. So too, in the case of English history, the late Elie Halévy[6] attributed great importance to the rise of Methodism and the Evangelical Movement in the eighteenth and nineteenth centuries, but for the opposite reason—that is, as one of the main causes of the nonrevolutionary character of the development of English society in the age of the French Revolution.

In all these ways the study of Christian culture is important to the historian. But above all, far outweighing any other consideration, there is the fact that Christian culture was identical

5. [Feodor Augustovich Stepun (1892–1965), Russian writer of the menshevik faction who fled to Germany during the Russian Revolution; Nicolay Alexandrovich Berdyaev (1874–1948), Russian political and religious philosopher. Among his influential books is *The Origin of Russian Communism* (1937).—Ed.]

6. [Elie Halévy (1870–1937), French social and political historian. His *History of the English People in the Nineteenth Century* was translated into English in 1949–52.—Ed.]

with Western culture during the centuries of formation and growth, and that it was the integrative force which first united the different peoples of Western Europe in a new community. What Hellenism was to the ancient world, Christendom has been to the modern. So that to attempt to understand the modern world without any study of Christian culture is as difficult as it would be to understand the Roman world without any knowledge of Hellenism.

6

Civilization in Crisis

W<small>E HAVE BECOME</small> accustomed to taking the secular character of modern civilization for granted. We have most of us never known anything else and consequently we are apt to think that this is a natural and normal state of things, so that whatever our own beliefs may be, we do not expect modern civilization to pay much attention to religion, still less to be based upon a religious conception of existence.

Actually, of course, this state of things is far from being normal; on the contrary, it is unusual and perhaps unique. If we look back and out over the world and across the centuries, we shall see how exceptional and abnormal it is. It is hardly too much to say that all civilizations have always been religious— and not only civilizations but barbarian and primitive societies also. For in the past man's social life has never been regarded as something that existed in its own right as a law to itself. It was seen as dependent on another more permanent world, so that all human institutions were firmly anchored by faith and law to the realities of this higher world. No doubt human life in the past was more insecure than it is today, more precarious and more exposed to violence and to the catastrophic accidents of famine and pestilence. But on the other hand this world of disorder and suffering was only a part of reality. It was balanced and compensated by the larger, more permanent world from which man came and to which he returned. So that a civilization was not just a highly organized form of social existence with its industry and art and scientific technique, it was both social and religious—two worlds of reality bound together by a visible fabric of institutions and laws, and by objective conceptions of justice and authority which gave them validity.

As I have shown in *Religion and Culture* and elsewhere, all the great civilizations of the ancient world believed in a transcendent divine order which manifested itself alike in the cosmic order—the law of heaven; in the moral order—the law of justice; and in religious ritual; and it was only in so far as society was co-ordinated with the divine order by the sacred religious order of ritual and sacrifice that it had the right to exist and to be considered a civilized way of life.

But today this ancient wisdom is forgotten. Civilization has cut adrift from its old moorings and is floating on a tide of change. Custom and tradition and law and authority have lost their old sacredness and moral prestige. They have all become the servants of public opinion and of the will of society. They have become humanized and secularized and at the same time unstable and fluid. As civilization becomes materially richer and more powerful, it becomes spiritually or religiously weaker and poorer. For a long time in Europe in the eighteenth and nineteenth centuries and to some extent in America today, this state of things was welcomed as a positive achievement. Individual freedom, political democracy and economic progress were regarded as ends in themselves, which would provide their own solutions to the problems that they created. It was believed that the secularization of culture was favorable to human freedom, since men would be freed from the incubus of authority in Church and State, and the functions of the latter would be reduced to that of a neutral guardian of order and security. In fact, however, the progress of scientific technique has led to the increasing concentration of power. Even the weakest and the mildest of modern governments possesses a universal power of control over the lives of its citizens which the absolute monarchies of the past never dreamt of.

Nevertheless this enormous concentration of power, which is to be seen alike in politics and economics and scientific technique, does not produce moral prestige as in the past. The politician and the civil servant do not possess the *mana* of the barbarian chief or the sacred majesty of ancient kingship, and it is the same with the industrialist and the scientific technologist. They are all regarded as ordinary men who have happened to succeed in their professions and have climbed to the top of the tree.

But it is questionable whether this state of things can last, for there is a glaring disproportion between the terrifying reality of power and the fragility and unimportance of the men who control it. And in fact during the last generation we have seen a violent reaction against the liberal ideology of the nineteenth century. First in Russia and then in Western Europe and in Eastern Asia, we have seen a series of attempts to unite the new forces of technology and scientific control with political absolutism and ideological orthodoxy. In this new totalitarian order individual freedom has been sacrificed, criticism has been outlawed, and science and technology have been forced to serve the will of authority and to justify the doctrines of the dominant ideology.

How does this affect the problem of secularization? Obviously its immediate direct effect is to cause an intensification of the process, since it makes it practically impossible for religious minorities to preserve their cultural autonomy or even to exist. The official ideology of the totalitarian state is itself completely secular and it is imposed compulsorily on the whole society, not only by party propaganda but by the convergent pressure of government action in every field of cultural and educational activity.

But indirectly and in the long run, all this may have a very different effect from that which was originally envisaged by the politicians. For when a revolutionary ideology is transformed from a minority protest into an official orthodoxy, it changes its nature and acquires many of the psychological characteristics of a religion.

Seen from this point of view its real *raison d'être* is not to carry on the process of secularization but to provide a substitute for religion, to stop modern civilization from drifting aimlessly and to anchor it again securely to absolute immutable principles which are beyond the reach of criticism.

It is difficult for us in the West to consider this aspect of totalitarianism dispassionately, since as Christians our objection to totalitarianism as a counter-religion is even greater than our objection as Westerners to the totalitarian suppression of individual liberty and the right of criticism. Nevertheless the sweeping victories of Communism in Asia and the growing unpopularity there of the Western democratic ideology make it a matter of life and death to understand the real nature of the totalitarian appeal, whether we call it religious or antireligious.

We must face the fact that Western political ideals—democracy, liberty, equality and the like—are the product of a particular cultural tradition and represent the experience and achievement of certain privileged peoples and classes—the citizen class in ancient Greece, the free estates of medieval Christendom, and the bourgeoisie and free churches of modern Europe and America. The greater part of the world has never known these things. In Asia and Africa life has been short and hard and uncertain. Constitutional government and individual political rights have been unknown and there has been no appeal or legal protection from the decrees of arbitrary power. The only alternative has been between a paternal despotism which protects the peasant in his life and his labor and a ruthless exploitation which leaves him at the mercy of the tax gatherer and the money-lender.

In such a world the evils of totalitarianism which shock the Western mind—its denial of personal liberty, of freedom of opinion and free enterprise—are less apparent than the evils of misgovernment and the oppression of class by class which it professes to cure. From the Oriental standpoint Communism represents the return to a familiar pattern—the traditional order of authoritarianism and mass responsibility. It demands everything—absolute loyalty, absolute obedience to the state and the utter subordination of the individual to the community; but in return it makes men feel that there is a power watching over them which is immune from human weakness and is based on an unchanging foundation of absolute principles.

A faith of this kind is a religion in the subjective sense—a way of salvation for man, though it is not religion in the objective theological sense.

But, it may be asked, if Communism is viewed in this light, why should it prove so attractive to Asians who are already well provided with real theological religions? The answer, I think, is that the great Oriental religions are no longer culturally active and that they have become divorced from social life and from contemporary culture. This explanation is borne out by a remarkable passage in the last volume of Mr. Koestler's autobiography in which he describes an interview he had when he was travelling in Central Asia many years ago with a blind Afghan immigrant into the U.S.S.R. I will quote it in full, as it gives a first-hand account of the impact of Communism on a completely un-Westernized Asian:

Do we all come from the same place? No—We come from many places and many tribes and one did not know of the other who was coming. Some are from the Chilchiqs and some from Afridi and some others from other tribes. We did not know of each other, but of the new religion and of the chasing away of the Beys and the Mullahs everyone knew in Afghanistan. Some say it is a good thing, and some say it is a bad thing, but they all speak about it, although it is forbidden.

No, I could not read, even when I had eyes, but I took much thought when I heard about this new religion—for I had much time to think during the famine, though it is forbidden to speak about these sacred matters. And now I will tell you the result of my thinking:

A fertile womb is better than the loveliest lips.

A well in the desert is better than a cloud over the desert.

A religion that helps is better than a religion that promises.

And this secret which I found will spread over there where we come from, and more and more will understand it and follow our way.

But others will stay where they are and embrace the new religion and preach it to the ignorant.[1]

There is no reason to doubt the genuineness of this report and it shows convincingly how a completely anti-religious secular ideology may take on the aspect of a new religion and may compete successfully with the established faiths of the ancient East. And it succeeds not because of its ideological truth but because of its immediate appeal. It is a new gospel in the elementary sense—good news of salvation here and now.

This appeal is not so strong in the West, because the situation here is so much less simple. The distinction between religion and politics is much more obvious and we are less inclined to accept the enormous claims of the totalitarian state as a matter of course. Nevertheless the success of the totalitarian ideologies in Germany and Central and Southern Europe has been sufficiently formidable to show that we are not immune to indoctrination and that in Western Europe also there are plenty of people who desire certainty and authority more than freedom. Certainly there is no doubt that the old nineteenth century liberal ideology has become generally discredited and is no longer the ruling faith of our civilization.

Where then does Christianity stand today? At first sight the prospects seem highly favorable, for its old enemy, the antireligious secularism of the liberal rationalists, has lost its power and its new enemy, the antireligious ideology of the Communists, has not yet taken its place. There is a spiritual vacuum and Christianity seems the only spiritual form that can fill it.

Now if Christianity was embodied in a living culture, as it was in the past, or if it was the living faith of modern Western

1. A. Koestler, *The Invisible Writing* (Boston: Beacon Press, 1954), p. 135.

culture, there is little doubt that it would be able to take advantage of this opportunity. But the situation is not so simple as this. For centuries now there has been a divorce between Christianity and Western culture which has led to that process of secularization to which I referred at the beginning of this chapter. This has not destroyed our religion but it has left it in a position of weakness and social isolation. No doubt the Communists attack Christianity as the ally of the capitalist system, but in actual fact no such alliance exists. Christians are isolated between two rival forms of secularism, one of which is openly hostile while the other is indifferent or negatively hostile. In fact Christians are fighting a war on two fronts, each of which requires its own tactics and strategy.

The conflict with Communism (and the other totalitarian ideologies also) is by far the easiest to understand, owing to the fact that their opposition to Christianity is clear, consistent and complete. They have a creed and a dogma, they have an ideology and a social philosophy, and a code of ethics and moral values. Finally they form a secular church, a community of believers with its own very highly organized hierarchy of institutions and authorities.

But the other and liberal form of secularism has none of these characteristics. It does not possess any formulated creed and its *raison d'être* is to be undogmatic and anti-authoritarian. There was a time—two hundred years ago or rather less, during the period of the Enlightenment—when Freemasonry attempted to create a sort of liberal Church, but the attempt broke down about the time of the French Revolution and since then liberal secularism has been an unorganized and amorphous movement. Nevertheless it does possess a sort of ideology and social philosophy and a set of moral ideals if not a consistent system of ethics. In the past this liberal ideology and moral idealism has exerted a very powerful influence on the Western mind, and though its principles are now regarded as platitudes they continue to be repeated on a thousand platforms and in hundreds of thousands of publications, so that they have become part of the democratic way of life, something in the atmosphere which

millions of men inhale every day when they read the newspapers
or partake of political discussions.

This is a difficult situation for Christians to deal with. They
know where they are when they are faced with the aggressive
challenge of Communism, but they have no clear idea of where
they stand with regard to this other type of secularism. They
are quite ready to join with their fellow citizens in democratic
states to affirm their allegiance to general principles like the
Four Freedoms, yet when they do so they are using the same
words in a different sense. There is an unresolved misunderstanding on general principles. I think it is true to say that
the average English or American Christian shares the general
atmosphere of modern secularized Western culture and feels no
difficulty about it until he is suddenly brought sharply up by
some concrete issue, such as religious education, contraception,
divorce and so on.

The result is that the secularist regards the Christian as illib-
eral and intolerant. Possibly the best known example of this
secularist reaction is the work of Mr. Paul Blanshard[2] and his
comparison of Catholicism and Communism as two different
forms of totalitarianism. Of course, if it is totalitarian to claim
authority over the whole of human life, then Christianity is
totalitarian and so are all the other world religions. But this is
a misuse of terms, for totalitarian is essentially a political concept and implies a totalitarian state, whereas the fundamental
distinction which Christians make between Church and State
and spiritual and temporal authority is the opposite of totalitarian and is perhaps the only ultimate defense of man's spiritual
freedom against the totalitarian challenge and the growing pressure of the secular state. And this is especially true of the issue
with which Mr. Blanshard is concerned. For in claiming the
right to maintain separate schools and to teach its own principles to its own people, the Church is the champion of freedom

2. [Paul Blanshard (1892–1980), American writer and controversialist. His best
known work on this topic is *Communism, Democracy and the Catholic Power*
(1951).—Ed.]

in the most vital matter, and even the liberal democratic state is becoming totalitarian when it asserts the principle of the single school and claims a universal monopoly of teaching.

It is in this field that the secularist danger is most formidable. In politics Christianity can accommodate itself to any system of government and can survive under the most severe forms of despotism and autocracy. And in the same way, it is not bound to any economic system and has in the past existed and expanded in a world of slavery as well as in a world of freedom, under feudalism and capitalism and state socialism. But if it loses the right to teach it can no longer exist. The situation was entirely different in the past when most people were not educated and when church and chapel provided the only channel of popular instruction. But today, when the whole population of every civilized country is subjected to an intensive process of schooling during the most impressionable years of their lives, it is the school and not the church that forms men's minds, and if the school finds no place for religion, there will be no room left for religion elsewhere. It is no accident that the introduction of universal compulsory state education has coincided in time and place with the secularization of modern culture. Where the whole educational system has been dominated by a consciously antireligious ideology, as in the Communist countries, the plight of Christianity is desperate, and even if there were no persecution of religion on the ecclesiastical level, there would be little hope of its survival after two or three generations of universal Communist education. Here however the totalitarian state is only completing the work that the liberal state began, for already in the nineteenth century the secularization of education and the exclusion of positive Christian teaching from the school formed an essential part of the programs of almost all the progressive, liberal and socialist parties everywhere.

Unfortunately, while universal secular education is an infallible instrument for the secularization of culture, the existence of a free system of religious primary education is not sufficient to produce a Christian culture. We know only too well how little effect the religious school has on modern secular culture and how easily the latter can assimiliate and absorb the products of the religious educational system. The modern Leviathan is such a formidable monster that it can swallow the religious school system whole without suffering from indigestion.

But this is not the case with higher education. The only part of Leviathan that is vulnerable is its brain, which is small in comparison with its vast and armored bulk. If we could develop Christian higher education to a point at which it meets the attention of the average educated man in every field of thought and life, the situation would be radically changed. In the literary world something of this kind has already happened. During my lifetime Christianity has come back into English literature, so that the literary critic can no longer afford to ignore it. But the literary world is a very small one and it does not reflect public opinion to anything like the degree that it did in Victorian times. The trouble is that our modern secular culture is sub-literary as well as sub-religious. The forces that affect it are in the West the great commercialized amusement industries and in the East the forces of political propaganda. And I do not think that Christianity can ever compete with these forms of mass culture on their own ground. If it does so, it runs the danger of becoming commercialized and politicized and thus sacrificing its own distinctive values. I believe that Christians stand to gain more in the long run by accepting their minority position and looking for quality rather than quantity.

This does not mean that Christianity should become an eso-teric religion for the learned and the privileged. The minority is a religious minority and it is to be found in every class and at every intellectual level. So it was in the days of primitive Chris-tianity and so it has been ever since.

The difference is that today the intellectual factor has become more vital than it ever was in the past. The great obstacle to the conversion of the modern world is the belief that religion has no intellectual significance; that it may be good for morals and satisfying to man's emotional needs, but that it corresponds to no objective reality. This is a pre-theological difficulty, for it is impossible to teach men even the simplest theological truths if they believe that the creeds and the catechism are nothing but words and that religious knowledge has no foundation in fact. On the other hand I do not believe that it is possible to clear the difficulty away by straight philosophical argument, since the general public is philosophically illiterate and modern philosophy is becoming an esoteric specialism. The only remedy is religious education in the widest sense of the word. That is to say, a general introduction to the world of religious truth and the higher forms of spiritual reality.

Now the Christian world of the past was exceptionally well provided with ways of access to spiritual realities. Christian culture was essentially a sacramental culture which embodied religious truth in visible and palpable forms: art and architecture, music and poetry and drama, philosophy and history were all used as channels for the communication of religious truth. Today all these channels have been closed by unbelief or choked by ignorance, so that Christianity has been deprived of its means of outward expression and communication.

It is the task of Christian education at the present time to recover these lost channels of communication and to restore contact between religion and modern society—between the world of spiritual reality and the world of social experience. Of course this is not what is commonly meant by education, which is usually confined within the narrow limits of schools and examinations. But instruction cannot achieve much unless it has a culture behind it; and Christian culture is essentially humanist, in as much as there is nothing human which does not come within its sphere and which does not in some way belong to it.

Thus Christian culture is a very rich and wide culture: richer than modern secular culture, because it has a greater spiritual depth and is not confined to a single level of reality; and wider than that of any of the Oriental religions because it is more catholic and many-sided. For the average modern man, however, it is more or less a lost world and one from which even the modern Christian has been partially estranged by his secular environment and tradition. Consequently Christians have a double task: first, to recover their own cultural inheritance, and secondly to communicate it to a sub-religious or neo-pagan world. I do not believe that the second of these is as difficult as it appears at first sight, because people are becoming more and more aware that something is lacking in their culture; and there are many who are still far from positive religious belief but who possess a good deal of intellectual curiosity about religion which may become the seed of something more.

Apart from the Communist and dogmatic secularist, there exists a growing consciousness of the inadequacy of rationalism, alike as a philosophy of life and as a method of education. The influence of modern psychology above all has made men realize that their behavior is never entirely determined by rational motives, and that the power of enlightened self-interest—and even of class interest—is far less extensive than the nineteenth century believed. Hence we are no longer satisfied with an education which confines the mind entirely to the sphere of rational consciousness, which cultivates the intelligence and starves the emotions, which ignores the existence of the unconscious forces in psychological life and concentrates its attention on the surface activity of the mind. For such an education inevitably produces an internal schism in personality and culture which is ultimately disastrous. Sooner or later the forces that have been ignored and repressed take their revenge and destroy the rational unity of the personality and the culture by their violent eruption into the sphere of consciousness.

It is true that the psychologists themselves have had their own form of rationalism and materialism which has led them to concentrate their attention on a single aspect of the unconscious—the repression of the sexual impulses—and to neglect the rest. But this is easy enough to explain, since modern psychology began as a form of individual psychiatry and was not primarily concerned with the problems of society and culture.

But it is impossible to understand these social problems in terms of the Freudian dualism between unconscious impulse and rational consciousness. Human life—and especially the life of man in the higher cultures—involves three different psychological levels. There is first the sub-rational life of unconscious instinct and impulse which plays such a large part in human life, especially the life of the masses. Secondly there is the level of conscious voluntary effort and rational activity which is the sphere of culture, *par excellence*. And finally there is the super-rational level of spiritual experience, which is the sphere not only of religion but of the highest creative forces of cultural achievement—the intuitions of the artist, the poet and the philosopher—and also of certain forms of scientific intuition which seem to transcend the sphere of rational calculation and research.

Now in the past all the great civilizations of the East and the West have recognized this world of spiritual experience as the supreme end of human culture in general and of education in particular. It is only during the last two centuries that Western man has attempted to deny its existence and to create a completely secular and rationalized form of culture. For a time the experiment succeeded, but only so long as it was carried on by men who had been trained in the tradition of the old humanist culture and who accepted its moral values and intellectual ideals with almost religious conviction.

But as soon as this minority culture gave way to the rule of the masses, with the coming of universal education and universal suffrage and universal mechanization, the new secular culture proved unable to control the sub-rational forces which are always present below the surface of culture. During the present century these forces have manifested themselves in a succession of revolutions and wars which have steadily increased in violence and destructiveness until they endanger the existence of Western civilization itself.

The true cause of this phenomenon is neither political nor economic, but psychological. It is the direct result of the onesided rationalization of modern culture and of the starvation and frustration of man's spiritual nature. In reality the conflicts of human nature and society cannot be solved either on the material or on the rational plane. The divergent forces of unconscious impulse and rational purpose can only be reconciled by the subordination of both of them to a higher spiritual principle.

For the third psychological plane which I have mentioned—the plane of spiritual experience and religious faith and intuitive vision—is also the center of unity for man and society. It is here that a culture finds its focus and its common spiritual ends; and here also is the source of the higher moral values which are accepted not merely as rules imposed by society for its own welfare but as a sacred law which finds its tribunal in the human heart and the individual conscience.

In the last resort every civilization depends not on its material resources and its methods of production but on the spiritual vision of its greatest minds and on the way in which this experience is transmitted to the community by faith and tradition and education. Where unifying spiritual vision is lost—where it is no longer transmitted to the community as a whole—the civilization decays. "Where there is no vision, the people perish."

This vital element in human life has been denied or forgotten during the triumphant expansion of modern secular civilization during the last century. It is only by the rediscovery of this lost dimension of culture and by the recovery of man's spiritual vision that it is possible to save humanity from self-destruction. This is the real task before modern education—a task so great and so different from what men have been accustomed to look for from education that there are many who will deny that it is possible. Yet there can be no doubt that in the past, not only in Europe but in every great civilization, the higher forms of culture were always orientated toward this ideal of spiritual knowledge, and there were few who would have denied that the true object of education was the cultivation of man's spiritual faculties.

However at the present day the very success of our civilization in terms of material wealth and technical achievement has led modern culture further and further from its spiritual center and has destroyed our sense of spiritual community. This divorce of culture from its spiritual foundations is the malady of our age and it may well be fatal to the society which gives way to it completely. Nevertheless there is no reason to believe that the disease is inevitable or incurable. The deeper levels of the human consciousness have not been lost by the changes of the last one hundred and fifty years; they have only been obscured or overlaid by surface activities. The time has come for a movement in the reverse direction—a movement from the circumference to the center—which will restore the lost balance between the outer world of mechanized activity and the inner world of spiritual experience.

It seems to me that the time has come when the universities should consider whether it is not possible to do more for Christian studies. The Christian culture of the past was an organic whole. It was not confined to theology; it expressed itself also in philosophy and literature, in art and music, society and institutions; and none of these forms of expression can be understood completely unless they are seen in relation to the rest. But under existing conditions this is impossible. One can study some parts of the whole in detail but never the whole itself. To understand the development of Christian culture it must be studied in all its three major phases—Ancient, Medieval and Modern; Patristic, Scholastic and Humanist; Byzantine, Gothic and Baroque.[3] At the most it is possible to study one of the first two parts of these triads in isolation from the rest, while the third cannot be studied at all. The result of this situation is that we tend to view Christian culture exclusively in one of its phases only. Thus the men of the nineteenth-century Catholic revival saw it exclusively in its medieval phase, so that they identified Christian culture with medieval culture, and especially with the culture of the thirteenth century, while others

3. But each of these phases is further divisible into two ages as I have shown in detail in Chapter 3.

have followed the same course with the culture of the Patristic age. And the effect has been to narrow our whole conception of the subject so that we fail to see how it transcends the limitations of any particular age or social environment.

Of course it may be objected that the subject is too vast a field to be studied as a whole. But the same may be said more or less of any great culture—such as Hellenism or Islam or the civilization of China—yet in those cases any specialized study of the past must be accompanied by a general study of the whole.

This gap in our education caused by the absence of any systematic study of Christian culture is now more and more being recognized by the specialists themselves. In a recent American survey on the place of religion in higher education sponsored by the American Council of Education, the writer of the section on Music, Paul E. Langer, asserts:

The great problems underlying the relation of art and religion are seldom touched upon in the literature of the subject. As a rule most writers confuse religious thought and its manifestations in art with the mere existence of church music. . . .

Many writers, even those excellent in the technical aspects of their field, echo the somewhat naïve popular conceptions of the utter decadence of the Church of Rome during the High Renaissance. Nothing is said about the Catholic Reform, of the thousands of great religious paintings, masses and motets that were produced in profusion during this supposedly godless era. And nothing is said about the manner in which the old church met the challenge of the new, the artistic effects of the Counter-Reformation, the role of the Jesuits, etc. The regenerated force of Catholic dogma, the first artistic affirmation of the Counter Reformation that are summed up in the work of the Palestrina, are recognized but not explained.

These criticisms were made with particular reference to *The Oxford History of Music.* But the same criticism could be made in every field; above all in history, where a great standard work like *The Cambridge Modern History* ignores the whole subject of Baroque culture. No doubt things are better today than when the Cambridge volumes were first published. The tide of opinion has changed, but even so the general study of Christian culture is ignored both in university curricula and by educated opinion at large. Until this has been changed, the secularization of modern civilization will go on unchecked. Christians can only react successfully through cultural and educational channels and they are unable to do so unless they possess either their own institutes of higher education or reasonable opportunities for the study of Christian culture within the existing system.

It is true that Christians do not always recognize this. There are many who look on Christianity and culture as alien from one another and who regard the world of culture as part of "this world," the world that lies in darkness under the dominion of evil. In their extreme forms such views are irreconcilable with Catholicism. Nevertheless there is a kind of Catholic Puritanism which separates itself as far as possible from secular culture and adopts an attitude of withdrawal and intransigency. Now this attitude of withdrawal is perfectly justifiable on Catholic principles. It is the spirit of the Fathers of the Desert and of the martyrs and confessors of the primitive church. But it means that Christianity must become an underground movement and that the only place for Christian life and for Christian culture is in the desert and the catacombs. Under modern conditions, however, it may be questioned if such a withdrawal is possible. Today the desert no longer exists and the modern state exerts no less authority underground in the subway and the air raid shelter than it does on the earth and in the air. The totalitarian state—and perhaps the modern state in general—is not satisfied with passive obedience; it demands full co-operation from the cradle to the grave. Consequently the challenge of secularism must be met on the cultural level, if it is to be met at all; and if Christians cannot assert their right to exist in the sphere of higher education, they will eventually be pushed not only out of modern culture but out of physical existence. That is already the issue in Communist countries, and it will also become the issue in England and America if we do not use our opportunities while we still have them. We are still living internally on the capital of the past and externally on the existence of a vague atmosphere of religious tolerance which has already lost its justification in contemporary secular ideology. It is a precarious situation which cannot be expected to endure indefinitely, and we ought to make the most of it while it lasts.

And I believe that it is the field of higher education that offers the greatest opportunities; first on the ground of economy of effort, because a comparatively small expenditure of time and money is likely to produce more decisive results than a much greater expenditure at a lower level. And secondly because this is the sphere where there is most freedom of action and where the tradition of intellectual and spiritual freedom is likely to survive longest. Moreover the need for action is especially urgent in this field, because the social changes of the last half century have extinguished the old tradition of independent private scholarship to which these studies owed so much in the past. But today the disappearance of the leisure class makes this kind of unorganized individual scholarship impossible. Either the church or the universities must carry on the tradition and make themselves responsible for the maintenance of these studies or the work will not be done at all.

As I have pointed out elsewhere, every turning point in European history has been associated with a change in education or a movement of educational reform. We are today in the presence of one of these turning points of history and consequently the time is ripe for a new movement of educational reform.

This reform can be conceived in two alternative ways. On the one hand it can be seen as a return to the tradition of Christian education which has always been one of the main sources of Western culture and which still remains today as the representative and guardian of the spiritual tradition in our civilization. On the other hand it can be seen in terms of psychology as a movement to bring modern education into closer relation with the psychological bases of society and to re-establish the internal balance of our culture.

But these two alternatives are not in contradiction to one another. They are rather two different aspects of the same process. It is necessary to extend the range of modern education not so much in width as in depth, and the obvious way to do this is by a better understanding of the Christian tradition as the spiritual source and the moral basis of our culture.

Christianity and Western Culture

THE SURVIVAL OF a civilization depends on the continuity of its educational tradition. A common educational system creates a common world of thought with common intellectual values and a common inheritance of knowledge, which makes a society conscious of its identity and gives it a common memory of its past. Consequently any breach in the continuity of the educational tradition involves a corresponding breach in the continuity of the civilization; so that if the breach were a complete one, it would be far more revolutionary than any political or economic change, since it would mean the birth of a new civilization, or at any rate the death of the old one.

I do not know how far these facts are generally admitted, or whether they would be regarded as a platitude or as a paradox. Certainly I do not think that modern opinion fully realizes the immense antiquity and persistence of the great educational traditions. Perhaps it is easier to see this in the case of the more remote and alien civilizations than in that of our own, for example in the case of China where the continuity of the Confucian tradition of education and learning has always impressed the Western observer. But I do not think we give sufficient consideration to the parallel phenomenon of the tradition of liberal education in Western culture which is practically as old as the Confucian tradition in China and which has played such an essential part in forming the mind and maintaining the continuity of Western civilization. Only the specialists in classical studies (and by no means all of them) realize the full significance of that great tradition which had its origins twenty-four centuries ago in ancient Athens, and which was handed down from the Latin rhetoricians to the monks of the West, from the medieval church to the humanists of the Renaissance, and from the humanists to the schools and universities of modern Europe and America.

The failure to recognize the importance of this element of educational tradition in our civilization is the more serious because everywhere today civilization is being subjected to the growing pressure of revolutionary forces which threaten it with complete disintegration. In the East, above all in China, the issue is a comparatively simple one. There the tradition of an ancient and intensely conservative culture has been violently interrupted by the sudden invasion of a new political order, a new social system and a new ideological doctrine, all of them closely related to one another.

But in the West the situation is a much more complicated one. Western culture has never rejected change as such. It has given birth again and again to critical and revolutionary movements and it has been strong enough to overcome them and even to profit by them. And so our problem is not that of an alien invasion but rather of an internal revolt and a schism between the divergent tendencies in our own culture.

What makes the present situation different, and more serious than in the past, is that European civilization is suffering from a sense of discouragement and a loss of faith in its own values, such as we have never experienced before.

Now it must be admitted that this reaction is neither incomprehensible nor unjustifiable. For more than a century Western man was inspired by a boundless faith in the absolute superiority of Western civilization and in its inevitable progress to higher and higher stages of social perfection. It was only during the lifetime of the present generation that these utopian hopes have been suddenly dissipated by the bitter realities of the two world wars and their sequel. It is true that these disasters have been mainly political and economic. There is little real evidence that the internal resources of European culture, in science and literature and intellectual activity, have declined in the catastrophic way in which the intellectual culture of the classical world declined during the later centuries of the Roman Empire.

No doubt the nineteenth-century faith in Western civilization and progress was so largely based on material considerations of wealth and power and external expansion that it was not fitted to cope with the situation which has arisen from Europe's sudden loss of her position of world hegemony. But the disillusionment caused by the present crisis of European culture is not confined to a reaction against the nineteenth-century idolatry of material progress; it also affects the permanent values of Western culture and extends to the even more fundamental tradition of Western Christendom. To some extent this is the inevitable result of the sudden extension of the Western democratic ideology to peoples who in other respects possessed a totally different tradition of culture. The old nationalisms were the children of Europe. They all shared the same background of Western culture and Christian moral traditions. But the new nationalisms of Asia and Africa have no such common background. They belong to different cultural worlds—some, like China and India, of immense antiquity and complexity; others, like the peoples of Africa and Oceania, only barely emerging from the darkness of barbarism, but all eager to claim cultural as well as political equality in the new cosmopolitan society of nations.

There is a tendency in the present day to extend the democratic principle from politics to culture. As men are equal in the democratic state, so the peoples should be equal in the international organization of the new world, and if the peoples are equal then their cultures must be equal also. Hence any claim on the part of the ancient world-cultures to possess a tradition of universal validity represents a kind of cultural imperialism which is no less unpopular than the military and economic imperialism of the Great Powers. In its extreme form this idea of "cultural democracy" is obviously inacceptable. We cannot regard the culture of a particular Melanesian people or even the Melanesians as a whole as in any sense equivalent to the culture of China or India. Nevertheless the tendency to cultural relativism is just as strong among the scholars who have made a lifetime's study of the problems of civilization. We see a striking example of this in the case of Dr. Arnold Toynbee, whose whole work is based on the principle of the philosophical equivalence of cultures and who rejects the idea of the unity of civilization as a one-sided simplification of history due to the pride and provincialism of Western historians. The unification of the world by Western civilization is a fact that he does not deny, but it is a purely technological achievement which is entirely independent of cultural and spiritual values. In the new world-unity all the great historic spiritual and cultural traditions will have equal shares. As he writes in a striking passage of his Creighton lecture of 1947: "our own descendants are not going to be just Western like ourselves." They are going to be heirs of Chinese philosophy as well as of Hellenism, of Buddhism as well as Christianity, heirs of Zoroaster and Mohammed as well as of the Hebrew prophets and the Christian apostles.[1]

Thus Dr. Toynbee's historical relativism is not limited to the material and political aspects of culture; it extends even more explicitly to its spiritual traditions. His doctrine of the philosophic equivalence of the different world civilizations is carried further to the theological plane and seems to involve the spiritual equivalence of the different world religions.

Now it is obvious that Christians cannot accept this historical relativism when it is carried into the sphere of theology. But

1. On "The Unification of the World and the Change in Historical Perspective," reprinted in *Civilization on Trial*, pp. 62–97.

is it any more acceptable on other intellectual levels? Philosophy and science also involve objective intellectual values and it is difficult to see how these are to be reconciled with a thoroughgoing historical relativism which leaves no room for any judgment of values as between different civilizations.

It seems clear that we must look for some middle way between the blind faith of the nineteenth century in the superiority of Western culture and the scepticism regarding the ultimate values of Western culture which result from the relativist view of the philosophic equivalence of cultures. From this point of view it is instructive to consider the views propounded by Cardinal Newman in Dublin almost a century ago in his inaugural lecture on "Christianity and Letters" which is the first of his "Discourses on University Subjects."

In this lecture Newman states in the most unequivocal form his belief in the unique value of the Western tradition of culture. After speaking of the multiplicity of human societies and the apparent chaos of the ebb and flow of history, he goes on:

But there is one remarkable association which attracts the attention of the philosopher, not political nor religious, or at least only partially and not essentially such, which began in the earliest times and grew with each succeeding age, till it reached its complete development, and then continued on vigorous and unwearied, and which still remains as vigorous and unwearied as ever it was. Its bond is a common civilization; and though there are other civilizations in the world, as there are other societies, yet this civilization, together with the society which is its creation and its home, is so distinctive and luminous in its character and so utterly without a rival upon the face of the earth, that the association may fitly assume to itself the title of Human Society and its civilization the abstract term "Civilization."[2]

At first sight this may seem a typical example of the nineteenth-century liberal attitude toward European culture with its belief in the unilinear continuity of social progress and its

2. *Idea of a University*, p. 251, cf. the whole passage, 250–54.

uncritical acceptance of its own standards and values as universally valid. The remarkable thing is that it comes from a man who was the lifelong adversary of liberalism, and who fully realized the fallacies of the creed of secular progress and the deceptive character of the material power and prosperity of the modern Western civilization.

Moreover he does not identify the great central tradition of human civilization with Christian civilization or even with the tradition of Christendom. For he goes on to speak of Christianity as the second great social tradition of humanity, analogous to and to a certain extent parallel with the first, but possessing its own independent principles of life and law of development. So that while these two associations are never exactly coincident, they occupy approximately the same field in space and time and have continued to co-operate with and react on one another throughout the course of their histories.

Now if I understand Newman's thought aright, he believes that his analogy of Christianity and Western civilization is no accident but a part of the providential order of history. The inchoate world community of Western culture provided the natural preparation and foundation for the diffusion of the new spiritual society in which the human race was finally to recover its lost unity. It is this Christian philosophy of history that underlies the whole of Newman's doctrine on education. And in fact nothing shows more clearly the relation between these two traditions both in their theoretical independence and their practical co-operation than the history of Christian education. It was the union of the classical tradition of human letters—as represented by the liberal arts—with the Christian tradition of religious doctrine—as represented by the faculty of theology— which gave birth to the European universities. More than that, it was the dominant factor in the formation of Western thought and one which no historian of European philosophy or literature or culture can afford to disregard for a moment.

This then is Newman's conclusion: The two traditions are different in origin and operation but their

heir and successor is one and the same. The grace stored in Jerusalem and the gifts which radiate from Athens are made over and concentrated in Rome. This is true as a matter of history. Rome has inherited both sacred and profane learning—she has perpetuated and dispensed the traditions of Moses and David in the supernatural order, and of Homer and Aristotle in the natural. To separate their distinct teachings, human and divine, which meet in Rome, is to retrogress; it is to rebuild the Jewish temple and to plant anew the groves of Academus.[3]

Newman's theory has been described by a distinguished Catholic educator as "a philosophy of severance." The passage that I have quoted shows how unjust this criticism is. For, more perhaps than any man of his generation, Newman stood for the principle of unity in education, in religion and in culture. It is true that today no one can ignore the schism in Western educational and intellectual traditions. In that sense perhaps we are all of us "philosophers of severance." For the separation which Newman condemned had already taken place and has been going further and deeper ever since. First the liberal arts were separated from theology by the secularization and religious divisions of modern culture. The Reformation rebuilt the Jewish temple and the Renaissance replanted the groves of Academus. Secondly the science of nature took the place of theology as the queen of the sciences or rather as Science in the absolute sense. And finally the liberal arts themselves have been ousted by the growth of a new series of technical disciplines which have reduced higher education to a jungle of competing specialisms.

Newman saw the first and second phases of this process and he makes a very interesting parallel between the temporary dethronement of the arts by theology in the thirteenth century and the utilitarian and scientific reaction against classical education which was characteristic of nineteenth-century liberalism. What he did not foresee was that science itself was destined to be dethroned not by a revival of humanism but by the emergence

3. *Ibid.*, p. 265.

of political ideology as the final authority in the sphere of education and culture. The new totalitarian ideologies have nothing in common with either the Christian or the humanist traditions but they are also no less opposed to that disinterested pursuit of knowledge and truth which inspired the scientific movement of the past three centuries. They regard education as a general technique for influencing human behavior, and science as a series of special techniques which must be strictly subordinated to the economic and military plans of the State.

Now this totalitarian demand for the political control of science and education finds its natural allies in the modern instrumentalist view of science and the disintegration of higher education into a mass of unrelated specialisms. Since he social importance of science and education has steadily increased while the cultural leadership of Christianity and humanism has diminished, it was inevitable that some other power should be called in to provide the directive element which modern technology itself cannot supply. And where was this power to be found except in the State?

Thus totalitarianism only accentuates a tendency to political control which is inherent in the nature of technological civilization. Even in Western democratic society, which consciously rejects the totalitarian solution, the element of state control and political direction inevitably tends to increase, owing to the fact that the State has taken the place of the independent organs of culture as the paymaster and controller, first of universal public education, and eventually of higher education and scientific research. Hence it is not surprising that some leading representatives of democratic educational theory, like the late Professor Dewey, go as far as the Communists in their subordination of education to the needs of the political community. In Professor Dewey's view the function of education is not to communicate knowledge or to train scholars in the liberal arts: it is to serve Democracy by making every individual participate in the formation of social values and contribute to what he calls "the final pooled intelligence" which is the democratic mind.

No doubt Dewey's democratic community is not so crudely political as that of the totalitarian ideologies. What he has in mind is not the political organization of the state but the community of popular culture. But it is no less fatal to the traditional concept of culture since it reverses the natural relation between the teacher and the taught and subordinates the higher intellectual and moral values to the mind of the masses. It is indeed difficult to see on these principles how any of the higher forms of culture could ever have arisen. For even the most primitive and barbarous peoples known to us achieve Dewey's ideals of social participation and communal experience no less completely by their initiation ceremonies and tribal dances than does the modern democratic educationalist with all his elaborate programs for the integration of the school with life.

The original founder of democratic educational theory, Jean-Jacques Rousseau, who was more consistent than his descendants, might not have objected to my criticism since he believed that civilization was rather a mistake and that the human race would have been better without it. But the modern democrat, like Professor Dewey, usually has a whole-hearted and naïve faith in the value of modern civilization, and he wishes to accept the inheritance of culture while rejecting the painful process of social and intellectual discipline by which alone that inheritance has been acquired and transmitted.

The Christian educationalist who does not share these democratic illusions, but who equally rejects the totalitarian simplification that reduces culture to a political instrument, is therefore faced with two very definite problems: how to maintain the unity of culture in an age of technical specialization, and how to preserve the tradition of Christian culture in an age of secularism.

No doubt the two ancient traditions of Christian theology and classical humanism still remain but they have themselves become specialized studies which are confined to a comparatively small minority, and they no longer dominate the university and the whole system of higher education as in the past.

Yet some unifying study is absolutely necessary if higher education is not to be entirely disintegrated into an inorganic mass of technical specialisms.

This need has been strongly felt in recent years in the United States where the development of specialization and utilitarian vocational courses has proceeded further and faster than in Europe. In some American universities there has been for many years now a course in contemporary culture which is compulsory for all freshmen. But I do not feel that a course of this kind really provides the unifying principle that we need. Where a civilization has lost its internal unity, as ours has done, it also loses its intelligible unity and the field of study becomes practically unlimited. For example the two volumes of sources which are the textbook for this course at Columbia University amount to more than two thousand pages and they include such diverse material as the Bull *Unam Sanctam* and the Communist Manifesto, Magna Carta and the Weimar Constitution, St. Augustine's views on Original Sin and William James's views on pragmatism; the Hat Act of 1732 and *Quadragesimo Anno*. No first-year student can possibly absorb such a pabulum. It needs a lifetime to digest it. And the same difficulty stands in the way of all attempts to find the necessary principle of unity in an encyclopedic subject like World History or the History of Science.

The success of the old classical education was largely due to the fact that it limited itself to a single cultural tradition and was able to study it thoroughly. Nevertheless, as we have seen, the classical tradition was not the only unifying element in Western culture. The tradition of Christian culture is even more important and reaches far deeper into the European consciousness. For it is this and not science or humanism which was the spiritual bond that transcended the divisions and antagonisms of race and class and nationality and created that society of peoples which was the community of Western Chrisendom.

Why has this essential factor not received more recognition in our educational system? No doubt to some extent it is due to the tendency of modern historians to concentrate their whole attention on the development of their own national traditions, both political and cultural, and to ignore or to take for granted the existence of that wider spiritual community out of which the national cultures have sprung. But this is a comparatively recent phenomenon, and the source of the difficulty is much older. It goes back at least four hundred years and has its origin in the one-sided classicism of the humanist educators who treated the previous thousand years of Western culture as a kind of cultural vacuum which educated men could afford to ignore.

But to do this is not only to ignore the value and achievement of Christian culture, it is to destroy the intelligible unity of Western civilization. For it is only in the light of this unbroken tradition that we can understand the nature of Western unity and the spiritual forces which have influenced and enriched the life of all the peoples of the West.

Now it seems to me that it is in the study of this unjustly neglected tradition that we can find that unifying principle which modern education requires. Unlike the new encyclopedic studies of which I have spoken, it is a manageable subject with a clearly defined field of study. Unlike the old discipline of classical studies, it has a direct relevance to the modern world and to the needs of men today. For although the old order of Christendom no longer exists, we Christians are not a negligible minority, and every Christian, whatever his special vocation and technique, has a general interest in the Christian past and a common responsibility for the preservation of the inheritance of Christian culture.

The main objection to such a solution is that it is impracticable, owing to the vagueness of its terms of reference and the width of its field of study. But as I have said, it is far less vague and indefinite than the new encyclopedic subjects like "modern civilization" or world history which have been actually introduced into university curricula.

No one denies the existence of Christian history, Christian philosophy, Christian literature and Christian institutions. And though these have never been studied as part of an integrated whole in the same way as classical history, philosophy and literature have been, there is no reason why they should not be.

In fact the lack of an integrated study of this kind makes the detailed study of any particular aspect of European culture extremely difficult. For example it is impossible to understand the development and interrelation of the different European vernacular literatures unless we have studied the common Western tradition of medieval Latin culture by which all the early vernacular literatures were so deeply influenced. This has been fully demonstrated by Dr. E. R. Curtius in his very important book on *European Literature and the Latin Middle Ages* which was published in 1948. And if his conclusions are not more widely known and have not made a deeper impression on educated opinion, this is because there can be no public for such works so long as the study of Christian culture is nobody's business and finds no place in the curriculum of the modern university.

Nevertheless, it is difficult to exaggerate the educative value of such a study. It opens new avenues of approach to the civilization of the ancient world in which Christianity was born and to the civilization of the modern world which, however secularized it may be, still retains an organic relation to the Christian past. And between the two there stands not the cultural vacuum of a Dark Age of medieval barbarism but the historic reality of Christendom as a social and cultural unity.

The more deeply the student penetrates into this great religious and cultural unity the more aware he will become of the essential continuity of Western civilization and of the spiritual dynamism and fecundity of the Christian tradition.

No doubt the development of an integrated study of this kind involves the co-operation of scholars and specialists in many different fields. But the same is true of the old classical education. The school of Litterae Humaniores, which dominated university studies at Oxford so long and so effectively, was itself a most comprehensive study, since it covered the cultural development of the ancient world from Horner to the age of the Antonines and involved a comparatively thorough study of ancient philosophy and history as well as literature.

It is no more difficult in principle to conceive of a unified study of Christian culture which would include Christian philosophy, Christian literature and Christian history, studied in close relation with one another. In both cases the field of study comprises three successive cultural epochs[4]: first the period of formation—the Homeric age of Greece and the Patristic period of Christian culture; secondly the classical age—the fifth and fourth centuries B.C. and the twelfth and thirteenth centuries A.D.; and thirdly the age of transmission and diffusion—the Roman Hellenistic period in the ancient world and the age of the formation of the vernacular literatures and cultures in Western Europe.

From the traditional humanist point of view it will perhaps seem absurd and shocking to regard the great centuries of the Middle Ages as the classical age of our culture. But the more we study Western culture as a whole the more impossible it becomes to accept the valuation of Christian culture which has been the orthodox view of the educated world since the Renaissance. The age of St. Thomas and Dante is more central and more universal than the age of Leo X and Luther or than that of Descartes and Corneille or that of Locke and Dryden. And I think historians are more and more coming to realize the eccentric and one-sided character of the Renaissance theory of culture.

Far more serious however are the practical objections to a study of Christian culture such as I have suggested. I fear it must be admitted that the introduction of a new basic integrative study of this kind is not practical politics. Modern education has become such a vast and highly organized system that the teacher is not as free as in the past to choose his own path—at least that is the case in England and, I believe, on the Continent. Nevertheless we can at least hold it in mind as a goal for the future and attempt to direct and co-ordinate our

4. See note 3, p. 79.

studies in this direction. In any case I believe that it is impossible to overestimate the importance of this problem, for it is only by some such study that we can overcome the schism between religion and culture which began in the age of the Renaissance and Reformation and was completed by the Enlightenment and the Revolution. This schism is the great tragedy of Western culture. It must be solved if Christian culture is to survive. And the survival or restoration of Christian culture involves not only the fate of our own people and our own civilization but the fate of humanity and the future of the world.

8

Is the Church Too Western?

URING THE LAST four or five centuries, the expansion of
Christianity in the non-European world has been associated with the expansion of Western colonial power. The missionaries went hand in hand with the European explorers and traders
and conquerors who sailed unknown seas and discovered new
continents or found new contacts with ancient peoples; indeed
to a great extent the missionaries were themselves the pioneers
in the work of discovery. Consequently it was inevitable that
the peoples of the Far East and Africa and the island world of the
Pacific should have seen Christianity as something essentially
Western, as the religion of the foreigners, the Sahibs in India,
the Hairy Barbarians in China and the White Man in Africa and
Oceania. And so it is not surprising that the rise of the modern
nationalist movement in Asia and Africa with its slogans of
anticolonialism and antiimperialism, and the reassertion of the
traditions of oriental culture against the West, should be accompanied by a reaction against the influence of Western missionaries and often against Christianity itself. As a rule this reaction
has not been a violent one like that which produced the great

persecution of the Christians in Japan in the seventeenth century. It has been political and cultural rather than religious. It has been directed mainly against proselytization and education by foreign missionaries, but it has also led to a demand for a strictly national organization of oriental Christianity and its emancipation from all forms of Western or external control, as we see in the report of the government commission on Christian missions in Madya Pradesh, which proposed that all the Christian Churches in the region should be fused in a single national or provincial body which would be completely autonomous.

Now it is obvious that proposals of this kind are irreconcilable with the fundamental principles of Catholicism. If nationalism—whether in the East or the West—denies the right of the Church to exist as a universal autonomous spiritual society, it is a challenge to the law of God and the kingship of Christ. But this does not mean that the Church is essentially Western. On the contrary, the same principle that forbids us to make the Church a national organization also prevents us from identifying it with a particular civilization. The mission of the Church is essentially universal and it is common to all nations and races— to those of the East equally with those of the West.

We must however distinguish between this ideal universality and the practical limitations imposed by history on the circumstances of the Church's apostolate. By the nature of the case, the missionary is in some sense a stranger to the nation and the culture that he evangelizes. He comes from outside bringing a new doctrine and initiating men into a new society. But however supernatural is his mission, he is a human being who has been born and educated in some particular society and brings his own cultural traditions with him, and hence in some degree his native habits and prejudices. In this sense it is true the missionary tends to be too Western, so that it is his duty to divest himself of his natural prejudices and become assimilated to an alien environment and culture. As he must translate the Christian Gospel into a new language and speak with strange tongues, so too he must learn to think in terms of an alien culture and accept its social standards and values.

Yet this is not the real point at issue. For when men talk, as they do today, about the Church's being too Western they are not thinking of this inevitable but accidental dependence of the missionary on his particular cultural background; they mean rather that the Church herself has become occidentalized: that her philosophy and theology, her liturgy and devotion have been so deeply influenced by fifteen hundred years of association with Western culture that she has become estranged from the Oriental world and no longer speaks to it in terms that the peoples of Asia can understand.

Before we consider what grounds there are for such an assertion it is necessary to determine what we mean by the word "Western." On the one hand there is our modern Western civilization, which has spread so rapidly through the world during the last century. This civilization is indubitably Western, since it owes its distinctive features to the revolutionary changes which originated in Northwestern Europe and North America during the last two centuries. On the other hand there is the ancient tradition of the Catholic Church, which may also be described as Western, in so far as it is the tradition of the Western Church and looks to Rome, the ancient metropolis of the West, as its center and head. Nevertheless it is also a universal tradition, since it first arose at the point where East and West met and it derived its inheritance from them both. And if we look at the Catholic tradition in detail we shall see how this duality runs through all the different aspects of its life.

The Church itself, though it bears a Greek name, Ecclesia, derived from the Greek civic assembly, and is ordered by the Roman spirit of authority and law, is the successor and heir of an Oriental people, set apart from all the peoples of the earth to be the bearer of a divine mission.

Similarly the mind of the Church, as expressed in the authoritative tradition of the teaching of the Fathers, is neither Eastern nor Western but universal. It is expressed in Western languages—in Greek and Latin—but it was in Africa and Asia rather than in Europe that it received its classical formulation.

Greek theology was developed at Alexandria and Antioch and in Cappadocia, while Latin theology owes its terminology and its distinctive character to the African Fathers—Tertullian, Cyprian and above all St. Augustine.

While these men wrote in Latin, it was not the Latin of the Romans; it was a new form of Christian Latin which was developed, mainly in Tunisia, under strong Oriental influence.

And the same is true of the new Christian Latin poetry and of the Latin liturgy itself. No doubt the Roman rite which has outlived and absorbed the other Latin rites bears an indelible mark of the Roman spirit in its simplicity, its severity and its concision. But this does not mean that it is only adapted to the worship of modern Western man, or that its spirit is alien from that of the East. On the contrary it gives it a classical, universal and supertemporal character which is accentuated by its music, which is so remote from the modern West. For what has the Mass to do with Western culture? It is the eternal offering of an eternal priesthood—"without father, without mother, without genealogy, having neither beginning of days, nor end of life, but like the Son of God, continuing a priest for ever" (Heb. 7:3).

It is impossible for us to understand the Church if we regard her as subject to the limitations of human culture. For she is essentially a supernatural organism which transcends human cultures and transforms them to her own ends. As Newman insisted, the Church is not a creed or a philosophy but an imperial power, a "counter Kingdom" which occupies ground and claims to rule over those whom this world's governments had once ruled over without rival. But if the Church is an objective social reality she is not bound to conform herself to cultural divisions. She can take whatever forms and institutions she needs from any culture and organize them into a new unity which is the external expression of her spirit and the organ of her mission to the world. If this is the case, the question we have to ask is not whether the particular elements of this unity are derived from East or West—but whether they are fit instruments of the Church's supernatural purpose. If so, they entirely transcend the sphere of political nationalism and national culture.

Let us take the case of a typical Catholic institution—a religious Order for example. Here the original institution of Christian monasticism was of purely Oriental origin and came into existence in the Egyptian desert in the fourth century. Almost immediately, however, the Church accepted this new way of life as an essential expression of the Christian spirit and spread it East and West from the Atlantic to the Black Sea and the Persian Gulf. And as it grew it adapted itself to the life of the different peoples amongst whom it came, though it remained fully conscious of its origins and of the continuity of its tradition.

It was, however, in the West that this development of monasticism produced the most remarkable fruits. It was here, in the course of the Middle Ages, that there arose the idea of the religious Order as a specialized organ of the Church, dedicated to the performance of some particular spiritual task—preaching or study or the care of the poor and the sick, or the redemption of captives. Since these Orders are specialized some of them are more adapted to one culture than to another, and it may well be that an Order that has been founded to fulfill some special task in medieval Italy or modern America is "too Western" for India or China. But this is not necessarily the case. The essential principle of the Western religious Order has become part of the common tradition of the Church and is capable of being applied to the special circumstances of the East, no less than the West.

There is therefore no need to undo the work of the Christian past and to attempt to create a new type of oriental monasticism modeled on Hindu or Buddhist patterns, for East and West already coexist in the tradition of Christian monasticism, and the same tradition can bear new fruits wherever it is planted. The vital point is not the nationality or the cultural background of the founders but the timeless ideals of prayer and contemplation and the universal spirit of the apostolate for which they are founded.

This I think is the secret of the whole matter. The Church as a divine society possesses an internal principle of life which is capable of assimilating the most diverse materials and imprinting her own image upon them. Inevitably in the course of history there are times when this spiritual energy is temporarily weakened or obscured, and then the Church tends to be judged as a human organization and identified with the faults and limitations of its members. But always the time comes when she renews her strength and once more puts forth her inherent divine energy in the conversion of new peoples and the transformation of old cultures. At no time can we expect this work to be unopposed, for the very fact that the Church represents something entirely different—the intervention of a supernatural principle and the coming of a divine Kingdom—must inevitably arouse the fierce opposition of all those human societies and powers which claim absolute power over man and refuse to admit a superior or rival. One of the strongest and most aggressive of these forces in the modern world is nationalism, and here Christians cannot expect to avoid a conflict. But the conflict is not really one between East and West: it is the old conflict between the spiritual and temporal powers, which was formerly confined largely to the Western world and has now emerged as a burning question in the East, largely owing to the introduction of the political ideologies of the West into Asia and Africa. But East or West, it is basically the same conflict, and alike in East and West the Church stands neither for East nor West but for the universal spiritual society which is destined to embrace them both: "And the nations shall walk in the light of it: and the kings of the earth shall bring their glory and honour into it" (Apoc. 22:24).

PART TWO

Selected Essays

I

The Study of Christian Culture

THE FOLLOWING ESSAYS[1] cover so wide a field in space
and time that it may be difficult for the reader at first sight
to grasp their connection with one another. True, they all deal
with some aspect of "medieval" culture, but the word medieval
is in itself unsatisfactory or insignificant. It was coined by post-
Renaissance scholars to cover the gap between two periods of
positive achievement which were regarded as the only ones worthy of the attention of the educated man—the classical civilization of Greece and Rome and the civilization of modern Europe.
But this conception is the very opposite of that on which this
book is based. What I am concerned with is not the interim
period between two civilizations, but the study of *Christian
Culture*—a culture which is not only worthy of study for its
own sake, but is the source of the actual sociological unity
which we call Europe.

If, as I believe, religion is the key of history and it is impossible to understand a culture unless we understand its religious

1. [This essay appeared as the introduction to *Medieval Essays* (Image, 1959).
—Ed.]

roots, then the Middle Ages are not a kind of waiting-room between two different worlds, but the age which made a new
world, the world from which we come and to which in a sense
we still belong.

But the concept of Christian culture is far wider than that of
the Middle Ages, not only potentially and ideally but actually
and historically. It is true that there have been many Christian
cultures and there may be many more. Nevertheless the main
stream of Christian culture is one and should be studied as an
intelligible historical unity.

The present volume does not, of course, attempt to deal with
this whole subject. It is limited to particular aspects of the
formative process of Christian culture. Even so this formative
process involves three distinct phases of evolution and three
different cultural situations.

In the first place there is the situation of a new religion in
an old culture. This was the situation of Christianity in the
Roman Empire of which I write in the essay on "The Age of
St. Augustine".[2] This process of conflict and conversion produced the first phase of Christian culture—the society of the
Christian Empire and the age of the Fathers. This form of Christian culture was preserved almost unchanged in the Byzantine
world, while in the West it provided a kind of classical standard
or ideal towards which later ages have looked back.

Secondly there is the situation in which the Church entered
the barbarian world not only as the teacher of the Christian
Faith but also as the bearer of a higher culture. This double
impact of Christian culture on the barbarian world which had
its own tradition of culture and its own social institutions produced a state of tension and conflict between two social traditions and two ideals of life which has had a profound influence
on the development of Western culture. Indeed it has never
been completely resolved, since with the coming of modern

2. [A Monument to Saint Augustine (1936). In Medieval Essays, a version of
this essay appeared as "The Christian West and the Fall of the Empire." —Ed.]

nationalism we have seen a conscious attempt to undo the medieval synthesis and to reassert the old pre-Christian national traditions in an idealized form.

In the third place we have the situation in which Christianity inspires a new movement of cultural creativity, in which the new life of the new peoples finds a new expression in consciously Christian forms. This is the medieval synthesis which is the characteristic achievement of the Middle Ages, in the narrower sense of the expression. It would, however, be more correct to describe it as the age of the Western Renaissance for it is essentially the birth of a new world culture. It is to this movement that most of these essays are devoted, since it is the decisive moment in the history of Western culture and since it is possible to study it at first hand in the new vernacular literatures which are its living voice.

Finally I have devoted an essay to the great rival cultures of Western Islam, the influence and importance of which have hitherto been so insufficiently recognized by the Western historians of medieval culture.[3] It is sometimes said that the emphasizing of the Christian character of Western culture makes us blind to the value of other civilizations. I believe that the case is just the contrary. The more we understand Christendom, the more we shall understand Islam, and the more we underestimate the religious element in our own culture the less we shall appreciate the cultures of the non-European world.

At the present time it is exceptionally difficult to realize this affinity between the world cultures because we have become accustomed to think of them primarily in racial and geographical terms; we see Western civilization as the civilization of the white man against the civilization of Asiatics and coloured men. To some extent this was always so and it is easy to find signs of racial antipathy in the Western accounts of the Huns or the Mongols and in Moslem accounts of the Franks. Nevertheless

3. ["The Moslem East and the Oriental Background of Later Medieval Culture," *Medieval Essays.* —Ed.]

the essential principle of the great world cultures of the past (with the partial exception of India and China) was to be found not in the community of race but in the bond of a common religious faith, or as Moslems and medieval Christians put it, in a common *law*. Both in the North and South, on the Baltic and in the Western Mediterranean, the frontiers of Christendom cut across the geographical and racial frontiers, so that the pagan Lithuanians and the Moslem Spaniards belonged to different cultural and spiritual worlds. While on the other hand, the Christians of Asia, however remote they might be in speech and behaviour, were felt to be in some sense fellow-citizens in the great society of Christendom.

This sense endured longer in the East than in the West. Armenian poets were still composing elegies on the destruction of the Christian Kingdom of Jerusalem[4] when the descendants of the Crusaders themselves were destroying Christendom in the interests of power politics; while at the extreme limit of the Christian world, the little kingdom of Karthli still fought a lonely crusade against overwhelming odds and maintained the tradition of Christian chivalry down to the age of Voltaire.[5] The existence of this culture which was to such a large extent common to East and West and of the great society of Christendom which was its bearer, is one of the main facts of world history which no historian can ignore without falsifying his whole understanding of the past. That it is so largely ignored or forgotten at the present day is one of the most serious faults in our present system of education. No doubt there are many reasons which explain though they do not excuse it.

4. Cf. The elegy on the conquest of Jerusalem in 1187 composed by Nerses Mokatzi in 1622. [Mokatzi (d. 1625) was an Armenian monk whose many works recounted the troubles of exiled Armenians and related them to biblical themes. —Ed.]

5. The great martyr queen, St. Kethevan, suffered at Shiraz in 1624 and the author of the last heroic epic or *chanson de geste*—the *Guramiani*—survived until the beginning of the nineteenth century. [St. Kethevan (Catherine) was killed by order of Abbas I, king of Persia. Karthli was in present-day Bulgaria. —Ed.]

A secularized society must inevitably be unfavourable to the study of Christian culture, since its own way of life and its beliefs and ideals are totally alien. We see this most clearly in the case of Communist society which is professedly antireligious and regards the history of Christian culture as nothing but the story of an illusion which has led mankind down a blind alley for 1,700 years. And a similar attitude is also to be found in a less extreme form in the educational theory of democratic idealists like the late Professor Dewey, who believe that education is essentially an instrument for creating a common democratic mentality and that all study must be directed towards sharing the experience of contemporary democratic society and creating new democratic values.

But even before our society had undergone the extreme process of secularization in recent times, the study of Christian culture had never received the attention that it deserved. It was at once ignored and taken for granted: ignored by the Humanists who concentrated their attention on the study of classical antiquity, and taken for granted by the theologians whose energies were devoted to strictly ecclesiastical studies and paid little attention to the non-theological aspects of Christian culture. The Humanists may have been good Christians, and the theologians may have been good humanists, but between them they left vast fields of Christian culture and history uncultivated and disregarded.

The leaders of the Catholic revival in the early nineteenth century—men like Goerres and Ozanam and Montalembert[6]—made a serious attempt to remedy this neglect and to promote the study and appreciation of Christian culture, but their efforts were too sporadic and too uncritical to be entirely successful. The age saw indeed a great renaissance of medieval studies but the ultimate beneficiary was not Christian culture but the mod-

6. [Johann Joseph von Goerres (1776–1848), Antoine Frédéric Ozanam (1813–1853) and Charles-Forbes-René, comte de Montalembert (1810–1870), were Catholic writers and politicians. Goerres was German, Ozanam and Montalembert French. —Ed.]

ern cult of nationalism which has had such a vast influence on the whole development of modern education and modern historical studies.

It is generally agreed today that this influence has not been altogether wholesome. In its extreme forms, as in the nationalist ideology imposed on school and university by National Socialism, it has been one of the most destructive forces that have threatened the existence of Western culture. But even the milder forms of nationalist history, such as prevailed generally in Europe and America in the second half of the nineteenth century, were also unfavourable to the cause of civilization, inasmuch as they tended to widen the gulf that divides nation from nation and to minimize or ignore the elements that are common to Western culture as a whole.

Nevertheless it is useless to look for a remedy to the opposite ideology of Communism with its cosmopolitan ideals of world revolution and the international solidarity of the workers. For it produces just the same subordination of culture to politics and the same compulsory imposition of an exclusive party ideology on society which characterize the rival forms of totalitarianism. Whatever the faults of the old humanist culture, it was wider in sympathy, richer in values and more civilized in its social attitude than the new political faiths. Nevertheless it is hard to see how it can survive in the harsh climate of a world that is subject to the pressures of total war and mass propaganda. It was essentially the culture of a privileged class and of a society that possessed not only leisure, but a kind of moral security which did not depend on political freedom or material wealth but on universally accepted standards of personal honour and civilized behaviour.

From this point of view the world of Christian culture is nearer to our own than is the world of Humanism. The former was always at grips with the problem of barbarism. It had to face the external threat of alien and hostile cultures, while at the same time it was in conflict with barbaric elements within its own social environment which it had to control and transform. And in this work it could not rely on the existence of common standards of civilization or common moral values. It had to create its own moral order before it could achieve an ordered form of civilized existence.

The study of such a culture with its problems, its failures and its achievements, involves a much deeper level of human experience than either the self-centered and self-regarding political ideologies or the self-assured humanism of the Enlightenment. St. Augustine is a better guide for our age than Gibbon or Marx, but he is so remote from us and speaks such an alien tongue that we cannot learn what he has to teach unless we know something of the tradition of Christian culture as a whole. And this is not easy because, as I have said, the study of Christian culture has never hitherto been given a recognized place in university studies or in the curriculum of Western education.

But we cannot afford to neglect it any longer. Though Christians today may be only a minority, they are a very considerable minority, and they are quite strong enough to carry out a programme of Christian studies, if they wish to do so. What is needed, it seems to me, is a comprehensive course of studies which would deal with Christian culture in the same integrative and objective way in which the humanist educators dealt with Classical culture. For the Humanist was not merely a grammarian and a philologist, he studied the whole course of ancient civilization from Homer to Marcus Aurelius in all its manifestations—its languages and literatures, its history and institutions, its religion and philosophy, its architecture and art. From the point of view of the scientific specialist, the field of study was too wide; yet as a form of education it was by no means impracticable or ineffective, and has survived down to our own time in such forms as the school of *Litterae Humaniores* at Oxford. And it was, above all, its non-specialized character—the way in which it used the parallel studies of literature and philosophy and history to support and illuminate one another—that was the source of its educational success.

Now it is true that the field of Christian culture is even more extensive than that of Classical culture, since it involves a longer historical development and a larger number of vernacular languages. But this is largely compensated by the fact that every European people possesses its own approach to the common culture of Christendom through its literature and history. I have given a specimen of this approach in my essay on Piers Plowman,[7] and every European literature provides similar opportunities.

Apart from this problem of the vernaculars, a comprehensive study of Christian culture is no more difficult than that of classical antiquity, and it offers the same educational advantages. Professor E. R. Curtius has shown in his book on *European Literature and the Latin Middle Ages* how our ignorance of the common language and literature of Western Christendom has vitiated our interpretation of the origins of our own literary traditions. And the same thing is true in other fields. It is difficult to separate the study of medieval political institutions from that of medieval political ideas, and we cannot understand the latter without a knowledge of medieval philosophy which is part of the central tradition of Christian culture. It is impossible to treat the various national traditions and national cultures as self-sufficient and self-explanatory entities, for they are all of them rooted in the common tradition of Christendom–a tradition which has its own history and its own laws of development. Thus behind all the divergencies and idiosyncracies of the national developments, we have the three great phases of the Christian culture itself which are organically related to one another.

First the growth of the Christian culture on the soil of the Græco-Roman world which had been fertilized by the accumulated remains of so many older cultures. Secondly its transplantation to the virgin soil of the West, and finally its new flowering in the vernacular cultures of the European world.

Each of these phases has its own social and institutional history, its own form of education and learning and its own literature and art. But the continuity of the tradition as a whole

7. ["The Vision of Piers Plowman," *Mediaeval Essays.* —Ed.]

is unbroken and even in the seventeenth century the thought of St. Augustine still exercises a living influence on the thought and life of the new peoples. Nor is this continuity confined to the higher levels of culture. Down to the age of the French Revolution, and sometimes even later, the Church remained the centre of the life of the common people, and even today we see in the case of survivals like the Passion Play of Oberammergau how the peasant no less—perhaps even more—than the scholar retained for ages a vital contact with the spiritual and artistic traditions of the Christian culture.

But what is the situation today when such survivals, in so far as they still exist, can be regarded as no more than picturesque archaisms? It is clear that contemporary culture can no longer be regarded as Christian, since it is probably the most completely secularized form of culture that has ever existed. Nevertheless the Christian religion still survives and there seems to be little likelihood that it will disappear. In fact it is more widely distributed than ever before. Nor is it confined to the more backward peoples or to the more uneducated sections of society, as was the case with the religions and religious cultures of the past when they were in a state of decline. Indeed today Christians take a more active part than they did two centuries ago in the higher cultural activities of society: in science, literature and art.

This anomalous situation offers both obstacles and opportunities for the study of Christian culture. On the one hand it involves the whole subject in a controversial atmosphere, since the secularist is exceptionally sensitive to the intrusion of religion and religious ideas into the field of education which he regards as neutral ground. But on the other hand, the more secularized a society becomes the more necessary is this study, since without it the thought and literature of the past will become increasingly unintelligible to the modern mind.

But for the modern Christian the advantages of this study are obvious since it is the study of his own spiritual tradition. Without it he will suffer from a sense of cultural inferiority and estrangement in the modern world, and the more attached he is to his religion, the greater will be the danger of his adopting a negative sectarian attitude which will narrow his sympathies and contract his social activities. This has always been a danger for religion and not least for Christianity. In the past it has produced a thousand sectarian aberrations, from Tertullian to Jansenius, and from the Puritans to modern pietist groups such as Edmund Gosse described in his own youth[8]; and the danger is no less today, though it takes new and less introverted forms. Nevertheless nothing could be more opposed to the nature of Christianity. For the Christian spirit is essentially dynamic and diffusive, penetrating every form of human life and influencing every human activity.

Nowhere do we see this character more clearly than in the development of the culture of Western Christendom. For Medieval Christianity, for all its other-worldliness, its supernaturalism and its moral asceticism, never lost sight of its world mission and its cultural responsibilities, so that there has never been an age in which the transforming power of religion manifested itself so universally in so many different fields. The community of faith expressed itself in the community of thought and the community of life and found media of artistic and literary expression which became the common possession of all the Western peoples.

This simultaneous flowering of Christian culture in thought and art and social life makes the thirteenth century a classical age in the strict sense of the word—one of those ages which in the words of Voltaire "vindicate the greatness of the human spirit and compensate the historian for the barren prospect of a thousand years of stupidity and barbarism". For this reason alone it deserves to be studied as the humanists have studied the age of Pericles or Augustus. But to the Christian it means still more. To him figures like St. Francis and St. Thomas Aqui-

8. [Sir Edmund William Gosse (1849–1928), British poet and literary critic. —Ed.]

nas are not just classical types of a culture that has disappeared centuries ago but creative powers whose influence lives on in the spiritual society which produced the Christian culture of the past and will produce the new Christian culture of the future.

The old order of Western Christendom has passed away, but the tradition of Christian culture is inseparable from the tradition of Christian life and of the Christian faith. Consequently our interest in the Christian culture of the past can never be a purely historical or literary one. It is relevant to the problem of Christian culture today in spite of the immense changes that have transformed the modern world. Medieval Christendom is the outstanding example in history of the application of Faith to Life: the embodiment of religion in social institutions and external forms; and therefore both its achievements and its failures are worthy of study. No doubt to the secularist the strength of the religious element in medieval culture may only tend to make it more unintelligible, since it is a case of an incomprehensible ideology expressed through a remote and unfamiliar social medium. But the Christian who possesses the ideological key will appreciate the medieval achievement the more in proportion as he recognizes the social limitations of the age. If the semi-barbarous society of feudal Europe could create such a remarkable cultural unity under the influence of Christian ideas, what might the modern world achieve with its vast resources of knowledge and power which are now running to waste or being perverted into instruments of social destruction?

2

The Modern Dilemma

THE MODERN DILEMMA is essentially a spiritual one, and every one of its main aspects, moral, political and scientific, brings us back to the need of a religious solution. The one remaining problem that we have got to consider is where that religious solution is to be found. Must we look for some new religion to meet the new circumstances of the changing world, or does the Christian faith still supply the answer that we need?

In the first place, it is obvious that it is no light matter to throw over the Christian tradition. It means a good deal more to us than we are apt to realise.

As I have pointed out, it is the Christian tradition that is the most fundamental element in Western culture. It lies at the base not only of Western religion, but also of Western morals and Western social idealism. To a far greater extent than science or philosophy, it has determined our attitude to life and the final aims of our civilisation. Yet on the other hand we cannot fail to recognise that it is just this religious element in Western culture that is most challenged at the present day. The majority of men, whatever their political beliefs may be, are prepared to accept science and democracy and humanitarianism as essential elements in modern civilisation, but they are far less disposed to admit the importance of religion in general and of Christianity in particular. They regard Christianity as out of touch with modern life and inconsistent with modern knowledge. Modern life, they say, deals with facts, while Christianity deals with unproved and incomprehensible dogmas. A man can indulge in religious beliefs, so long as he treats them as a private luxury; but they have no bearing on social life, and society can get on very well without them.

Moreover, behind this vague tendency to treat religion as a side issue in modern life, there exists a strong body of opinion that is actively hostile to Christianity and that regards the destruction of positive religion as absolutely necessary to the advance of modern culture. This attitude is most in evidence in Soviet Russia, where, for the first time in the history of the world, we see a great state, or rather a world empire, that officially rejects any species of religion and has adopted a social, and educational policy inspired by militant atheism. But this tendency is not confined to Russia or to the followers of communism. Both in Europe and America there is a strong anti-religious movement that includes many of our ablest modern writers and a few men of science. It seeks not only to destroy religion, but also to revolutionise morals and to discredit the ethical ideals which have hitherto inspired Western society.

This, I think, is one of the most significant features of the present situation. Critics of religion in the past have, as a rule, been anxious to dissociate the religious from the moral issue. They were often strict moralists, like the late John Morley,[1] who managed to clothe atheism in the frock coat and top hat of Victorian respectability. But today the solidarity of religion and morals is admitted on both sides. If Europe abandons Christianity, it must also abandon its moral code. And conversely the

1. [John Morley (1838–1923), first Viscount Morley; editor of the *Pall Mall Gazette* and author of lives of Edmund Burke, Oliver Cromwell, and William Gladstone.—Ed.]

modern tendency to break away from traditional morality strengthens the intellectual revolt against religious belief.

At first sight it seems as though the forces of change in the modern world were definitely hostile to religion, and that we are rapidly approaching a purely secular state of civilisation. But it is not so easy to get rid of religion as we might imagine. It is easy enough for the individual to adopt a negative attitude of critical scepticism. But if society as a whole abandons all positive beliefs, it is powerless to resist the disintegrating effects of selfishness and private interest. Every society rests in the last resort on the recognition of common principles and common ideals, and if it makes no moral or spiritual appeal to the loyalty of its members, it must inevitably fall to pieces.

In the past, society found this unifying principle in its religious beliefs; in fact religion was the vital centre of the whole social organism. And if a state did not already possess a common religious basis, it attempted to create one artificially, like the official Caesar-worship that became the state religion of the Roman Empire. And so, today, if the state can no longer appeal to the old moral principles that belong to the Christian tradition, it will be forced to create a new official faith and new moral principles which will be binding on its citizens.

Here again Russia supplies the obvious illustration. The Communist rejection of religion and Christian morality has not led to the abandonment of social control and the unrestricted freedom of opinion in matters of belief. On the contrary, it has involved an intensification of social control over the beliefs and the spiritual life of the individual citizen. In fact, what the Communists have done is not to get rid of religion, but merely to substitute a new and stricter Communist religion for the old official orthodoxy. The Communist Party is a religious sect which exists to spread the true faith. It has its Inquisition for the detection and punishment of heresy. It employs the weapon of excommunication against disloyal or unorthodox members. It possesses in the writings of Marx its infallible scriptures, and it reveres in Lenin, if not a God, at least a saviour and a prophet.

It may be said that this is an abnormal development due to the excesses of the Russian temperament. But it is abnormal only in its exaggerations. The moment that a society claims the complete allegiance of its members, it assumes a quasi-religious authority. For since man is essentially spiritual, any power that claims to control the whole man is forced to transcend relative and particular aims and to enter the sphere of absolute values, which is the realm of religion. On the other hand, if the state consents to the limitation of its aims to the political sphere, it has to admit that its ideal is only a relative one and that it must accept the ultimate supremacy of spiritual ideals which lie outside its province.

This is the solution that Western society has hitherto chosen, but it implies the existence of an independent spiritual power, whether it be a religious faith or a common moral ideal. If these are absent, the state is forced to claim an absolute and almost religious authority, though not necessarily in the same way that the Communist state has done. We can easily conceive a different type of secularism that conforms to the needs of capitalist society: indeed, we are witnessing the emergence of something of the kind in the United States, though it is still somewhat coloured by survivals from the older Protestant tradition.

And so too in Western Europe the tendency seems all towards the development of a purely secular type of culture which subordinates the whole of life to practical and economic ends and leaves no room for any independent spiritual activity. Nevertheless a civilisation that fails to satisfy the needs of man's spiritual nature cannot be permanently successful. It produces a state of spiritual conflict and moral maladjustment which weakens the vitality of the whole social organism. This is why our modern machine-made civilisation, in spite of the material benefits that it has conferred, is marked by a feeling of moral unrest and social discontent which was absent from the old religious cultures, although the lot of the ordinary man in them was infinitely harder from the material point of view.

You can give men food and leisure and amusements and good conditions of work, and still they will remain unsatisfied. You can deny them all these things, and they will not complain so long as they feel that they have something to die for.

Even if we regard man as an animal, we must admit that he is a peculiar sort of animal that will sacrifice his interests to his ideals—an animal that is capable of martyrdom. The statesman sees this when he appeals to the ordinary man to leave his home and his family and to go and die painfully in a ditch for the sake of his country; and the ordinary man does not refuse to go. The Communist recognises this, when he calls on the proletarian to work harder and to eat less for the sake of the Five-Year Plan and the cause of world revolution. But when the soldier comes back from the war, and the Communist has realised his Utopia, they are apt to feel a certain disproportion between their sacrifices and the fruits of their achievements.

Now it is the fundamental contradiction of materialism that it exalts the results of human achievement and at the same time denies the reality of the spiritual forces that have made this achievement possible. All the highest achievements of the human spirit, whether in the order of thought or action or moral being, rest on a spiritual absolute and become impossible in a world of purely economic or even purely human values. It is only in the light of religious experience and of absolute spiritual principles that human nature can recognise its own greatness and realise its higher potentialities.

There is a world of eternal spiritual realities in which and for which the world of man exists. That is the primary intuition that lies at the root of all religion, even of the most primitive kind. The other day I came upon a very good illustration of this, rather unexpectedly, in a passage in one of Edgar Wallace's novels[2] in which he is describing a religious discussion between

2. [Edgar Wallace (1875–1932), English novelist.—Ed.]

a white officer and a West African medicine-man. The former says "Where in the world are these gods of whom you are always talking?" and the savage answers, "O man, know that the Gods are not in the world; it is the world that is in the Gods."

In our modern civilised world this truth is no longer obvious; it has become dim and obscured. Nevertheless it cannot be disregarded with impunity. The civilisation that denies God denies its own foundation. For the glory of man is a dim reflection of the glory of God, and when the latter is denied the former fades.

Consequently the loss of the religious sense which is shown by the indifference or the hostility of the modern world to Christianity is one of the most serious weaknesses of our civilisation and involves a real danger to its spiritual vitality and its social stability. Man's spiritual needs are none the less strong for being unrecognised, and if they are denied their satisfaction through religion, they will find their compensation elsewhere, often in destructive and anti-social activities. The man who is a spiritual misfit becomes morally alienated from society, and whether that alienation takes the form of active hostility, as in the anarchist or the criminal, or merely of passive non-co-operation, as in the selfish individualist, it is bound to be a source of danger. The civilisation that finds no place for religion is a maimed culture that has lost its spiritual roots and is condemned to sterility and decadence. There can, I think, be little doubt that the present phase of intense secularisation is a temporary one, and that it will be followed by a far-reaching reaction. I would even go so far as to suggest that the return to religion promises to be one of the dominant characteristics of the coming age. We all know how history follows a course of alternate action and reaction, and how each century and each generation tends to contradict its predecessor. The Victorians reacted against the Georgians, and we in turn have reacted against the Victorians. We reject their standards and their beliefs, just as they rejected the standards and beliefs of their predecessors.

But behind these lesser waves of change there is a deeper movement that marks the succession of the ages. There are times when the whole spirit of civilisation becomes transformed and the stream of history seems to change its course, and flow in a new direction. One such movement occurred sixteen hundred years ago, when the ancient world became Christian. Another occurred in the sixteenth century with the coming of the Renaissance and the Reformation, which brought the mediaeval world to an end and inaugurated a new age. And the forces of transformation that are at work in the world today seem to betoken the coming of another such change in the character of civilisation, which is perhaps even more fundamental than that of the sixteenth century.

All the characteristic movements that marked the culture of the last four centuries are passing away and giving place to new tendencies. We see this not only in politics and the material organisation of life, but also in art and literature and science; for example, in the tendency of modern art to abandon the naturalistic principles that governed its development from the Renaissance to the nineteenth century in favour of new canons of style that have more in common with the art of Byzantium and of the ancient East.

We are not, indeed, going back to the Middle Ages, but we are going forward to a new age which is no less different from the last age than that was from the mediaeval period.

But if this is so, may it not be that religion is one of the outworn modes of thought that are being abandoned and that the new age will be an age of rationalism and secularism and materialism? This is, as we have seen, the current belief, but then the current beliefs are always out of date. It is difficult to realise how much of current thinking belongs to the past, because it is natural for men's minds to be soaked in the mental atmosphere of the last generation, and it needs a considerable effort to see things as they are and not as other people have seen them. The artist and the philosopher and the scientist, each in his own way, sees life direct, but the majority of men see it at second-hand through the accepted ideas of their society and culture. And consequently, the tendencies that we regard as characteristic of the age are often those that are characteristic of the age that is just passing away rather than of that which is beginning.

Thus in fact the tendencies that are hostile to religion and make for secularism and materialism are not new tendencies. They have been at work in Europe for centuries. The whole modern period from the Renaissance to the nineteenth century was a long process of revolt in which the traditional order of life and its religious foundations were being undermined by criticism and doubt. It was an age of spiritual disintegration in which Christendom was divided into a mass of warring sects, and the Churches that resisted this tendency did so only by a rigid discipline which led to religious persecution and the denial of individual freedom. And this again brought religion into conflict with the spirit of the age; for it was an age of individualism, dominated by the Renaissance ideal of liberty of thought, the Reformation ideal of liberty of conscience, the individualist ideal of economic liberty and the romantic ideal of liberty of feeling and conduct. It was an age of secularism in which the state substituted itself for the Church as the ultimate authority in men's lives and the supreme end of social activity. And finally it was an age which witnessed the triumphant development of scientific materialism, based on a mechanistic theory of the world that seemed to leave no room for human freedom or spiritual reality.

Today this process of revolution has worked itself out, so that there is hardly anything left to revolt against. After destroying the old order, we are beginning to turn round and look for some firm foundation on which we can build anew. Already in social life we are witnessing the passing of individualism and the recovery of a sense of community. In economics for example, the nineteenth-century ideal of unrestricted freedom and individual initiative has given place to an intense demand for social organisation and social control.

Looked at from this point of view, socialism and communism are not purely revolutionary and negative movements. They mark the turn of the tide. Karl Marx was among the first to feel the insufficiency of the liberal revolutionary tradition and the need for a new effort of social construction. And so he built on what seemed to his age to be an ultimate foundation—the bed-rock of scientific materialism. But today we realise that the materialistic theory of the nineteenth century was no more final than the scientific theories that it superseded. Science, which has explained so much, has ended by explaining away matter itself, and has left us with a skeleton universe of mathematical formulae. Consequently the naive materialism that regarded Matter with a capital M as the one reality is no longer acceptable, for we have come to see that the fundamental thing in the world is not Matter but Form. The universe is not just a mass of solid particles of matter governed by blind determinism and chance. It possesses an organic structure, and the further we penetrate into the nature of reality the more important does this principle of *form* become.

And so we can no longer dismiss mind and spiritual reality as unreal or less real than the material world, for it is just in mind and in the spiritual world that the element of form is most supreme. It is the mind that is the key of the universe, not matter. In the Beginning was the Word, and it is the creative and informing power of the Word that is the foundation of reality.

And if this is true of the world of nature, it is still more true of the world of society and culture. We must abandon the vain attempt to disregard spiritual unity and to look for a basis of social construction in material and external things. The acceptance of spiritual reality must be the basic element in the culture of the future, for it is spirit that is the principle of unity and matter that is the principle of division.

And as soon as this truth is admitted, religion will no longer appear as an unessential and extraneous element in culture, but as its most vital element. For religion is the bond that unites man to spiritual reality, and it is only in religion that society can find the principle of spiritual union of which it stands in need. No secular ideal of social progress or economic efficiency can take the place of this. It is only the ideal of a spiritual order which transcends the relative value of the economic and political world that is capable of overcoming the forces of disintegration and destruction that exist in modern civilisation. The faith of the future cannot be economic or scientific or even moral; it must be religious.

This is just where the new artificial manmade religions, like Positivism, fail. They lack the one thing that is necessary, namely, religious faith. It is a complete mistake to think that we can bring religion up-to-date by making it conform to our wishes and to the dominant prejudices of the moment. If we feel that modern society is out of touch with science, we do not call on the scientists to change their views and to give us something more popular. We realise that we have got to give more thought and more work to science. In the same way the great cause of the decline of religion is that we have lost touch with it, either by abandoning religion altogether, or by contenting ourselves with a nominal outward profession that does not affect our daily life and our real interests. And the only way to bring religion into touch with the modern world is to give it the first place in our own though and in our own lives. If we wish to be scientific, we must submit to the authority of science and sacrifice our easy acceptance of things as they seem to the severe discipline of scientific method. And in the same way, if we wish to be religious we must submit to religious authority and accept the principles of the spiritual order. In the material world, man must conform himself to realities, otherwise he will perish. And the same is true in the spiritual world. God comes first, not man. He is more real than the whole external universe. Man passes away, empires and civilisations rise and fall, the stars grow old; God remains.

This is the fundamental truth which runs through the whole of the Bible. There is, of course, a great deal more than this in Christianity. In fact, it is a truth that Christianity shares with practically all the religions of the world. Nevertheless it is just this truth that the modern world, like the ancient world before it, finds most difficult to accept. You even find people who reject it and still wish to call themselves Christians. They water down religion to a series of moral platitudes and then dignify this mixture of vague religiosity and well-meaning moral optimism with the respectable name of Christianity.

In reality Christianity is not merely a moral ideal or set of ideas. It is a concrete reality. It is the spiritual order incarnated in a historical person and in a historical society. The spiritual order is just as real as the material order. The reason we do not see it is because we do not look at it. Our interests and our thoughts are elsewhere. A few exceptional men, mystics or philosophers, may find it possible to live habitually on a spiritual plane, but for the ordinary man it is a difficult atmosphere to breathe in. But it is the function of Christianity to bring the spiritual order into contact and relation with the world of man. It is, as it were, a bridge between the two worlds; it brings religion down into human life and it opens the door of the spiritual world to man. Its ideal is not a static and unchanging order like that of the other world religions. It is a spiritual society or organism that has incorporated itself with humanity and that takes into itself as it proceeds all that is vital and permanent in human life and civilisation. It aims at nothing less than the spiritual integration of humanity, its deliverance from the tyranny of material force and the dominion of selfish aims, and its reconstitution in spiritual unity.

And thus there are two principles in Christianity which though they sometimes appear contradictory are equally essential as the two poles of the spiritual order. There is the principle of transcendence, represented by the apocalyptic, ascetic, world-denying element in religion, and there is the principle of catholicity, which finds expression in the historic, social, world-embracing activity of the Church. A one-sided emphasis on the former of these leads to sectarianism, as we see in the history of the early Christian sects that refused all compromise with secular civilisation and stood aside in an attitude of negative and sterile isolation. But the Catholic Church rejected this solution as a betrayal of its universal mission. It converted the ancient world; it became the Church of the Empire; and it took up into itself the traditional heritage of culture that the puritanism of the sectaries despised. In this way the Church overcame the conflict between religion and secular culture that had weakened the forces of Roman society, and laid the foundations of a new civilisation. For more than a thousand years society found its centre of unity and its principle of order in Christianity. But the mediaeval synthesis, both in its Byzantine and mediaeval form, while it gave a more complete expression to the social function of Christianity than any other age has done, ran the risk of compromising the other Christian principle of transcendence by the immersion of the spiritual in the temporal order—the identification of the Church and the World. The history of mediaeval Christendom shows a continuous series of efforts on the part of orthodox reformers and Catharist and "spiritual" heretics against the secularisation and worldliness of the Church. And, as the wealth and intellectual culture of Western Europe increased, the tension grew more acute. It was the coming of the Renaissance and the whole-hearted acceptance by the Papacy of the new humanist culture that stretched the mediaeval synthesis to breaking-point and produced a new outburst of reforming sectarianism. It is true that Catholicism met the challenge of the Reformation by its own movement of spiritual reform. But it failed to recover the lost unity of Christendom and was forced to lose touch with the dominant movements in secular culture. Thus Christianity withdrew more and more into the sphere of the individual religious life and the world went its own way. European civilisation was rationalised and secularised until it ceased even nominally to be Christian. Nevertheless it continued to subsist unconsciously on the accumulated capital of its Christian past, from which it drew the moral and social idealism that inspired the humanitarian and liberal and democratic movements of the last two centuries. Today this spiritual capital is exhausted, and civilisation is faced with the choice between a return to the spiritual traditions of Christianity or the renunciation of them in favour of complete social materialism.

But if Christianity is to regain its influence, it must recover its unity and its social activity. The religious individualism of the last age, with its self-centred absorption in the question of personal salvation and private religious emotion, will not help us. The Christianity of the future must be a social Christianity that is embodied in a real society, not an imaginary or invisible one. And this society must not be merely a part of the existing social and political order, like the established churches of the past; it must be an independent and universal society, not a national or local one. The only society that fulfills these conditions is the Catholic Church, the most ancient yet, at the same time, the most adaptable of all existing institutions. It is true that Catholicism has suffered grievously from the sectarian division and strife of the last four hundred years, but it has succeeded in surmounting the long drawn-out crisis that followed the dissolution of the mediaeval synthesis, and it stands out today as the one remaining centre of unity and spiritual order in Europe. If Christianity is necessary to Europe, the Catholic Church is no less necessary to Christianity, for without it the latter would become no more than a mass of divergent opinions dissolving under the pressure of rationalist criticism and secularist culture. It was by virtue of the Catholic ideal of spiritual unity that the social unity of European culture emerged from the welter of barbarism, and the modern world stands no less in need of such an ideal if it is to realise in the future the wider unity of a world civilisation.

But though Christianity is necessary to civilisation, we must not forget the profound difference that there is between them. It is the great paradox of Christianity, as Newman so often insisted, that though Christianity is a principle of life to civilisation even in secular matters, it is continually at issue with the world and always seems on the verge of being destroyed by it. Thus the Church is necessary to Europe, and yet any acceptance of the Church *because* it is necessary to society is destructive of its real essence. Nothing could be more fatal to the spirit of Christianity than a return to Christianity for political reasons.

But, on the other hand, any attempt to create a purely political or social religion is equally destined to fail. Nothing is more remarkable than the collapse of all the efforts to create an artificial religion to meet "the needs of the age." Deism, Saint-Simonianism, Positivism and the rest have all ended in failure. It is only a religion that transcends political and economic categories and is indifferent to material results that has the power of satisfying the need of the world. As Newman wrote eighty years ago:

The Catholic Church has accompanied human society through one revolution of its great year; and it is now beginning a second. She has passed through the full cycle of changes in order to show that she is independent of them all. She has had trial of East and West, of monarchy and democracy, of peace and war, of times of darkness and times of philosophy, of old countries and young.

And today she still stands as she did under the Roman Empire, as the representative in a changing world of an unchanging spiritual order. That is why I believe the Church that made Europe may yet save Europe, and that, in the great words of the Easter liturgy,

The whole world may experience and see what was fallen raised up, what had grown old made new, and all things returning to unity through Him from whom they took their beginning.

3

Europe and the Seven Stages
of Western Culture

THE EXISTENCE OF EUROPE is the basis of the historical development of the modern world, and it is only in relation to that fact that the development of each particular state can be understood. Nevertheless it is a submerged reality of which the majority of men are only half conscious. For the last century and more, the whole trend of education and politics and public opinion has tended to develop the consciousness of nationality and to stress the importance of the nation-state, while leaving Europe in the background as a vague abstraction or as nothing more than a geographical expression. The main reason for this is, of course, the cult of nationalism which, owing to its double appeal to political passion and to cultural idealism, exerts an exceptionally strong influence in the popular mind. But behind this there is a further cause which has not perhaps been sufficiently recognized. This is the tradition of education which has provided the framework of Western thought, and in this tradition the conception of Europe has never held a definite place. On the one hand, there was the history of the ancient world—of classical Greece and Rome—which was regarded as an essential part of education: on the other, and on a very much lower plane, there was the history of a man's own country and people, which every educated person was supposed to be familiar with but which did not possess the same prestige as classical history or humane letters or even natural science. A transition from one to the other was provided by such works as Gibbon's *Decline and Fall of the Roman Empire,* and it was books of this kind, which were the nearest approach to a study of Europe that the old tradition of education provided. But they were obviously partial and unsatisfactory, so that the consciousness of Europe as an historical reality was something which somehow had to be picked up on the road that led from ancient Rome to modern England (or whatever one's country might be), and it was only an exceptionally enterprising mind which troubled to enquire where and how it made its first appearance and what was its essential character.

From this defect in our education all modern culture has suffered. In fact the bitter harvest we are reaping to-day was in large measure the fruit of this initial error.

To ignore Europe and to concentrate all our attention on the political community to which we belong, as though it were the whole social reality, leads in the last resort to the totalitarian state, and National Socialism itself was only this development carried out with Germanic thoroughness and Prussian ruthlessness.

The democratic states have, on their part, no doubt refused to accept the extreme consequences of the nationalist heresy. They have preserved some contact with the tradition of Natural Law and a real sense of international obligation. Yet they also have ignored the existence of Europe as a social reality and oscillated between the reality of the nation-state and the ideal of a cosmopolitan liberal world order which was theoretically co-extensive with the human race, but was in practice dependent on the economic realities of international trade and finance. Yet apart from Europe, neither the one nor the other would have existed. For Europe is more than the sum of the nations and states of the European continent, and it is much more than a subdivision of the modern international society. In so far as a world society or a world civilization can be said to exist, it is the child of Europe, and if, as many peoples believe to-day, this ideal of world civilization is being shipwrecked before it has achieved realization, then Europe remains the most highly developed form of society that humanity has yet known.

What then is Europe? Europe is a community of peoples who share in a common spiritual tradition that had its origins three thousand years ago in the Eastern Mediterranean and which has been transmitted from age to age and from people to people until it has come to overshadow the world. The tradition as a whole cannot, therefore, be strictly identified with the European continent. It has come into Europe and has passed beyond it, and what we call "Europe" in the cultural sense is really only one phase of this wider development.

As I have argued in the previous chapter, we can only understand Europe and its historical development by the study of Christian culture, for this forms the centre of the whole process, and it was as Christendom that Europe first became conscious of itself as a society of peoples with common moral values and common spiritual aims.

Viewed from this centre, the whole development of Western culture falls into three main stages—Christian, pre-Christian and post-Christian, each of which may in turn be divided into two or three subordinate phases.

There are first the two phases of classical Mediterranean culture: (1) Hellenism and (2) the Roman world. Next there are the three central periods of Christian history; (3) the formation of Western and Eastern Christendom; (4) Mediaeval Christendom, from the eleventh to the fifteenth century; and (5) the age of religious division and humanist culture, from the sixteenth to the eighteenth century. Finally, we have (6) the age of Revolution—the later eighteenth and the nineteenth centuries, when

European culture became secularized, and (7) the disintegration of Europe, which is both the cause and the result of the two World Wars in whose shadow we live to-day.

1. The first of these three stages is pre-Christian and even pre-European, since it originated in the Aegean and remained to the end a predominantly Mediterranean development. But it was emphatically Western, and all the later stages of European culture have looked back to it as the source of their intellectual and often of their social traditions.

For Western civilization was born when the Greeks first became conscious of their separation from the Asiatic world at the time of the Persian war, when they realized that they possessed a different way of life and a different standard of values from those which were embodied in the great archaic civilizations of the ancient East. These new ways of life and thought were already fully manifested in the great creative achievement of Hellenic culture during the seventh and sixth centuries B.C., the age that saw the development of the city-state and its political institutions, the great colonial expansion of the Greeks round the shores of the Mediterranean and the Black Sea, and the origins of the Greek scientific and philosophical movement. But during this earlier period the Ionians and the other Greeks of Asia Minor were the leaders of Hellenic culture, and European Greece held a relatively inferior position. The wars with Persia changed all that, not only by securing the European leadership of the Greek world, but still more by increasing the self-consciousness and unity of the whole Greek world against the oriental world empire that threatened its independence. For in spite of the jealous regionalist patriotism of the Greek city-states, they also acquired an intense loyalty to the wider unity of "Hellenism", so that the dualism of state and culture which was a characteristic feature of mediaeval and modern Europe already finds its prototype in the Greek world.

Thus the two poles of Greek civilization were the free city and the common culture. It was as "free men", as members of a self-governing community, that the Greeks felt themselves to be different from other men, and it was as members of the wider society of Hellenism which embraced a hundred cities and was in contact with every part of the Mediterranean world that they developed their cooperative work of thought and rational enquiry which was the source of Western philosophy and science. In the same way, they developed their own distinctive system of education—*Paideia*—which was essentially different alike from the traditional learning of the oriental priest and from the warlike discipline of the barbarian tribesman and was the origin and pattern of the Western tradition of liberal education. In short, it was the Greeks who created the Western idea of Man and that conception of humanist culture which has become one of the formative elements in the European tradition.

But though the Greeks were the real creators of the Western tradition, they had little direct influence on continental Europe. The second great wave of Hellenic expansion and colonization which began in the fourth century was directed to the East, and during the Hellenistic period Western and Central Asia, from the Mediterranean to the Oxus and the Indus, was covered by a network of Greek cities under the protection of the Graeco-Macedonian dynasties, which regarded the extension of Hellenic culture as the basis and justification of their power. Thus Hellenism became a real world-wide civilization which influenced the culture of all the peoples of Asia as far east as North-West India and Turkestan. But this movement of imperial expansion in the East was accompanied by the decline of Greek power in Europe itself, and the same age that saw the conquest and Hellenization of the East by Alexander and his successors witnessed the rise of a new power in the West which was destined to act as the intermediary between the Hellenistic civilization of the East and the barbaric peoples of Western Europe.

2. This process forms the second phase in the history of Western culture. It covers a period of six or seven centuries— three hundred years from Alexander to Augustus and three hundred years from the death of Augustus to the conversion of Constantine. During those centuries Rome gradually grew from

a peasant state in Central Italy to a world empire which embraced the whole Mediterranean world and extended from the Atlantic to the Euphrates and the Caucasus, and from the Rhine and the Danube to the Sahara and the Arabian desert. Thus for the first and last time in the history of Western culture the whole civilized world east of Persia and India was united in a single state ruled by one master, administered by a common law and defended by a uniform military system. At first sight there seems little in common between the Roman spirit and that of Hellenic culture. The Romans were a people of soldiers and organizers, lawyers and engineers, road-makers and land-surveyors, whose achievement is summed up in the lapidary sentence "Balbus built a wall". They had none of the genius for abstract speculation and the creative artistic imagination of the Greeks, and their vast empire, built up by harsh military discipline and ruthless political planning, seems as inferior to Periclean Athens as the Colosseum is inferior to the Parthenon. Nevertheless their work was extraordinarily enduring, and it served the cause of Western culture better than the more spectacular achievements of Alexander and his successors. While the latter were content to conquer the civilized East and cover it with a veneer of Hellenistic urban culture, the Romans drove their roads like a plough through the virgin soil of Western Europe and laid the foundation of new cities where none had stood before. Though they were not the creators of Western culture they diffused and defended it, and the walls that Balbus built on the Northumbrian moorland and round the posts in the Libyan desert were the shield which protected the westward advance of the classical Mediterranean culture. The Greeks themselves, like Polybius and Strabo, were the first to recognize the nature of the Roman achievement as the indispensable continuation and completion of the achievement of Hellenism.

Thus the second phase of Western culture was in fact a cooperative effort which was common to the two great Mediterranean peoples. The Roman genius built the fabric of civilized society in Western Europe which still subsists to-day, at least in

Italy and Gaul and Spain, in spite of the changes of later centuries. But this social order provided a channel for the transmission and diffusion of the Hellenic traditions. Latin literature and education as represented by Cicero and Livy, Horace and Quintilian, represent a simplified version of Hellenistic culture which was better suited to the needs of the new peoples of the West than the Greek original. Thus Latin endured as the common language of the educated world in the West for more than a thousand years after Greek ceased to be the common language of the civilized East. The strength of the Latin element in Western culture is no doubt due as much, or more, to the influence of the Catholic Church as to that of the Roman Empire. For the Church came to the Western barbarians with all the prestige of Latin culture and Roman authority. As Rome had acted as the intermediary between Hellenism and the West, so the Church acted as intermediary between the Latin West and the new peoples of Northern Europe. The last service which the Roman Empire performed in the development of Western culture was to provide the sociological and juridical basis for the organization of the new religious society with its ecclesiastical hierarchy and its Canon Law.

This task was only achieved by a long and costly struggle. Christianity is the one element in Western culture which is completely non-Western in origin, and which transplanted into the Roman-Hellenistic world a sacred tradition of immemorial antiquity, preserved intact by the one people that had held out indomitably against the pervasive influence of Hellenistic world culture.

Christianity came out of this unknown oriental world into the full light of Roman-Hellenistic culture with a new faith and a new standard of spiritual values which aspired to change human life and inevitably aroused the opposition of Greek culture and the persecution of the Roman state. In a single generation it spread from Syria through the cities of Asia Minor and Greece to Rome itself, and then proceeded, rapidly in the East and much more slowly in the West, to permeate the whole civilized world. For three centuries it had to fight for its existence, until it was finally recognized as the universal religion of the world empire. In the Eastern Mediterranean it maintained this position for more than a thousand years, but in the West it was hardly established before the Empire broke up under the pressure of the barbarians. Nevertheless the Western Church was strong enough not only to survive the fall of the Empire, but also to maintain the tradition of higher culture and to become a city of refuge for the conquered peoples.

3. The formation of Western Christendom by the conversion of the barbarians and the transmission to them of the tradition of Mediterranean culture by the Church marks a new stage in the Western development and the birth of the new European society of nations. It was a slow process, since it was interrupted in the ninth century by a fresh wave of barbarian invasion from the north and the east and by the Moslem conquest of Spain and the Western Mediterranean, so that it was not completed until the Vikings of Scandinavia and the Magyars of Hungary had been converted and brought into the society of Christian Europe. But during these five or six centuries the foundations of a new Christian society were firmly laid by the cooperation between the Catholic Church and the barbarian kingdoms and by the missionary activity of the Irish and Anglo-Saxon monks, whose foundations were the centres of Christian culture and education in lands where no city had ever existed.

The focus of the new European development during these centuries was the Frankish kingdom, which included the greater part of France, Belgium and Western and Central Germany. This was the formative centre towards which the living forces of Western culture converged and in which the first deliberate attempt was made to realize the social unity of Western Christendom. This unity was based on the alliance of the new Frankish dynasty of the Carolingians with the Papacy, an alliance which was consummated and consecrated by the coronation of Charlemagne as Emperor at Rome on Christmas Day, A.D. 800. But it was primarily the work of the reforming party in the Church, as represented above all by Anglo-Saxon missionaries and scholars like St. Boniface and Alcuin. It was their ideals which inspired the new Carolingian legislation and the far-reaching programme for the revival and reform of learning, liturgy and script. All these activities were dominated by the conception of Christendom as an all-embracing unity which was both Church and state and in which the ruler had a sacred character as the anointed leader of the Christian people.

This conception survived the political collapse of the Carolingian Empire, which broke down under the stress of the Viking and Magyar invasions. It was inherited by the new society which grew up from its ruins;—the new Empire that was founded by the Saxon Kings of Germany in the tenth century, the feudal states that made up the Kingdom of France, and even by the Anglo-Saxon Kingdom of England which was founded by King Alfred and his successors. Mediaeval Christendom was in a real sense an extension and fulfilment of the Carolingian Empire and culture.

4. During these formative centuries, Western Europe had remained a relatively backward area on the extreme frontier of the civilized world. It occupied less than a third of the European continent and was by no means the richest or the most civilized part. But in the eleventh century Western culture began to expand from its Carolingian nucleus in all directions, and during the next three or four centuries it transformed Europe from a barbarian hinterland into a centre of world culture which equalled the older oriental civilizations in power and wealth and surpassed them in creative energy. These centuries saw the rise of the European city and the European state; they created a new art, a new poetry, a new philosophy, as well as new social, cultural and religious institutions: the order of chivalry, the estates of parliament, the religious orders and the universities.

All this cultural activity was inspired by the Carolingian conception of Christendom as a social unity, the society of the Christian people, which included and transcended the lesser unities of nation and kingdom and city. But this conception now found its primary expression, not in a universal empire but in the universal order of the Church as reorganized by the reforming movement of the eleventh and twelfth centuries. The Pope took the place of the Emperor as the head of the international society of Christendom and the ruler of the Christian people.

It is true that the Carolingian ideal of a universal Christian empire still survived, and even in the fourteenth century it was strong enough to inspire the work of the greatest of mediaeval poets—Dante. But by this time it was little more than a utopian ideal, whereas the international authority of the Papacy was a reality embodied in the law and institutions of Christendom and enforced by an effective system of centralized control. Thus mediaeval Christendom during its central period, from the time of Gregory VII to that of Boniface VIII (c. 1075–1300), was a kind of theocracy in which the whole social hierarchy of Christendom was dominated by the authority of the spiritual power.

This theocratic internationalism manifests itself in almost every aspect of mediaeval culture—in the crusades which were, at least in theory, international enterprises against the common enemies of Christendom; in the religious and military orders which were the international organs of Christendom; in the universities, like Paris and Bologna, which were international centres of higher studies for the whole of Western Europe. Moreover, the unity of European culture was reinforced by the use of Latin as the sacred language of the liturgy and the common language of learning, by the symbolism and imagery of a common religious art, and by the common ideals and conventions of aristocratic behaviour embodied in the cult of chivalry.

All these influences extended far beyond the frontiers of the Latin South and the Carolingian West. For it was during these centuries that Central and Eastern Europe as far as Poland and Lithuania and Hungary were brought into the society of Western Christendom.

But while this development was taking place in the West, the old centres of civilization in the East were beginning to decline

under the pressure of new warrior peoples from the steppes. The
Mongols destroyed the Bagdad Khalifate and conquered China,
Persia and Russia, while the Ottoman Turks established themselves in Asia Minor and the Balkans and ultimately destroyed
the Byzantine Empire. As a result of these changes, the axis of
world culture gradually shifted westward, and the East began to
lose its position of cultural leadership. Italy took the place of
Greece as the most advanced country in Europe in art and learning and economic development. Indeed the city-states of Italy
in the later Middle Ages rivalled those of sixth-century Greece
in the intensity of their social and intellectual life.

5. At the same time, the progress of Western culture during
the later Middle Ages was unfavourable to the unity of mediaeval Carolingian culture which was based on the alliance of the
Papacy with the movement of ecclesiastical reform in France
and Germany and with the ruling classes in the North which
supported it and which also provided the driving force of the
crusading movement. The renaissance of Mediterranean culture
separated these elements, so that the reforming spirit which was
still strong in the North became the enemy instead of the ally
of the Papacy, while the latter became increasingly Italianized
and was the leading patron of the new humanist culture. The
theocratic unity of mediaeval Christendom was destroyed, and
Europe became a society of sovereign states in which the temporal power of the prince either abolished or severely limited the
spiritual power of the universal Church.

From the religious point of view this loss of Christian unity
was a tragedy from which Christendom has never recovered. But
it did not destroy the unity of European culture, since the influence of the new humanist culture which spread from Italy to
the rest of Europe in the later fifteenth and the sixteenth centuries provided a bond of intellectual and artistic unity between
the two halves of divided Christendom and between the sovereign states and nations of Europe.

Thus, although Latin had ceased to be the common sacred
language of liturgy and religion, it was more than ever the com-

mon language of education and learning. Moreover, the importance of the classical tradition in European culture was now reinforced and extended by the recovery of the Hellenic tradition, which from the fifteenth century onwards had an increasing influence on Western education and Western thought. This re-Hellenization of Western culture had its origins far back in the Middle Ages with the recovery of Greek science and philosophy from the Arabs by the translators of the twelfth century, and with the Aristotelian revival which had such a profound influence on Western thought in the later Middle Ages. But it was not until the Renaissance had restored a direct contact with Hellenic culture that the movement bore fruit in the great advance of scientific thought inaugurated by Copernicus and Kepler and Galileo. From the sixteenth century onwards Europe was to surpass the Greeks in the originality and boldness of its cosmological speculation. Every generation extended the boundaries of science, and Western man began to acquire a knowledge and control of nature which seemed to open unlimited possibilities of progress for mankind.

Meanwhile the external relations of European culture had already been profoundly changed. Before Western science had discovered the new world of knowledge, Western man had discovered and conquered a new geographical world. The defeat of the last crusades by the Turks at Nicopolis and Varna, and their control of the great historic trade routes to Asia and Africa, compelled Europe to seek new fields for expansion and new channels for trade. The maritime discoveries of the Portuguese in Africa which opened the new oceanic route to India and the Far East, and the discovery and conquest of the new world of America by the Spaniards, involved a general reorientation of Europe from the Mediterranean to the Atlantic and from the old continental trade routes to the new oceanic sea ways. The resultant development of economic activity and the oceanic expansion of European trade and colonization prepared the way for the world hegemony of Western civilization in the following age, but it also intensified the political rivalry of the European

powers which was characteristic of this age and which was complicated by the religious conflicts of the post-Reformation period. The attempt to prevent this struggle for power from destroying the European state system led to the elaboration of
the system of the Balance of Power, which was the product of
Renaissance statecraft and reflects the tension of conflicting
forces within the limits of a common culture. While the struggle
for power was a revolutionary and destructive force, its agents
were the most traditional and formal institutions in Europe—
the courts of the great powers—which all tended to share in
the same humanist culture and imitate the same patterns of
social behaviour. Thus in spite of the disruptive effects of national rivalries, European war and diplomacy themselves produced an international society of a limited kind, so that Western
statesmen and diplomats and generals during this period belonged to the same world and shared the same ways of thought
and the same style of conversation and manners and dress.

6. This highly stylized aristocratic civilization of post-Renaissance Europe, which reached its full development in the age of
Louis XIV, differed from the earlier phases of European development in its lack of religious foundations. The stronger became
the culture of the courts, the weaker became the culture of the
Churches, so that by the eighteenth century European society
began to undergo a process of rapid secularization which changed
the whole character of Western culture. The alliance of the courts
with the humanist culture and with the scientific movement
which was still predominantly humanist in spirit generated the
new ideals of enlightened despotism and of the rationalization of
human life by the diffusion of scientific knowledge. The movement was strongest in France, where it possessed a consciously
anti-Christian character and carried on a crusade of enlightenment against the dark forces of fanaticism and superstition which
it saw embodied in the Church and the religious orders. From
France the movement spread with extraordinary rapidity throughout continental Europe, using the courts and the aristocratic sa-
lons as its channels of diffusion, and extending even as far as Russia and Portugal.

Only in England did the movement take a different form. Here alone in Europe the court culture was relatively unimportant and the centre of power had passed to the great landowners who ruled the country through parliamentary institutions and were practically emancipated from royal and ecclesiastical authority. Under their rule, English society also underwent a process of secularization, but it was less complete and far less revolutionary than that of the Continent. The main energies of English society were directed to practical ends—to commercial and industrial expansion and to the revolution of economic life by capitalism and scientific invention. There was no sudden breach with religious tradition. Indeed in England, unlike the Continent, the eighteenth century witnessed a popular movement of religious revival which had a deep effect on the common people and the middle classes of English society. Thus in England the movement towards the secularization of culture followed a very uneven and irregular course. There was no sharp conflict between religious tradition and the scientific enlightenment, but a number of dissident sectarian or party movements which broke up the traditional unity of religion and culture and created their own separate creeds and ideologies.[1] Some of these movements, like the Unitarians, were in close sympathy with the Enlightenment and were led by philosophers and scientists like Joseph Priestley; others, like the Wesleyans, were inspired by the ideal of personal sanctity and evangelical simplicity. But they all acted, consciously or unconsciously; as a ferment of social change, and prepared the way for the reforming movements of the following century.

On the Continent, and especially in France, where these intermediate sectarian groups did not exist, the secularization of culture was far more complete, and the conflict between the movement of Enlightenment and the forces of tradition was far more acute. By degrees the Enlightenment became transformed

---

1. The foundations of this development had been already laid in the seventeenth century, in the age of the Puritan Revolution, and some of the seventeenth-century leaders like Roger Williams, the founder of Rhode Island, had already developed theories of the complete separation of Church and State.

into a kind of counter-religion, and the spiritual forces which were denied their traditional religious expression found their outlet in the new revolutionary cult which was embodied in the Declaration of the Rights of Man and was inspired by an irrational faith in Reason and by boundless hopes for the progress of humanity when liberated from the age-long oppression of priests and kings. Political democracy and economic liberalism were the practical corollaries of these beliefs, and the attempt to realize them by a drastic breach with the past and the introduction of new rational institutions led to the French Revolution and the Reign of Terror and the Caesarian imperialism of Napoleon.

The Napoleonic Empire was a bold attempt to re-establish the unity of Europe on new foundations, and for a moment it seemed as though a new Caesar had arisen, capable of transforming the ramshackle edifice of the *ancien régime* into an ordered unity by his military genius and his powers of organization. But the classical symmetry of the *style empire* was little more than a plaster façade which hardly concealed the heterogeneous character of the underlying structure. There was an inherent contradiction between the military authoritarianism of the Empire and the liberal idealism of the Revolution, and the stubborn resistance of the two most independent Western peoples, the British and the Spaniards, ultimately aroused the dormant forces of European nationality and caused the downfall of Napoleon and the dissolution of his Empire. Nevertheless the revolutionary quarter-century from 1789 to 1814 had changed the face of Europe and the character of Western culture. It had swept away the venerable relics of mediaeval Christendom—the Holy Roman Empire, the territorial power of the Church with its ecclesiastical principalities and endowments, the hierarchical order of society and the sacred character of kingship. The *ancien rèime* had suffered such a fall that all the powers of the Holy Alliance and all the statesmen of the Congress of Vienna were unable to put it together again.

In spite of all this, the work of the statesmen of Vienna was infinitely superior to that of their successors at Versailles in

1919 or at Dumbarton Oaks and San Francisco in 1944-45. For they faced the problem of European unity in a sane constructive spirit, without utopian illusions or nationalist prejudices. Their attempt to transform the old antagonistic principle of the Balance of Power into a practical system of international cooperation which was embodied in the Law of Treaties and the Concert of Europe was fundamentally sound, and it gave Europe a longer period of peace than it has ever known before or since. Its failure was due not to any inherent defect, but to the lack of any common spiritual principle strong enough to overcome the centrifugal forces in European culture. The revolutionary idealism which found expression in the secret societies and in national liberalism and democratic socialism was too strong to be restrained by the rigid conservatism of the restored monarchies. There was a glaring contrast between the repressive traditionalism of the minor German and Italian states and the immense progress of wealth and population and scientific technique that was taking place in the Atlantic world. Thus the new world of America became the promised land of the European peasant and artisan; and the balance between the two worlds was held by England, the workshop and bank of the world, the ruler of the seas and the home of parliamentary institutions. This world-wide economic and colonial expansion of Western culture, which was mainly the work of the two English-speaking peoples, provided a safety valve for the frustrated and repressed elements in Europe, like the political refugees of 1848 and the far more numerous victims of famine and industrial depression. But at the same time it strengthened the centrifugal tendencies in nineteenth-century culture, so that the expansion of Europe was also a flight from Europe. In spite of the genuinely pacific aims of the Vienna settlement and the Concert of Europe, the Holy Alliance was everywhere regarded by liberals and democrats as a conspiracy of kings against peoples and of despotism against liberty.

Consequently at the very time when the external prestige of European culture was at its highest and the world was being conquered and transformed by European science and wealth and power, Europe itself was being torn asunder by the increasing violence of its internal conflicts. In England the bloodless victory of constitutional reform in 1832 inaugurated a long period of social peace and economic progress inspired by the ideology of Victorian Liberalism. But on the Continent the conflicting forces were too extreme and too evenly matched to admit of such a compromise. The traditions of revolutionary liberalism, nationalism, and social revolution all helped to undermine the restoration settlement and to destroy the Holy Alliance, but they were incapable of combining to create a new European order. The ultimate victor in the struggle was the centralized and militarized national state, like the new German Empire which represented an alliance between the old tradition of Prussian militarism and the new ideology of German nationalism. But neither of those elements was favourable to the ideal of European unity, and the Bismarckian era witnessed a spiritual decline of European culture which was in sharp contrast to the increasing economic power and military efficiency of the European state.

7. In the last period of our survey, from 1914 to 1950, this internal disintegration of European culture manifested itself in the new phase of war and revolution which has destroyed the European society of peoples and has deprived Europe of its world leadership.

During this period the threat of German military imperialism united the rest of the world against her and forced first Britain and then the United States to abandon their traditional isolation from continental Europe and to convert their economic and financial power to military ends. The result of the First World War was to destroy the three great military empires of Central and Eastern Europe and thus to clear the ground for a new social and political system. But the attempt of the Western powers to reorganize Europe and the world on liberal democratic principles did not succeed in meeting the needs of the situation or controlling the revolutionary forces that had been released. On the ruins of the military empires there arose the new totalitarian states of Soviet Russia and National Socialist Germany, which alike by their conflict and their collaboration destroyed the emergent democratic national states of Eastern Europe and precipitated a Second World War.

This second war was even more disastrous in its effects on European culture than the first. Europe has been not only economically ruined and morally weakened; it has been cut in two by the new frontier between Western Europe and the Communist-controlled East. This frontier, which passes through the heart of Central Europe, is not merely a political boundary; it is a line of division between two alien worlds which excludes the possibility of social intercourse and cultural communication, so that the man who wishes to pass from one part of Europe to the other is forced to abandon his citizenship and become a fugitive and an exile. Thus the old European society of states, which even fifty years ago was still the focus of world power and the leader of world civilization, has become a truncated fragment too small and too weak to exist without the military protection and economic aid of America.

Must we conclude from all this that Europe no longer exists and that the problem of European unity is no longer relevant to the present situation? Not necessarily so, since the present division of Europe is so recent and so artificial that it is difficult to believe in its final character. But in any case it is impossible to exaggerate the seriousness of the present crisis both for Europe itself and for the world. The division and impoverishment of Europe must inevitably lead to the division and impoverishment of the world, for Western Europe has played and still plays such an important part in world commerce and industry, and still more in science and thought, that its decay would inflict a more serious blow to world civilization than the fall of the Roman Empire or any other of the historic catastrophes which have caused the decline of some particular centre of higher culture. The very suddenness of the decline of Europe suggests that it may be a temporary crisis rather than a final catastrophe, since the fall of cultures in the past has usually been preceded, as in the case of the Roman Empire, by a slow process of decline and sterility lasting for centuries, whereas the present crisis of European culture took place when the social and economic activity of Western culture was at its highest pitch of development. It is due not to any decline of physical or social vitality, but to the internal division of Europe by an intensive process of revolutionary criticism which affected every aspect of Western culture. This process did not consciously aim at the destruction of European unity. At each successive stage it was inspired by a belief in social progress and the hope of a new European order. In fact the European revolutionary movement as a whole was not a symptom of social decadence, but an expression of the energy and optimism of an age of social and economic expansion. But the revolutionary ideal of a new European order was frustrated by the conflicting aims of the different revolutionary movements—liberal, socialist and nationalist—so that the revolutionary movement became destructive of European unity and hostile to European culture itself. In the bitter intensive struggle of parties and ideologies the deeper spiritual foundations of Western culture were forgotten or rejected until the movement which had begun with the worship of liberty and the Declaration of the Rights of Man ended in the concentration camps of the totalitarian state and the mass suicide of total war.

The process of European revolution has thus reached an absolute conclusion. There is no going forward on this path. If the peoples of Europe desire to survive, they must seek a new way. The age of revolution was also an age of world expansion when Europe was threatened by no external enemies, so that each of the great powers was a law to itself. During the last forty years this situation has been completely reversed and the peoples of Western Europe find themselves in a position of relative inferiority as a minority group exposed to the pressure of stronger and more united non-European world powers.

This catastrophic change must inevitably have a powerful effect on the immediate future of the peoples of Europe. But it may operate in two opposite directions. It may lead to discouragement, pessimism and despair, or alternatively it may make the European peoples realize their common interests and the need to restore the broken unity of European culture. If world expansion has led to cultural disintegration, then we might expect that external pressure would promote internal unity. But the essential problem is not the political issue of European federation or the practical question of European economic organization. The vital question is how to preserve the spiritual inheritance of Europe and restore a common purpose to Western civilization. The great world civilizations of the East were based on a sacred law of immemorial antiquity embodied in an unchanging pattern of institutions and customs. But Western culture has always owed its strength to the persistence of a dynamic purpose which has enabled it to change the world, to widen the frontiers of human knowledge and extend the range of human activity, without losing the continuity of its spiritual tradition and the community of its moral values. If this dynamic purpose can be restored, the spirit of Europe will survive and the unity of Western culture will reassert itself in some new form. For these fundamental issues belong to the plane of religion rather than to that of politics or economics, and these planes do not coincide. An age of material prosperity may often be an age of spiritual decline, while a dark age of material destruction and economic decline may see the birth of new spiritual forces.

4

The Classical Tradition
and Christianity

IF EUROPE OWES its political existence to the Roman Empire
and its spiritual unity to the Catholic Church, it is indebted
for its intellectual culture to a third factor—the Classical Tradition—which is also one of the fundamental elements that have
gone to the making of the European unity.

It is indeed difficult for us to realise the extent of our debt,
for the classical tradition has become so much a part of Western
culture that we are no longer fully conscious of its influence on
our minds. Throughout European history this tradition has been
the constant foundation of Western letters and Western thought.
It was first diffused through the West by the cosmopolitan culture of the Roman Empire. It survived the fall of Rome and
remained through the Middle Ages as an integral part of the
intellectual heritage of the Christian Church, and in the age of
the Renaissance it arose with renewed strength to become the
inspiration and model of the new European literatures and the
basis of all secular education.

Thus for nearly two thousand years Europe had been taught in the same school and by the same masters, so that the schoolboy and undergraduate of the nineteenth century were still reading the same books and conforming their minds to the same standards as their Roman predecessors eighteen hundred years before.

It is almost impossible to overrate the cumulative influence of so ancient and continuous a tradition. There is nothing to be compared with it in history except the Confucian tradition in China, and it is curious to reflect that both of them seem finally in danger of coming to an end at the same moment and under the influence of the same forces.

But the classical tradition of Europe differs from that of China in one important particular. It is not of indigenous origin, for though it is so closely linked with the Roman tradition Rome was not its creator, but rather the agent by which it was transmitted to the West from its original home in the Hellenic world. The classical tradition is, in fact, nothing else than Hellenism, and perhaps the greatest of all the services that Rome rendered to civilization is to be found in her masterly adaptation of the classical tradition of Hellenism to the needs of the Western mind and the forms of Western speech, so that the Latin language became not only a perfect vehicle for the expression of thought but also an ark which carried the seed of Hellenic culture through the deluge of barbarism. And thus the great classical writers of the first century B.C., above all, Cicero, Virgil, Livy and Horace, have an importance in the history of Europe that far outweights their intrinsic literary value, great as this is, for they are the fathers of the whole Western tradition of literature and the foundations of the edifice of European culture.

At the very moment when Rome had succeeded in extending her Empire over the Hellenistic world, the empire of the Greek classical tradition over the Western mind was assured by the Latin literature of the Augustan age, and the influence of Hellenism continued to increase and spread throughout the first two centuries of the Roman Empire. On the one hand, the first and second centuries A.D. witnessed a renaissance of the Hel-

lenic tradition in its strictly classical form throughout the Greek
world; and on the other, the Latin form of Hellenism, which
had already reached its full development in the first century
B.C., above all in the work of Cicero, was communicated to the
Western provinces and became the foundation of their culture.
Classical education was widely diffused throughout the Empire,
and not only great cities like Rome and Antioch and Alexandria
and Carthage, but provincial towns such as Madaura in Africa,
Autun and Bordeaux in Gaul, Cordova in Spain, and Gaza and
Berytus in Syria became the centres of an intense educational
activity. Juvenal writes of the universal mania for education
which was extending even to the barbarians:—

> Nunc totus Graias, nostrasque habet orbis Athenas,
> Gallia causidicos docuit facunda Britannos,
> De conducendo loquitur jam rhetore Thule.[1]

This culture was indeed purely literary. Science had little
place in it, except at Alexandria. The rhetorical ideal of education, inaugurated by Gorgias and the Sophists of the fifth century B.C. and developed in the schools of the Hellenistic world,
was completely dominant, and the successful rhetorician was
the idol of the educated public. But rhetoric had a much wider
scope than anything which we understand by the name. It was
the culmination of the whole cycle of liberal studies—arithme-
tic, geometry, astronomy, music, grammar, rhetoric and dialectic—the so-called "artes liberales," which were the fore-runners
of the mediaeval Quadrivium and Trivium.[2] Even apart from this

---

1. *Sat.* xv, 110–112. [Editor's translation: "Now the whole world has Greeks—
each our own Athens. Eloquent Gaul instructs the Britons in argument and even
Thule speaks of importing professors."]

2. This ideal of a liberal education dates from the Sophists themselves, above
all from Hippias of Elea, but it was not until the time of Martianus Capella and
the writers of the later Empire that the number of the Liberal Arts was definitely
fixed. The subdivision between the Trivium and the Quadrivium is later still,
and is probably due to the Carolingian Renaissance. On the other hand, the
mediaeval idea of the Liberal Arts as essentially propaedeutic—a preparation for
theology—is very ancient, since it goes back to Posidonius and Philo, from
whom it passed to the Christian scholars of Alexandria. Cf. Norden, *Die antike
Kunstprosa*, pp. 670–679.

wide ideal of oratory, which was upheld by Cicero and Tacitus, the pure rhetorician, such as Quintilian or Aristides, was far from being a mere pedant. He aimed at something wider than technical scholarship—at a broad literary culture which is nothing less than humanism. In fact, the humanist ideal of culture, which has dominated modern education since the Renaissance, owes its existence to a deliberate revival of the old rhetorical training. But even in the Middle Ages the latter survived to a far greater extent than is usually realised; indeed there is no period of European history in which its influence is not perceptible. The very type of the publicist—the man of letters who addresses himself to the educated public in general—a type which is almost unknown in other cultures, is a product of this tradition: Alcuin, John of Salisbury, Petrarch, Erasmus, Bodin, Grotius and Voltaire[3] were all of them the successors and disciples of the ancient rhetoricians, and this is but one aspect of that classical tradition which has been one of the chief creative forces in European culture.

In the fourth century, however, the supremacy of the classical tradition seemed gravely threatened by the victory of the new religion. Christianity was founded on an oriental tradition which had nothing in common with Hellenism, and its spirit and ideals were sharply opposed to those of the pagan rhetorician and man of letters. The Christians acknowledged no debt to the classical tradition. They had their own classics—the Christian Scriptures—which were so fundamentally different in form and spirit from pagan literature that there was at first no room for mutual comprehension. "What has Athens to do with Jerusalem?" writes Tertullian, "what concord is there between the Academy and the Church?" St. Paul himself expressly disavowed all claim

3. [Alcuin (d. 804), British monk and confidant of Charlemagne; John of Salisbury (d. 1180), pupil of Abelard and bishop of Chartres; Francesco Petrarch (1304–1374), Italian poet and man of letters; Desiderius Erasmus of Rotterdam (1466–1536), Dutch humanist and reformer; Jean Bodin (1530–1596), French political philosopher; Hugo Grotius (1583–1645), author of *De Jure Belli et Pacis*, an early treatise on international law; Francois Marie Arouet Voltaire (1694–1778), philosopher and a leading figure of the French Enlightenment.—Ed.]

to the graces of style and the wisdom of secular philosophy. "Where is the wise? Where is the scribe? Where is the disputer of this world? Hath not God made foolish the wisdom of this world? For the Jews require signs, and the Greeks seek after wisdom; but we preach Christ crucified, unto Jews a stumbling-block and unto the Gentiles foolishness; but with them that are called, both Jews and Greeks, Christ the power of God and the wisdom of God."[4]

Thus Christianity made its appeal not to the sophisticated and sterile mind of cultivated society, but to the fundamental needs of the human soul and to the religious experience of the common man. "Stand forth, O soul, and give thy witness," says Tertullian. "But I call thee not as when, fashioned in schools, trained in libraries, fed up in Attic academics and porticoes, thou belchest forth thy wisdom. I address thee simple and rude and unlettered and untaught, such as they have thee who have thee only, that very thing, pure and entire, of the road, the street, the workshop."[5]

In fact the early Christians were for the most part men of little education and culture. In the cities they belonged mainly to the lower and lower middle classes, while in the country they were often drawn from a peasantry which was almost unaffected by classical culture and which preserved its native Syriac or Coptic or Punic speech. In these circumstances it was but natural that the official representatives of the classical tradition should look on Christianity as the enemy of culture and, like the Emperor Julian or Porphyry, should identify the cause of Hellenism with that of the old religion. The "golden mediocrity" of the classical scholar could have little sympathy with the fanaticism of the martyrs and the desert monks, who condemned everything that made life delightful and proclaimed the approaching doom of all secular civilization. Maximus of Madaura, the pagan rhetorician who corresponded with St. Augustine, speaks of Christianity as a resurgence of oriental barba-

4. *Corinthians* i, 20–27.
5. Tertullian. *De Testimonio Animae,* i (Translated by Roberts and Donaldson.)

rism which sought to replace the worship of the gracious figures of the classical deities by the cult of executed criminals with horrid Punic names.[6]

Nevertheless, though it was ignored by the leaders of culture, there was going on all the time a process of assimilation by which the Church was preparing for the reception of the classical tradition and for the formation of a new Christian culture. As early as the second century, educated converts such as Justin Martyr and Athenagoras were beginning to address the cultivated public in their own language, and attempting to show that the doctrines of Christianity were in harmony with the rational ideals of ancient philosophy. The most remarkable of these attempts is the *Octavius* of Minucius Felix, a Ciceronian dialogue which is purely classical both in form and spirit. It is true that the greatest of the Latin apologists—Tertullian—wrote in a very different spirit, but even he, for all his neglect of the classical tradition, was a rhetorician to his very marrow, and appropriated the methods of the Roman barrister to the service of the new religion.

The tendency which is already visible in the Apologists to assimilate Hellenic thought and culture reaches its highest development in the school of Alexandria in the third century. Origen and his predecessor Clement were the first to conceive the mediaeval ideal of a hierarchy of sciences culminating in Christian theology. As the Greeks had treated the arts and sciences as a propaedeutic to rhetoric and philosophy, so Origen proposed to make philosophy itself a propaedeutic to theology— "that what the sons of the philosophers say about geometry and music and grammar and rhetoric and astronomy—that they are the handmaidens of philosophy—we may say of philosophy itself in relation to theology."[7] He taught, writes his disciple, Gregory Thaumaturgus, "that we should philosophies and collate with all our powers every one of the writings of the an-

6. Aug. *Epist.* XVI. [Maximus (d. 370) was a Neoplatonist and member of the court of Emperor Julian. Madaura was a provincial center in Africa.—Ed.]
7. *Philocalia* XIII, i. (Trans. W. Metcalfe.)

cients, whether philosophers or poets, excepting and rejecting nothing," save the writings of the atheists, "but giving a fair hearing to all."[8] The result of this programme was a far-reaching synthesis of Christianity and Hellenic thought which had a profound influence in the whole subsequent development of theology, but which from the first provoked considerable opposition on the ground that it was inconsistent with traditional orthodoxy, as indeed in some respects it certainly was. It is, however, important to note that this opposition to Origen did not necessarily imply any hostility to Hellenic culture as distinct from Hellenic philosophy. There were Hellenists in both camps; in fact Origen's chief opponent, Methodius of Olympus, went further than Origen himself in his allegiance to the classical tradition.[9]

Thus, by the beginning of the fourth century, classical culture had gained a sure foothold within the Church, and the establishment of the Christian Empire was actually followed by a considerable literary revival. The leaders of this movement—the great rhetoricians of the fourth century, Himerius, Themistius and Libanius—were themselves pagans, but they found no lack of pupils and imitators among the Christians; indeed even from a purely literary point of view the Christian writers of the period often surpassed their teachers. The Fathers of the fourth century, alike in the East and the West, were essentially *Christian rhetoricians* who shared the culture and traditions of their pagan rivals, but whose art was no longer an endless elaboration of the worn-out themes of the lecture-room, but had become the instrument of a new spiritual force. Three centuries earlier Tacitus had pointed out that rhetoric had become empty and unreal, because it no longer fulfilled a vital function in political life. "Great oratory, like fire, needs fuel to feed it and movement to fan it; it brightens as it burns."[10] Through the Church, rhetoric

---

8. Gregory Thaumaturgus, *Panegyric of Origen*, xiii. (Trans. W. Metcalfe.)

9. His chief work—the *Symposium of the Ten Virgins*—is an elaborate imitation of a Platonic dialogue.

10. *Dialogus de claris oratoribus* 30.

had recovered this vital relation to social life: in place of the old *ecclesia* of the Greek city it had found the new ecclesia of the Christian people. Once more the most profound issues were debated with passionate earnestness before an audience drawn from every class; as when St. John Chrysostom delivered his great homilies to the people of Antioch, while the fate of the city was hanging in the balance. Even the most abstruse theological questions were a matter of burning interest to the man in the street, and the man who could speak or write of them with eloquence and skill was assured of an almost world-wide influence.

This, of course, is primarily true of the Greek-speaking world, the world of Athanasius and Arius, of Basil and Eunomius, of Cyril and Theodoret; but in the Latin West the rhetorical tradition was equally powerful, though it was the tradition of the Roman magistrate and orator rather than of the Hellenic sophist and demagogue. No doubt the Hellenic world still retained its cultural leadership. Eusebius of Caesarea, St. Basil and the two Gregories, of Nyssa and Nazianzus, possessed a wider and deeper culture, alike in literature and philosophy, than any of their Western contemporaries. They preserved the traditions of the school of Origen, whereas the Western tradition inherited something of the legal and authoritative spirit of Tertullian and Cyprian. But in the fourth century the rise of the new Christian culture tended to draw East and West together once more. St. Ambrose was a diligent student of Greek literature, and owes infinitely more to the writings of the Greek Fathers than to Tertullian and Cyprian, whom he entirely ignores. St. Jerome acquired his theological learning in the East as the pupil of St. Gregory Nazianzen and Apollinarius of Laodicea, and the student of Origen and Eusebius.

Moreover, the tendency of the Church to come to terms with secular culture and to assimilate classical literature and thought manifests itself in the West no less than in the East. St. Ambrose adorns his sermons with quotations from Virgil and Horace, and takes Cicero as his model and guide in his most famous

work, *De Officiis Ministrorum*. The Ciceronian tradition forms
an essential part of the new Christian culture and influences
patristic literature from the time of Lactantius to that of Augustine. St. Jerome, it is true, speaks strongly of the dangers of
pagan literature, and the famous vision in which he was condemned for being "a Ciceronian not a Christian" is often quoted
as an example of the hostility of Christianity to classical culture.[11] But the true significance of the episode is that Jerome's
devotion to classical literature was so intense that it had become
a spiritual temptation. Had he not reacted against it, he might
have become a rhetorician and nothing more. And in that case
the Middle Ages would have lost the greatest of their spiritual
classics—the Latin Vulgate. For in his translation of the Bible
Jerome makes no attempt to adhere to Ciceronian standards,
but allows the primitive grandeur of the Hebrew original to
reflect itself in his style, so that he enriched the Latin language
with a new range of expression. But though he attempted to
moderate his ardour, he never lost his passionate devotion to
the greatest of the rhetoricians—"Tullius qui in arce eloquentiae
romanae stetit rex oratorum et latinae linguae illustrator."[12]
Rufinus relates, not without malice, that he would in his later
years pay his copyists more highly for the transcription of Cicero's dialogues than for that of ecclesiastical works,[13] and that
he taught the children at Bethlehem to read Virgil and the poets.
In fact, far from being an enemy to the classical tradition, Jerome is of all the Fathers the most steeped in pagan literature
and the most deeply influenced by the rhetorical tradition. Even
the intolerance and pugnacity which have scandalised so many
modern critics do not spring from the fanaticism of a bigot, but
from the irascibility of a scholar, and his literary vendettas are

11. *Epist. XXII.* Cf. Rufinus, *Apol.* II, 6, and St. Jerome's answer. *Apol.* I,
30-31, III, 32.

12. [Editor's translation: "Tullius, who stood atop the Roman art of speaking,
king of orators and exemplar of the Latin tongue."] From the preface to the
Hebraicae Quaestiones in Genesim. Cavallera, St. Jerome, *app.* P., p. 105. "If
such a man as Cicero," he says, "could not escape criticism, what wonder if the
dirty swine grunt at a poor little man like me!"

13. Rufinus, *Apol.* II, 8.

often curiously similar to those of the humanists of the Renaissance, who were themselves among his warmest admirers.[14]

The influence of Jerome was indeed second to none, not even to that of Augustine, but it was the influence of a scholar, not of a thinker or a theologian. In him the two great spiritual traditions of the classics and the Bible meet together, and from him they flow out again in a single stream to fertilise the culture of the Middle Ages.

The influence of the classical tradition is even more clearly discernible in the rise of a new Christian poetry; in the East, however, save in the case of St. Gregory Nazianzen, the servile imitation of classical models destroyed all spontaneity of feeling and found its supreme expression in the attempt of Apollinarius of Laodicea and his son to translate the Bible into the forms and metres of classical poetry. In the West, the same tendency produced the Biblical paraphrases of Juvencus and the ingenious but misguided attempts to compose poems on Biblical subjects entirely made up of passages from Virgil detached from their context. But the West possessed a far more living poetical tradition than the East, and during the fourth and fifth centuries this tradition was fully assimilated by the new Christian culture. Paulinus of Nola, who found a kindred spirit in his English biographer, Henry Vaughan, was a genuine Christian humanist, the spiritual ancestor of Vida and Mantuanus.[15] He was not a

14. *E.g.*, Erasmus speaks of Jerome as "that heavenly man, of all Christians beyond question the most learned and the most eloquent. . . . What a mass there is in his works of antiquities, of Greek literature, of history! and then what a style! What a mastery of language, in which he has left not only all Christian authors far behind him, but seems to vie with Cicero himself."—*Ep.* 134, trans. Nichols (=*e.p.* 141 ed. Allen).

Like the humanists, Jerome pillories his opponents under sobriquets drawn from classical literature. Rufinus is Luscius Lavinius or Calpurnius Lanarius (from Sallust), Pelagius and his supporters are Catiline and Lentulus. In the famous quarrel between Poggio and Francisco Filelfo the latter actually appeals to the precedents of Jerome and Rufinus in order to justify the violence of his invectives. Cf. his letters, printed in the Appendix to Walser's *Poggius Florentinus*, Nos. 40 and 42.

15. [St. Paulinus of Nola (d. 431), bishop and writer; Henry Vaughan (1621–1695), English religious poet. His life of Paulinus appeared in 1645.—Ed.]

great poet, but he was a man of high culture and of noble and attractive character, and his influence did more even than that of Jerome or Augustine to popularise the ideals of the new Christian culture among the educated classes in the Western provinces.

But the greatest of the Christian poets was Paulinus' Spanish contemporary, Prudentius, whom Bentley termed "the Christian Virgil and Horace." Of all the Christian writers, Prudentius shows the fullest appreciation of the classical tradition in both its literary and its social aspects. He yields to none of the pagan poets in his civic patriotism and his devotion to the great name of Rome. He does not look on Rome with the eyes of Tertullian and Augustine as a mere manifestation of human pride and ambition. Like Dante, he sees in the Empire a providential preparation for the unity of mankind in Christ. The Fabii and the Scipios were the unconscious instruments of the divine purpose, and the martyrs gave their lives for Rome no less than the legionaries. The last words of St. Laurence in the *Peristephanon* are a prayer for Rome. "O Christ, grant to thy Romans that the city by which Thou hast granted to the rest to be of one mind in religion should itself become Christian. . . . May it teach lands far apart to come together in one grace; may Romulus become faithful and Numa himself believe."[16] Now this prayer had been fulfilled; the Rome of the consuls and the Rome of the martyrs had become one. "To-day the lights of the Senate kiss the threshold of the temple of the apostles. The Pontiff who wore the sacred fillets bears on his brow the mark of the cross, and the Vestal Claudia kneels before the altar of St. Laurence."[17]

In the poems of Prudentius and in those of Paulinus of Nola we see how the cult of the martyrs, which had its origins in the protest of the Christian mind against the anti-spiritual claims of the secular power, had become transformed into a social institution and a manifestation of civic piety. To Prudentius, the old

16. *Peristephanon*, II, 433.
17. *Peristephanon*, II, 517.

local patriotism of the city-state finds a new justification through the cult of the local saints. He shows us the cities of Spain presenting themselves before the judgment-seat of God, each bearing the relics of its native martyrs. The saint has become the representative and guardian of the city and imparts to it a share in his glory.

> Sterne te totam generosa sanctis
> Civitas mecum tumulis; deinde
> Mox resurgentes animas et artus
>   Tota sequeris.[18]

The reconciliation between Christianity and the classical tradition in the fourth and fifth centuries, which finds expression in the patristic culture and the new Christian poetry, had a profound influence on the formation of the European mind. The modern is apt to regard the whole rhetorical tradition as empty pedantry, and to dismiss Cicero himself as a pompous bore. But, as I have already pointed out, it is to the rhetorician and his educational work that we owe the survival of classical literature and the whole tradition of humanism. Without them European culture would not only have been poorer, it would have been fundamentally different. There would have been no tradition of secular learning, no secular literature, save that of the minstrel and the saga-writer. The higher culture would have been entirely religious, as it has tended to be in the oriental world outside China. The survival of classical literature and the rhetorical tradition not only made possible the rise of the modern European literatures; they also formed the European habit of mind, and rendered possible that rational and critical attitude to life and nature which is peculiar to Western civilization. The coexistence of these two spiritual and literary traditions—that of the

18. *Peristephanon*, IV, 197. ["Prostrate yourself here with me, noble city, / at the sacred tombs of your holy martyrs / Thence you will soon follow them risen once more / Body and Spirit." Trans. Sr. M. Clement Eagan, C.C.V.L., Fathers of the Church, vol. 43, (Washington, D.C.: The Catholic University of America Press, 1962).—Ed.]

Church and the Bible on the one hand, and that of Hellenism and the classics on the other—has left a profound mark on our culture, and their mutual influence and interpenetration has enriched the Western mind in a way that no single tradition, however great, could have done by itself.

It is true that this rhetorical and literary habit of mind has its defects, and it is perhaps partially responsible for that artificiality which is one of the greatest weaknesses of our civilisation. Moreover, the coexistence of two intellectual traditions of disparate origin has tended to produce a certain dualism and disharmony in European culture that is absent in civilisations of a simpler or more uniform type. Nor can it be said that the rhetorical tradition was a complete embodiment of the intellectual achievement of the ancient world. It was a partial and one-sided development, which represents one aspect of the Hellenic genius, but fails to do justice to its scientific and metaphysical achievements. The true responsibility for the failure of mediaeval culture to preserve the inheritance of Greek science rests not on the Church, but on the rhetoricians. The scientific tradition of the Greek world had become separated from the literary tradition of the rhetoricians during the Hellenistic period, and consequently it was never assimilated by the Latin West as was the literary side of Greek culture. The only Latin contributions to science were the encyclopaedias of cultivated amateurs like Varro and Pliny and the technical works of engineers and surveyors (gromatici). All the real scientific work of the age was due to Greeks, such as Galen and Claudius Ptolemaeus (Ptolemy) in the second century A.D., who were the last creative minds in ancient science; but it is significant that although Galen lived and worked at Rome, his writings were never translated into Latin until the Middle Ages.

The scientific tradition still survived during the later Empire, but it was confined to the East and flourished mainly in the schools of Alexandria and Athens, which were at this period almost monopolised by the Neoplatonists. It was the aim of the latter, from the fourth century onwards, to combine the whole body of Greek science in an organic unity based on their own metaphysical and theological doctrines. Above all they aimed at the reconciliation of Aristotle with Plato and Ptolemy with Aristotle, and consequently their energies were directed not to original research but to interpreting and commentating the older authorities. Their curriculum was based on the works of Euclid and Nicomachus, Ptolemy and Geminos, Aristotle and Plato, but the importance of Aristotle steadily increased and reached its climax in the Alexandrian philosophers of the sixth century—Ammonius, Simplicius, Damascius and the Christian John Philoponus, all of whom show an extraordinarily wide knowledge of ancient science. This Aristotelian revival, which had begun as early as the beginning of the third century with the great commentator Alexander of Aphrodisias, was of the greatest importance for the future; but it did not reach the Latin West, save in a very rudimentary form through Boethius, until the twelfth and thirteenth centuries.

But although the later scientific development of Greek culture failed to affect the West, later Greek philosophy, as represented by Neoplatonism, had a direct influence on the new Latin Christian culture. Up to this point, philosophy in the West had been represented mainly by the Stoic ethics embodied in the rhetorical tradition, above all in the writings of Cicero and Seneca. There had been no creative metaphysical thought and no original psychological observation. Now at the very close of the imperial epoch the Latin world produced in St. Augustine a profoundly original genius, in whose thought the new Christian culture found its highest philosophic expression. Augustine also was a rhetorician by profession, and it was from Cicero that his mind first received an impulse towards the study of philosophy. But the turning-point in his life was eleven years later, when he came under the influence of the writings of the Neoplatonists that had been translated into Latin by the converted rhetorician Marius Victorinus. By them he was first convinced of the objective existence of spiritual reality, and from them he derived the two fundamental principles which remained the poles of his philosophy—the idea of God as the source of being and intelligence, the Sun of the intelligible world; and the idea of the soul as a spiritual nature which finds its beatitude in the participation of the Uncreated Light.

But Augustine was not contented with the intellectualism of Greek philosophy. He demanded not a speculative theory of truth, but its experimental possession. "The Platonists," he says, "indeed saw the Truth fixed, stable, unfading, in which are all the forms of all created things, but they saw it from afar . . . and therefore they could not find the way by which they might attain to so great and ineffable and beatific a possession."[19]

This *way* he found only in Christianity—in the supernatural wisdom which not only shows man the truth, but gives him the means of attaining to its fruition. His philosophy acquired its final character from the experience of his own conversion, the realisation of the intervention of a spiritual power which was strong enough to change his personality and to transform the notional order of intelligence into a vital order of charity. The spiritual evolution which began with the *Hortensius* of Cicero ends in the *Confessions,* and the *sapientia* of the Roman rhetorician finds its fulfillment in the *contemplatio* of the Christian mystic.

Thus the philosophy of Augustine differs from that of Origen, the greatest Christian thinker of the Greek world, in its intensely personal character. It remains Hellenic in its insistence on the existence of a rational order pervading the world, and in its sense of the goodness and beauty of all created being.[20] But it was both Western and Christian in its moral preoccupations and by reason of the central position which it accords to the will.

The philosophy of Augustine is essentially a philosophy of spiritual experience, and as such it is the source of Western mysticism and of Western ethics, as well as of the Western tradition of philosophic idealism.

19. *Sermo,* 141.
20. Cf., *e.g., de Trinitate,* VIII, iii.

In the fifth and sixth centuries, the influence of Augustine became dominant throughout the Christian West. Orosius, Prosper of Aquitaine, Leo the Great, Fulgentius of Ruspe, were all of them Augustinians; and finally through St. Gregory the Great the Augustinian tradition in a simplified form became the intellectual patrimony of the mediaeval Church. But this theological tradition was accompanied by a growing alienation from classical culture. The very profundity of Augustinian thought tended to narrow the range of intellectual activity and to concentrate all attention on the two poles of the spiritual life—God and the soul. This religious absolutism left no room either for pure literature or for pure science. For, to St. Augustine, the knowledge "wherein men desire nothing but to know" is an unprofitable curiosity that distracts the mind from its one true goal—the knowledge and the love of God. It is better for a man to know God than to number the stars or to seek out the hidden secrets of nature. "Surely unhappy is he who knoweth all these and knoweth not Thee, but happy whose knoweth Thee, though he know not these. And whoso knoweth both Thee and them is not happier for them, but for Thee only."[21]

This view was destined to dominate the clerical and monastic culture of the Latin West for many centuries. Nevertheless, so long as the West preserved the Roman-Byzantine tradition of an educated bureaucracy trained in the schools of rhetoric, there was no risk of classical culture being undervalued. Even the temporary recovery of secular culture that accompanied the Byzantine revival of the sixth century was not without its counterpart in the West. This is especially the case in Africa, where the court of the last Vandal kings was frequented—surprisingly enough—by the swarm of minor poets whose verses are preserved in the four-and-twenty books of the Salmasian anthology, and where the subsequent period produced the respectable epic of Corippus—the *Johannis*—perhaps the last genuine representative of the classical tradition in Latin poetry. So, too, in Italy under the rule of Theodoric the civil administration was still in

21. Aug. *Confessions*, V, iii. Cf. X, xxxv.

the hands of highly cultivated officials like Boethius, Symma-
chus and Cassiodorus, and they did all that was in their power
to preserve the inheritance of classical learning. Boethius was
not only the last of the classics, he was also the first of the
scholastics, a great educator, through whom the mediaeval West
received its knowledge of Aristotelian logic and the rudiments
of Greek mathematics. His tragic death put an end to the work
of philosophical translation that he had planned, but in compensation it gave the world the *De Consolatione Philosophiae*—a
masterpiece which, in spite of its deliberate reticence, is a perfect expression of the union of the Christian spirit with the
classical tradition.

The same ideal inspired the work of Cassiodorus, who did
even more than Boethius to build a bridge between the culture
of the ancient world and that of the Middle Ages. In the first
part of his life, as a minister of state in the service of the Gothic
régime, he devoted himself to the promotion of religious unity
and the reconciliation of the Germanic invaders to Roman culture, while his later life was dedicated to the service of the
Church and to the reconciliation of classical culture with the
needs of the new ecclesiastical society and the ideals of the monastic life. It is as though he realised that the state could no
longer serve as an organ of the higher culture and that the
inheritance of classical civilisation could be saved only by being
placed under the tutelage of the Church. In the last years of
Gothic rule he planned, in co-operation with Pope Agapitus, to
found a Christian school at Rome which should perform somewhat the same function for the West that the catechetical school
of Alexandria had fulfilled in the East at an earlier period.

These plans were frustrated by the outbreak of the Gothic
wars, which had a more disastrous effect on Italian culture than
all the invasions of the previous century. But Cassiodorus refused to be discouraged. Though he was forced to abandon public
life and to take refuge in the cloister, he found an opportunity
for the realisation of his ideal in the monastery that he founded
in his great Calabrian estates at Vivarium. Here he collected a

library and drew up his two programmes of monastic studies—
the *Institutes of Divine and Secular Letters*—which are one of
the fundamental documents for the history of mediaeval culture.
The first and most important of these works deals with religious
learning and insists on the need for a high standard of scholarship in the study and reproduction of the Sacred Text; the second is an encyclopaedic compendium of the seven Liberal Arts,
especially grammar, rhetoric and dialectic. It is the old curriculum of the later Empire adapted to the needs of the new religious society. As with Gregory Nazianzen and Augustine, the
arts are regarded as an instrument of religious education, not as
an end in themselves. But they are a necessary instrument, since
the neglect of them involves the weakening and impoverishment
of the theological culture that they serve. Even the study of the
pagan poets and prose writers is regarded as legitimate and even
necessary, since without them it was impossible to receive a
complete training in the Liberal Arts.

Thus Vivarium was the starting-point of the tradition of monastic learning that was afterwards to become the glory of the
Benedictine Order. Western monasticism entered into the heritage of the classical culture and saved it from the ruin that
overwhelmed the secular civilisation of the Latin West at the
end of the sixth century. It is to the monastic libraries and
scriptoria that we owe the preservation and translation of almost
the entire body of Latin classical literature that we possess today. It is true that Italian monasticism was itself affected by
this collapse, and Cassiodorus left no successors in his own
land. His work was taken up and completed by the children of
a new world—the Irish and Anglo-Saxon monks, who prepared
the way for that revival of Christian classicism which finally
emerged in the Carolingian period.

5

The Secularization of Western Culture

IT IS NOT POSSIBLE to discuss the modern situation either from the point of view of religion or politics without using the word "culture." But the word has been used in so many different senses and is capable of so many shades of meaning that it is necessary to say something at the outset as to the sense in which I am going to use it, in order to avoid unnecessary confusion.

The Concise Oxford Dictionary gives three senses—tillage, improvement by mental or physical training, and intellectual development. None of these however is precisely the sense in which the word is used by anthropologists, sociologists, and now to an increasing extent also by historians and philosophers. From the date 1871, when Tyler in England published his famous book on Primitive Culture, and from a much earlier date on the Continent, the word has been extended to cover the whole complex of institutions and customs and beliefs, as well as arts and crafts and economic organization, which make up the social inheritance of a people. Thus it is almost interchangeable with the word civilization, except that the latter is as a rule restricted to the higher forms of culture, as there is an obvious objection to speaking of the "civilization" of an uncivilized people. I use Culture therefore as the wider and more inclusive term, and civilization as a particular type of culture in its higher and more conscious manifestations.

Thus it is possible to get behind or beyond civilization and study human nature in a relatively primitive state. But it is never possible to get beyond culture. The eighteenth century idea of a state of nature in which man existed before he got entangled in the meshes of the state and of organized religion, and into which he must think himself back in order to construct a rational order of society is of course completely mythical and unreal. Primitive man is just as much part of a social pattern, often a very elaborate one, and is just as much dependent on cultural traditions as civilized man, or even more so.

In the same way it is impossible to separate culture from religion, and the further we go back in history, or the lower we descend in the scale of social development, the more closely are they related to one another. It is easy to understand the reason for this which is inherent in the nature of religion itself. For religion is not, as the rationalists of the last two centuries believed, a secondary phenomenon which has arisen from the exploitation of human credulity, or as Hobbes put it "from opinion of Ghosts, Ignorance of second causes, Devotion towards what men fear and Taking of things Casuall for Prognostiques"; it lies at the very centre of human consciousness, in man's sense of his dependence on higher powers and of his relation to the spiritual world. The simpler a culture is the closer is its relation with religion, not of course because a low culture is more spiritual than the higher ones, but because the narrow limits of its control over nature increases man's sense of dependence, so that it seems impossible for society to exist without the help of the mysterious powers that surround him.

The relation between the higher and lower forms of religion has never been more perfectly stated than in the words of the Apostles to the simple Lycaonians, when they accepted Barnabas and Paul as Gods; "We preach that you should turn from these vanities to serve the living God who made heaven and earth and the sea and all things that are therein, who in times past suffered all nations to walk in their own ways. Nevertheless He left not Himself without witness in that He did good and gave us rains from heaven and fruitful seasons, filling our hearts with food and gladness." The religion of primitive man is concerned with just those things—food and rain and the course of the seasons. In them he sees the hand of God and the working of sacred and magical forces. Therefore the ways by which men live and the crises of their lives are inextricably interwoven with religious beliefs and practices to form the pattern of culture.

Nevertheless even the crudest and most primitive forms of religion are never completely restricted to this pattern; they always possess an element of transcendence without which they would cease to be religion. For since religion is the bond between man and God, between human society and the spiritual world, it always has a twofold aspect. To the outsider, whether he be a traveller or a rational critic, primitive religions seem like a dead weight of social convention and superstition which prevents the society from advancing; to the primitive himself, however, it is the way of the Gods, the traditional consecrated order which brings human life into communion with the higher powers; and we see from the history of more developed religions that the most simple and elementary religious practices are capable, not merely of becoming charged with religious emotion, but of becoming the vehicle of profound religious ideas, as for example the ritual of sacrifice in ancient India or the ceremonial ordering of the calendar in ancient China.

On the other hand, when we come to the higher religions where there is a conscious effort to assert the absolute transcendence of God and of the spiritual order, we still do not find any complete divorce between religion and culture. Even Buddhism, which seems at first sight to turn its back on human life and condemn all the natural values on which human culture is built, nevertheless has as great an influence on culture and impresses its character on the social life of the Tibetans or the Singhalese no less than a religion which adopts a frankly positive, or as we say "pagan" attitude towards nature and human life. Religions of this type do, however, bring out more clearly the element of tension and conflict in the relation between religion and culture, which it is easy to ignore in a primitive religion which seems completely fused and identified with the social pattern.

In neither type of culture therefore do we find anything that really corresponds to the problem that confronts us at the present day—the problem of a state of separation and dislocation between religion and culture; in other words the problem of a secularized culture. No doubt other cultures have passed through phases of relative secularization, e.g., China in the third century B.C., and Rome in the last age of the Republic. But these phases were confined to particular societies and almost certainly to small classes or elites in these societies. But today it is a world-wide phenomenon and, at least in the more advanced societies, it extends through the whole social structure and affects the life of the common people no less than the thought of the leading classes and groups.

Now it is easy enough to explain the universality of the present situation. It is due to the world-wide extension of Western civilization by imperial expansion, by material progress and by economic and intellectual penetration. But what is the relation between the immense extension of modern Western civilization and its secularization? Are they related as cause and effect? And if so is the extension the cause of the secularization, or vice versa?

There is no doubt that the rapid material progress and external expansion of Western culture has had a secularizing effect. World empires usually tend to lose touch with their spiritual roots, and the same is true of the expansion of a civilization by way of administrative and intellectual influence, as we see in the case of the Hellenistic world in the third and second centuries B.C. Nevertheless this is not the essential cause of the change. Western culture was becoming secularized before the great period of its expansion had begun. The fundamental causes of that process were spiritual and closely related to the whole spiritual development of Western Man. But the same causes which produced the secularization of culture were also responsible for its external expansion. They were, in fact, two aspects of a single process, a world revolution of such a tremendous kind that it seems to transcend history and create new categories with which our traditional standards of judgment are incapable of dealing.

It is with regard to the religious issue that the traditional methods of interpretation are most defective. For if we consider the problem from a Christian point of view we are faced by the paradox that it was a Christian culture and not a pagan one which was the source of this revolution. While the secular historian is brought up against the equally disturbing fact that the non-secular element in Western culture has been the dynamic element in the whole process of change, so that the complete secularization of culture by removing this element would bring the progressive movement to a full stop, and thus bring about a static society which has mastered social change to such a degree that it no longer possesses any vital momentum.

This is the greatness and misery of modern civilization—that it has conquered the world by losing its own soul, and that when its soul is lost it must lose the world as well. Western culture has never been a natural unity, like the great civilizations of the ancient east, like Egypt and China and India. It is a changing association of peoples and countries which owes its unity to the continuity of its tradition, a tradition which it did not even originate but which it inherited and transformed and enlarged until it became the source of a new world and a new humanity. For a thousand years the bearer of this tradition was the Christian Church, and during this formative period it was only by becoming members of the Church that the nations became partakers in the community of Western culture.

The importance of this factor has seldom been sufficiently appreciated by the historians. They recognized the influence of the Church on medieval history, and the way in which the religious unity of Christendom conditioned the development of the Western peoples. But, it seems to me, they have none of them fully realized the significance of the fact which is almost unique in world history, that Europe found its unity and cultural form not simply by the profession of a common faith, but by entering a spiritual community which was already existing and which possessed an independent principle of organization, with its own organs of authority and its own institutions and laws. The medieval Church was not a state within a state, but a super-political society of which the state was a subordinate, local, and limited organ. Ideally there was one great society—that of the Christian people—with a twofold hierarchy of spiritual and temporal ministers. And the spiritual conflict which occupied the medieval consciousness was concerned not merely with the relations of the two hierarchies to one another, but less consciously and more profoundly with the problem of reconciling this ideal order with the real world of territorial states and feudal principalities, which the descendants of the barbarians had built for themselves by the sword.

The existence of this double dualism—of Church and state and of Christian ideal and barbaric reality—is one of the main reasons why Western Christendom did not develop into a closed religious civilization like those of the ancient East. Instead, the unity of Christendom was broken and the cultural hegemony of the Church was destroyed by the religious revolution of the sixteenth century. But though this prepared the way for the secularization of culture, nothing could have been further from the mind and intention of the leaders of the movement. On the contrary, it seemed to them that they were working for the desecularization of the Church, and the restoration of Christianity to its primitive purity. They did not realize that the attempt to purify and separate religion from its cultural accretions, might find its counterpart in the separation of culture from religion and the increasing secularization of life and thought. And this was in fact what happened; though it was a gradual process which took centuries to complete itself.

Nevertheless the new lay humanist culture which was beginning to develop in the West in the fifteenth and sixteenth centuries was far from being entirely secular. As Burdach has shown the very conception of the Renaissance—or the rebirth of culture—was closely connected with the Reformation or the rebirth of Christianity. Both were influenced in their origins by the apocalyptic hopes of a spiritual renewal of Christendom, which was so widespread in the later Middle Ages and which found different forms of expression in Northern and Southern Europe. Neither the Humanists nor the Reformers dreamt of the destruction of Christendom. They believed, like Erasmus, that "the world was coming to its senses as if awakening out of a deep sleep," and they thought that religion and culture could slough off their old skins and could renew their youth by returning to their origins.

Thus the Renaissance achievement was like that of Columbus who discovered the new world by attempting to find his way back to the old world by a new route. The sudden removal of the fixed limits which had bounded the thought and action of medieval man, the opening of new worlds and the realization of the boundless possibilities of human reason caused a release of energies which gave Western culture a new world-embracing character. Though Western science was still in its infancy men like Leonardo da Vinci and Paracelsus and Campanella and Bacon had already begun to realize its world transforming possibilities.

Glory to Him who knows and can do all, writes Campanella:

O my art, grandchild to the primal Wisdom, give something of his fair image which is called Man.

A second God, the First's own miracle, he commands the depths; he mounts to Heaven without wings and counts its motions and measures and its natures.

The wind and the sea he has mastered and the earthly globe with pooped ship he encircles, conquers and beholds, barters and makes his prey.

He sets laws like a God. In his craft, he has given to silent parchment and to paper the power of speech and to distinguish time he gives tongue to brass.

The author of these verses is a striking example of the way in which the thought of the Renaissance united humanist and scientific culture with apocalyptic religious ideals and revolutionary hopes for a new order of society.

Throughout his long imprisonment of thirty years in the prisons of Spain and the Inquisition, Campanella continued to advocate his ideas of the coming of a new order which would unite mankind under the rule of nature. But even in its earliest and most revolutionary form Campanella's City of the Sun was far from being secular. It was a totalitarian communist theocracy governed by a priest king—the Metaphysician—elected by universal suffrage, and three magistrates representing the three divine hypostases—Power, Wisdom and Love—who deal respectively with war, science and education, and economics and eugenics. Neither property, marriage nor the family were admitted and the magistrates work according to aptitude, honours are given according to merit and food according to need and constitution.

At first sight the utopia of Campanella resembles that of Thomas More, but at the same time it differs profoundly in spirit and intention. It was not for the sake of utopia that Thomas More lost his head, but in defense of the traditional order of Christendom. But Campanella's utopianism had a definitely revolutionary character which showed itself in the fantastic attempt of a handful of friars and outlaws to overthrow the Spanish government in 1599, and to set up the City of the Sun on Mount Stilo in Catalonia. Thus I believe that Campanella more than Thomas More, and more than the Anabaptists of Muenster, should be regarded as the forerunner of modern revolutionary socialism, more especially as the idea of the organization and control of social life by natural science formed an essential part of his theory. Yet in spite of the revolutionary character of his thought, and in spite of its complete divorce from the cultural tradition of medieval Christendom, his ideal, as I have already said, was not a secular one. He looked back to the pagan identification of religion with culture, rather than forward to the modern secular state and the secularization of life. It was for this reason that he was so bitterly opposed to the Reformation, which he regarded as an individualist movement to desecularize religion inspired by the natural indiscipline of the Germanic people: in fact the new revolt of the barbarians.

For all his misunderstanding of the situation, there remains this element of truth: that in fact the chief cause of the secularization of Western culture was the loss of Christian unity—the dissolution of the community in which the peoples of the West had found their spiritual citizenship. The mere fact of this loss of unity created a neutral territory which gradually expanded till it came to include almost the whole of social life. The wars of religion and the long controversy concerning religious toleration, which produced such a prolific literature during the seventeenth century, especially in England, forced men to accept, at least as a practical necessity, the principle of common political and economic action by men who differed in their theological views and in their ecclesiastical allegiance; and when once men had admitted the principle that a heretic could be a good citizen (and even that an infidel could be a good man of business), they inevitably tended to regard this common ground of practical action as the real world, and the exclusive sphere of religion as a private world, whether of personal faith or merely private opinion.

In this way there arose the new liberal humanitarian culture which represents an intermediate stage between the religious unity of Christendom and a totally secularized world. On the continent it was at first the culture of the people; and in Catholic countries, at least, its permeation of society was accompanied by a violent revolutionary crisis. Only in England and North America did it proceed in the other direction—from below upwards—for there it found its inspiration not only in the rational idealism of the humanist tradition, but even more in the religious idealism of Puritanism with its conception of the Holy Community and of Christian Liberty.

But both these currents ultimately came together to form the liberal bourgeois culture of the nineteenth century, with its individualism and its Christian-humanitarian ethics, with its faith in reason and progress, in free trade and constitutional government. The place that religion held in this culture differed from country to country and from class to class. But on the whole I am inclined to think that there has been a tendency to underestimate its importance. In early Victorian England, for example, what struck the foreign observer was not simply the amount of religious observance, but the fact that Christianity influenced public policy. Thus a contemporary French statesman writes

Religious convictions are not with them mere rules for private conduct or simply intellectual indulgences: they enter into political life and influence the actions of public men, as conscience weighs upon single individuals. The dissenting sects are generally the first to stir themselves energetically for some object, which in their eyes religion commands them to pursue. The movement even extends through the entire Christian Church of the country, then into the different classes of civil society, and finally reaches the Government itself, which either coincides from approbation or resigns itself to follow. Thus the traffic in slaves has been abolished; thus the spirit of peace has predominated in England until the last few years, gathering power at once from the wisdom of material interests and the force of religious convictions; and imposed by the nation on the government, which on its part, during the progress of this interval, has not repulsed the public feeling but has voluntarily adopted it as the rule of state policy.[1]

The fact that Liberal culture was founded on Christian moral values rendered it accessible to religious influences, even in a secular age. Nevertheless the spiritual elements in the Liberal culture were not strong enough to control the immense forces which had been released by the progress of the applied sciences and the new economic techniques. The advent of the machine, which was in a sense the result of the liberal culture, proved fatal to the liberal values and ideals, and ultimately to the social types which had been the creators and bearers of the culture.

1. (Guizot, *Memoirs II*, 72. (English translation, 1859.)

The machine involved the increase of power, the concentration of power and the mechanization first of economic life and then of social life in general. It is true that in Britain and the United States the revolutionary effects of mechanization were reduced by the existence of unlimited colonial territories and foreign markets to absorb the new economic forces. It was only when mechanization was applied in the closed world of continental Europe that the revolutionary character became plain. And this was above all the case when it passed from the liberal bourgeoisie of the West into the hands of the bureaucratic monarchies of Eastern Europe, which approached the problems of the new order from the standpoint of power politics and military organization.

The great conflict, that has divided Europe in the twentieth century and has produced two world wars, is the result of the application of similar technique in an opposite spirit and for opposite ends: science and mechanization being used, in the one case, in a commercial spirit for the increase of wealth; in the other, in a military spirit for the conquest of power. And as the conflict proceeds, the more complete becomes the mechanization of life, until total organization seems to be the necessary condition of social survival.

Liberal culture sought to avoid the danger of complete secularization by insisting on the preservation of a margin of individual freedom, which was immune from state control and to which, in theory at least, economic life was subordinated. And within the zone of individual freedom, religious freedom was the ultimate stronghold which defended the human personality. But the progress of mechanization and the social organization which it entails, has steadily reduced this margin of freedom, until today in the totalitarian states, and only to a slightly less degree in the democratic ones, social control extends to the whole of life and consciousness. And since this control is exercised in a utilitarian spirit for political, economic and military ends, the complete secularization of culture seems inevitable. That religion still survives is due on the one hand to the fact that the technique of social control is still not fully developed, so that there are holes and corners in society and in the human personality which have somehow escaped the process of regimentation, on the other hand, because religion itself is being used by the state as an instrument for social control, in much the same way as Augustus revived the moribund rites and institutions of Roman paganism in order to add the prestige of antiquity and tradition to his new order. But a religion of this kind which is being used either as a means to a political end, or at best as an instrument of culture, has lost its transcendent character and has thereby ceased to be a religion in the full sense.

Thus as I have suggested, the progress of Western civilization by science and power seems to lead to a state of total secularization, in which both religion and freedom simultaneously disappear. The discipline that the machine imposes on man is so strict that human nature itself is in danger of being mechanized and absorbed into the material process. Where this is accepted as an ineluctable historical necessity we get a society that is planned in a strictly scientific spirit, but it will be a static and lifeless order, which has no end beyond its own conservation and which must eventually cause the weakening of the human will and the sterilization of culture. On the other hand, if a society rejects this scientific determinism, and seeks to preserve and develop human vitality within the framework of a totalitarian state, it is forced, as in Nazi Germany, to exploit the irrational elements in society and human nature so that the forces of violence and aggressiveness, which all the cultures of the past sought to discipline and control, break loose to dominate and destroy the world.

This is the dilemma of a secularized culture, and we cannot avoid it either by a humanitarian idealism which shuts its eyes to the irrational side of life, or by a religion of personal spirituality which attempts to escape into a private world which is rapidly being liquidated and drained away by the social engineer.

6

The Planning of Culture

THE CONCEPTION OF a planned society has had a revolutionary effect on social thought and political action during
the last twenty years and its importance is still hardly realized
by public opinion. Yet it is possible that it marks a change in
human civilization greater than anything that has occurred since
the end of the stone age and the rise of the archaic cultures of
Egypt and Mesopotamia and the valleys of the Indus and the
Yellow River.

No doubt it is implicit in the idea of applied science, as was
already perceived by the men of the Renaissance such as Leonardo
da Vinci, Campanella and Bacon. It is less evident in the following
period owing to the eighteenth-century belief in a pre-established
harmony between the natural and moral worlds which made
individual interest an infallible guide to social good and regarded
governmental action with suspicion. It was the nineteenth-
century Socialists, above all the St. Simonians, who first popu-
larized the idea and made it the basis of their social philosophy.

Finally it became a political reality in the twentieth century
with the Russian Revolution and the rise of the totalitarian

state. Above all the launching of the Five Year Plan by Stalin in 1928 aroused world-wide interest in the possibility of large-scale state planning and gave birth to a whole literature of propaganda and controversy on the subject.

The conception of social and economic planning was, however, by no means confined to Russia or to the Communists. It was accepted by the Western democracies as the solution of economic depression and unemployment and was the inspiration of President Roosevelt's New Deal in the United States; while in Germany it was applied with immense technical efficiency and ruthless force in order to remold the whole life of the nation according to Nazi ideas and to equip it for the task of world conquest and domination.

The revelation of the sinister possibilities of this scientific organization when it is exploited by totalitarian states has led to a certain reaction against the naïve idealization of planning as an infallible social panacea. There is a general recognition of the need to defend human freedom and spiritual values against the dehumanizing effects of a totalitarian organization of society. The original advocates of social planning in England and in America had been reformist socialists who still accepted liberal and humanitarian values and who did not look far beyond the elimination of the selfishness and confusion of the capitalist system. But when they saw it applied for very different ends of dictators and militarists, they were forced to revise their ideas. They began to realize that the liberal values that they had taken for granted were more closely related to the Christian values that they had discarded than they had believed, and that unless these values could be defended against the soul-destroying inhumanity of the new tyrannies all these achievements of scientific organization and social control would not only be worthless, but would be perverted into instruments of destruction and degradation. It is therefore time for us to reconsider the problem of planning in its wider implications.

The discussion has hitherto been mainly confined to the political and economic issues. The underlying problem of a planned culture has as yet hardly touched public opinion. And it is the instinctive recoil from a planned culture which is one of the strongest forces making against totalitarianism.

But one need not be a materialist in order to see that it is impossible to have a planned society without involving cultural as well as economic issues. You can limit your planning as the democratic states have done in the past, but then you also limit your economic planning. Any total economic planning means a planned society and therefore a planned culture. And it is this situation in which cultural planning is an extemporized affair that is forced on society by its planned economy without being willed or desired that is responsible for the crude and utilitarian character of modern culture.

For if we accept the principle of social planning from the bottom upwards without regard for spiritual values we are left with a machine-made culture which differs from one country to another only in so far as the process of mechanization is more or less perfected. To most people this is rather an appalling prospect, for the ordinary man does not regard the rationalization of life as the only good. On the contrary, men are often more attracted by the variety of life than by its rationality. Even if it were possible to solve all the material problems of life— poverty, unemployment and war—and to construct a uniform scientifically-organized world order, neither the strongest nor the highest elements in human nature would find satisfaction in it.

These views are usually dismissed by the progressive as reactionary. They are in fact the arguments of the conservative, the traditionalist and the romantic. They were first developed by Burke and the romantics against the social rationalism of Enlightenment and the French Revolution. But their criticism was based on a real sense of historical realities and they had, above all, a much clearer and deeper sense of the nature of culture than the philosophers whom they criticized.

They saw the immense richness and vitality of European culture in its manifold development in the different nations through the ages, and, in comparison, the philosophic ideal of a society founded on abstract rational principles seemed lifeless and empty.

And today even in spite of all the achievements of scientific technique and the increased possibilities of social control the problem still remains whether it is possible to produce by scientific planning a culture that will be as rich and varied and vital as one that has grown up unconsciously or half-consciously in the course of ages.

Comparing the modern planned society with the unplanned historical societies which it has succeeded we see that it is enormously superior in power and wealth, but it has two great weaknesses: (a) it seems to leave little or no room for personal freedom, and (b) it disregards spiritual values.

We see these twin defects most strongly marked in the totalitarian states, which have been absolutely ruthless in their treatment of personal rights. But wherever modern mechanized mass culture obtains, even in countries of liberal tradition, we find the freedom of the personality threatened by the pressure of economic forces, and the higher cultural values sacrificed to the lower standards of mass civilization. This is not simply a question of class conflict, for it is not only the life of the proletariat that is standardized. On the contrary, the most extreme forms of cultural standardization are to be found in the higher economic levels. The luxury hotel is the same all over the world and represents a thoroughly materialistic type of culture, while the inn which caters to the poorer classes has preserved its cultural individuality and national or local character to an exceptional degree.

The older type of culture was characterized by a great inequality in regard to individual freedom. Freedom was a manifold thing. There were all kinds of different freedoms. The noble, the bourgeois and the peasant each had his own freedom and his own constraints. On the whole there was a lot of freedom and no equality, while today there is a lot of equality and hardly any freedom.

Similarly the older type of culture had very little power over its environment, natural or social. But it had very clearly defined spiritual standards and was rich in cultural values. These were of course primarily religious, for religion was the supreme unifying force in the old type of society, but they were also cultural in the narrower sense, so that these societies had a much greater sense of style than our own.

Today we have made incalculable progress in the scientific control of our environment, but at the same time our culture has lost any clearly defined spiritual standards and aims, and our cultural values have become impoverished.

The old religiously orientated culture disintegrated two centuries and more ago, and now we see the same process of disintegration taking place with the liberal-humanist culture that was its successor and heir.

Nevertheless this disintegration of culture does not mean that modern social planning can ignore the cultural issue and content itself with economic and political reconstruction. On the contrary the fact that it has done so hitherto is one of the chief factors in cultural disintegration and this, in turn, is one of the main causes of disorder from which the modern world is suffering and which expresses itself in revolution and war.

A civilization which concentrates on means and neglects almost entirely to consider ends must inevitably become disintegrated and despiritualized.

Our democratic societies have done this, by devoting all their planning to the technical and industrial organization and leaving the sphere of culture to the private initiative of individuals, i.e. to unplanned activities. This was possible before the machine age, when the ruling class in society consisted of men of property in the old sense, men with a fixed economic background and a tradition of leisure, not unlike the citizen class of antiquity. But when this class had lost its economic foundation and was progressively absorbed into the machine order, it ceased to be culturally creative.

On the other hand the totalitarian states have instituted centralized planning for definite ends. But they have been even more crudely materialistic than the democratic states. Their plans are short-term plans, and consequently practical and utilitarian. In so far as they have undertaken cultural planning, they have subordinated it to these practical aims with the result that culture has been still further degraded and despiritualized. In the democracies there has undoubtedly been a loss and impoverishment of spiritual values. But in so far as they remain, they are free. We do not feel that religion and philosophy, art and science are being prostituted to serve the interests of a party or even of the state.

But it may be objected that this subordination of culture to statecraft is inseparable from the concept of planning. A free culture is an unplanned culture. The organization of culture means bringing it into the service of social ends and hence of the state.

This is the vital issue. Is it possible to develop a planned culture which will be free? Or does cultural planning necessarily involve a totalitarian state?

This is the question that Dr. Mannheim deals with in the final chapters of his book *Man and Society*. He points out that the origins of Totalitarianism are to be found in the military absolutism of the continent. "The army of the absolute states," he writes, "was the first great institution which not only devised rational methods for creating uniform mass behavior artificially by means of military discipline and other devices for overcoming fear, but also used these methods for educating large masses of men (who were taken for the most part from the lowest classes) to act and if possible to think in the way prescribed."[1]

This system of integrating a mass of individuals into a disciplined unity by compulsion is obviously the simplest and the most rudimentary, but peoples that have been trained in it are naturally more susceptible of totalitarian organization than the more democratic ones. So it is not surprising that the two great totalitarian societies of today are the revolutionary successors and heirs of the two greatest military monarchies of yesterday—

1. K. Mannheim, *Man and Society*, p. 255.

i.e. Russia and Prussia. Whereas the two great democratic societies—the British Commonwealth and the U.S.A.—are essentially *civilian* states, which have never known (except in rare moments of emergency) the universal regimentation which is imposed by a militarist system.

But though this method of enforcing uniform organization by compulsory discipline is the easiest and gives the quickest results, it is not the most effective in the long run, not only because it leaves too little scope for individual adjustment, but because a society that is based on discipline and blind obedience has less internal resources and less power of moral resistance than a free society. If it is possible for a people to organize itself freely it will be stronger than one that is organized by force. It is the old story of the citizen soldiers of ancient Greece against the armies of Persia.

Now in the case of a modern planned society the problem is whether we can replace the enforced *Gleichschaltung* of the totalitarian dictatorships by a free co-ordination of all the social elements, a process which Dr. Mannheim compares to the orchestration of a symphony. But a symphony involves a composer as well as a conductor—and where is the composer to come from? It is, it seems to me, the ideal of the Philosopher King or the lawgiver of a Platonic Republic.

But who is there today who is able to act as the legislator of the spiritual world? Dr. Mannheim would agree that this problem is still unsolved and that the biologist and the economist are not capable of providing an answer. He looks rather to the rise of a new science of Social Psychology which will guide the legislator in the task not merely of organizing existing culture but also of transforming human nature to meet the new conditions of a planned order, since "it is only by remaking man himself that the reconstruction of society is possible." "At the present stage of events," he writes, "we need a new kind of foresight, a new technique for managing conflicts, together with a psychology, morality and plan of action in many ways completely different from those that have obtained in the past."

"While hitherto no particular group has had the responsibility of creating social integration—for anything that happened was the result of haphazard compromise between conflicting tendencies—today there are indications that if the groups engaged in politics still refuse to look beyond their own immediate interests, society will be doomed."[2]

It seems to me that Dr. Mannheim's solution raises two difficulties.

A. That a social science such as he desiderates hardly exists as yet, though we can see its beginnings.

B. That the remoulding of human nature is a task that far transcends politics, and that if the state is entrusted with this task it will inevitably destroy human freedom in a more fundamental way than even the totalitarian states have yet attempted to do.

Those states do, however, show us the risks of a wholesale planning which sacrifices the liberties and spiritual values of the older type of culture for the sake of power and immediate success. The planning of culture cannot be undertaken in a dictatorial spirit, like a rearmament plan. Since it is a much higher and more difficult task than any economic organization, it demands greater resources of powers of knowledge and understanding. It must, in fact, be undertaken in a really religious spirit.

Now it is clear that in the past in so far as culture was directed by conscious aims, it was above all religion that did it. In the Middle Ages religion did in fact create the cultural institutions that guided and controlled the mind of society, so that all the higher activities of culture were if not scientifically planned at least given spiritual form and unity.

And in the Liberal-Humanist culture which formed the transitional stage between medieval Christendom and modern secular civilization, religion still retained great cultural importance. It was the source of the moral standards and spiritual values

2. Op. cit. p. 15.

which are essential to the Liberal tradition, though Liberals frequently ignored this and attempted to base them on abstract ideas. But the rational ideals of Liberalism were abstracted from a historical religious tradition, and the Liberal culture was strongest and most enduring precisely in those societies in which the Christian social and political consciousness was most alive.

Nevertheless Liberalism prepared the way for the complete secularization of society by making a sharp division between the public world of economics and politics and the private world of religion and intellectual culture. It confined planning to the lower sphere and left the higher entirely free and entirely unorganized. Hence with the extension of planning and organization to the higher sphere, we are forced either to take account of religion in our schemes of social organization and therefore to desecularize culture; or to plan without any regard for religion and therefore to produce a totally secular culture, such as the Communists have evolved on the basis of economic Materialism.

Now in the days when the European social order was consciously religious, it preserved a dual social organization: It was recognized that the sphere of religion and of intellectual culture transcended the state. It had its own organization or spiritual society: the Church. This dual principle of organization had a far greater importance for European culture than is usually recognized. It was, no doubt, to some extent a source of conflict and tension. But it was a vital and healthy tension, which contributed in no small measure to the freedom of Western society and the richness of its culture.

It is obvious that modern culture is too secular, and modern religion is too divided for it to be possible to restore this principle directly by making the Church once again the all-embracing spiritual community that it once was. Any attempt to do this externally as a measure of social restoration would be an artificial construction, not a living spiritual principle. The territory that was formerly the domain of the Church, is now largely derelict. Religion has withdrawn into isolated strongholds, where it remains on the defensive, surveying the land through the narrow loopholes in the fortifications.

And the position of intellectual culture is no better. In a way it is worse, since its disintegration is more recent, and it has not had time to organize its defences as religion has done.

In fact at the present time it looks as though we were beginning to witness a sort of persecution of culture, corresponding to the anti-clerical and anti-religious movement of the last century. Of course the culture that is being attacked is by no means the same thing as the culture that we have been discussing. It is a sort of devitalized intellectualism which no longer possesses a social function or a sense of social responsibility.

A culture of this kind is a decadent and dying form of culture, and it is bound to disappear. But that does not mean that society can exist without culture at all. It is all very well saying "To Hell with Culture," but that is just what has happened, and see where it has landed us! During the last thirty years the natural leaders of Western culture have been liquidated pretty thoroughly—on the battlefield, by firing squads, in concentration camps and in exile. A tough may be better than a highbrow, but a society that is dominated by toughs is not necessarily a tough society: it is more likely to be a disintegrated and disordered one. It is a phenomenon that is common enough in history, a typical phenomenon of periods of transition, and it is often followed by a sharp reaction which prepares the way for a spiritual renaissance.

Sooner or later, there must be a revival of culture and a reorganization of the spiritual life of Western society.

The more successful and complete is the process of economic organization the greater will be the need for a super-economic objective of social action. If man's increased control over his environment and his greater material resources are simply devoted to the quantitative multiplication of his material needs and satisfactions, civilization would end in a morass of collective self-indulgence. But the more natural and rational solution would be to devote the increased power and wealth and leisure that would emerge in a planned society towards cultural ends or, in other words, to the creation of a "good life" in the Aristotelian sense. For the higher culture is, after all, essentially the fruit of the surplus energy and resources of society. Cathedrals and theatres, universities and palaces—such things flower naturally from a healthy society as soon as it has acquired a bare margin of freedom and leisure.

It is obvious that the new planned society should be more and not less culturally creative than the societies of the past which accomplished such great things in spite of their poverty and weakness. The reason it has not been so hitherto has been due to our intense and one-sided preoccupation with the economic issue, which led to the starvation of all the non-economic functions and which also created the unemployment problem in the form in which we know it. But a planned culture which is the necessary complement to a planned economy would restore the balance of society since it would devote no less a degree of organized social effort and thought to the development of the non-economic functions. In this respect it would mark a return to the traditions of the pre-industrial age, which put a much higher social value on the non-economic functions than we have done in the West for the last century and more.

The question remains whether this task of cultural planning can be achieved, as Dr. Mannheim hopes, by a purely rational effort of scientific planning; or whether there is an element in culture and in human life which necessarily transcends planning, just as there are sub-rational and irrational ones which can only be planned mechanically.

In other words, will the culture of the future be completely secularized, or will it be religious in a new way?

From the standpoint of the older rationalism, there is no question of super-rational elements. Religion is simply an expression of the irrational element in human nature—a dark and sinister power which is the enemy of true culture no less than of science.

Modern rationalism, however, adopts a somewhat different attitude. Today the emphasis is laid not so much on the irrationalism of religion, as on its sublimation of the irrational, but it is also criticized as escapism, wish-fulfillment—an illusory substitute for reality. If this were true, it would be useless to look to religion as a source of spiritual power; on the contrary, it would be a source of weakness, a kind of collective neurosis which perverts and saps social energy.[3]

But is it possible to reconcile such a view with the facts of history? For religion has undoubtedly been one of the greatest motive powers in human history. It seems to have increased collective energy rather than diminishing it, and whenever humanity has been on the move, religion has been like the pillar of fire and the cloud that went before the Israelites in their desert journeyings.

It seems to me impossible to believe that the power of the spirit is nothing but a perversion and consequently a degradation of physical energy, yet this is the logical conclusion of the rationalist argument. It is as though one were to say that reason itself arises from the perversion of the irrational. It is a line of thought that leads to the blank wall of nihilism and nonsense. Yet on the other hand if we admit the opposite principles—the creative powers of reason and the primacy of the spirit—we shall have to leave room in our planned world for the intervention of a power which transcends planning. And the only place for this power in a planned society is at the summit as the source of spiritual energy and the guiding principle of the whole development. For as economic planning is impossible unless a society possesses a certain amount of physical vitality—a will to live which provides the motive power for work, so cultural planning requires an analogous principle of spiritual life without which "culture" becomes a pale abstraction.

3. This is the Freudian view. Freud writes: "The religions of humanity must be classified as mass delusions of this kind," viz., delusional transformations of reality based on the desire to obtain assurance of happiness and protection from suffering. S. Freud, *Civilization, War and Death*, tr. J. Richman (1939), p. 34.

The only way to desecularize culture is by giving a spiritual aim to the whole system of organization, so that the machine becomes the servant of the spirit and not its enemy or its master. Obviously this is a tremendous task, but it is one that we cannot avoid facing in the near future. If culture is not to be dynamized from below by the exploitation of the subrational animal forces in human nature, it must be activized from above by being once more brought into relation with the forces of Divine power and wisdom and love. The faith in the possibility of this divine action on the world is the foundation of Christian thought. We believe that to every fresh need there is an answer of divine grace, and that every historical crisis (which is a crisis of human destiny!) is met by a new outpouring of the Spirit. The task of the Church and the task of the individual Christian is to prepare the way for such divine action, to open the windows of the human mind and remove the curtains of ignorance and selfishness which keep humanity asleep. The Gospels teach us how religion can act as the ally of human stupidity and ill will, how it can blind men's eyes and stop their ears. But we cannot use the Gospels as an argument for the failure of religion. On the contrary they prove that the power of the Spirit can break down any obstacles and overcome the most elaborate defenses that human ingenuity can devise. And while the present situation in many respects seems more difficult than any in past history, it is at the same time also more unstable, less fixed in custom and less emotionally attached. In fact the mechanization of human life renders it more sensitive to spiritual influence in some respects, than the old unorganized type of culture: at the present time this response is most evident where the forces in question are most evil, but clearly this cannot be the only possibility, and the great problem that we have to face is how to discover the means that are necessary to open this new world of apparently soulless and soul-destroying mechanism, to the spiritual world which stands so near to it.

7

The Kingdom of God and History

THE DEVELOPMENT OF an historical sense—a distinct consciousness of the essential characteristics of different ages and civilizations—is a relatively recent achievement; in fact it hardly existed before the nineteenth century. It is above all the product of the Romantic movement which first taught men to respect the diversity of human life, and to regard culture not as an abstract ideal but as the vital product of an organic social tradition. No doubt, as Nietzsche pointed out, the acquisition of this sixth sense is not all pure gain, since it involves the loss of that noble self-sufficiency and maturity in which the great ages of civilization culminate—"the moment of smooth sea and halcyon self-sufficiency, the goldenness and coldness which all things show that have perfected themselves." It was rendered possible only by the "democratic mingling of classes and races" which is characteristic of modern European civilization. "Owing to this mingling the past of every form and mode of life and of cultures which were formerly juxtaposed with or superimposed on one another flow forth into us," so that "we have secret access above all to the labyrinth of imperfect civilizations and to every form of semi-barbarity that has at any time existed on earth."[1]

Yet it is impossible to believe that the vast widening of the range and scope of consciousness that the historical sense has brought to the human race is an ignoble thing, as Nietzsche would have us believe. It is as though man had at last climbed from the desert and the forest and the fertile plain onto the bare mountain slopes whence he can look back and see the course of his journey and the whole extent of his kingdom. And to the Christian, at least, this widening vision and these far horizons should bring not doubt and disillusionment, but a firmer faith in the divine power that has guided him and a stronger desire for the divine kingdom which is the journey's end.

It is in fact through Christianity above all that man first acquired that sense of a unity and a purpose in history without which the spectacle of the unending change becomes meaningless and oppressive.

"The rational soul," writes Marcus Aurelius, "traverses the whole universe and the surrounding void, and surveys its form, and it extends itself with the infinity of time and embraces and comprehends the periodical revolutions of all things, and it comprehends that those who come after us will see nothing new, nor have those before us seen anything more, but in a manner he who is forty years old, if he has any understanding at all, has seen by virtue of the uniformity that prevails all things that have been or that will be."[2]

This denial of the significance of history is the rule rather than the exception among philosophers and religious teachers throughout the ages from India to Greece and from China to Northern Europe. Even Nietzsche, who grew up in the tradition of the modern historical movement and himself possessed so delicate and profound an historical sense, could not escape the terrifying vision of The Return of All Things, even though it seemed to nullify his own evolutionary gospel of the superman.

---

1. F. Nietzsche, *Beyond Good and Evil*, 224.
2. *Marcus Aurelius*, xi, i, trans. G. Long.

"Behold," he wrote, "this moment. Two roads meet here and none has ever reached their end. . . ." "From this gateway a long eternal road runs back: behind us lies an eternity. Must not all things that can run have run this road? Must not all that can happen have already happened, have already been done and passed through? And if all has already been, what . . . of this moment? Must not this gateway also have been before? And are not all things knotted together in such a way that this moment draws after it all that is to come, and therefore also itself? For all that can run—even in this long road behind, must run it yet again.

"And this slow spider that crawls in the moonlight and this moonlight itself, and you and I whispering together in the gateway, must we not all have been before?

"And must we not come again and run that other long road before us—that long shadowy road—must we not return eternally?"[3]

As St. Augustine said,[4] it is only by Christ the Straight Way that we are delivered from the nightmare of these eternal cycles which seem to exercise a strange fascination over the human mind in any age and clime.

Nevertheless, Christianity does not itself create the historical sense. It only supplies the metaphysical and theological setting for history and an attempt to create a theory of history from the data of revealed truth alone will give us not a history but a theodicy like St. Augustine's *City of God* or the *Praeparatio Evangelica* of Eusebius. The modern historical consciousness is the fruit of Christian tradition and Christian culture but not of these alone. It also owes much to humanism, which taught the European mind to study the achievements of ancient civilization and to value human nature for its own sake. And it was the contact and conflict of these two traditions and ideals—Christianity and humanism—classical and mediaeval culture—that found expression in the Romantic movement in which the mod-

---

3. *Also Sprach Zarathustra*, 30:2, 2.
4. *De Civitate Dei*, XII, xx.

ern historical sense first attained full consciousness. For it was
only then and thus that the human mind realized that a culture
forms an organic unity, with its own social traditions and its
own spiritual ideals, and that consequently we cannot understand the past by applying the standards and values of our own
age and civilization to it, but only by relating historical facts to
the social tradition to which they belong and by using the spiritual beliefs and the moral and intellectual values of that tradition as the key to their interpretation.

Hence the essence of history is not to be found in facts but
in traditions. The pure fact is not as such historical. It only
becomes historical when it can be brought into relation with a
social tradition so that it is seen as part of an organic whole. A
visitor from another planet who witnessed the Battle of Hastings
would possess far greater knowledge of the facts than any modern historian, yet this knowledge would not be historical for
lack of any tradition to which it could be related; whereas the
child who says "William the Conqueror 1066" has already made
his atom of knowledge an historical fact by relating it to a
national tradition and placing it in the time-series of Christian
culture.

Wherever a social tradition exists, however small and unimportant may be the society which is its vehicle, the possibility
of history exists. It is true that many societies fail to realize
this possibility, or realize it only in an unscientific or legendary
form, but on the other hand this legendary element is never
entirely absent from social tradition, and even the most civilized
society has its national legend or myth, of which the scientific
historian is often an unconscious apologist. No doubt it is the
ideal of the modern historian to transcend the tradition of his
own society and to see history as one and universal, but in fact
such a universal history does not exist. There is as yet no history
of humanity, since humanity is not an organized society with a
common tradition or a common social consciousness. All the
attempts that have hitherto been made to write a world history
have been in fact attempts to interpret one tradition in terms
of another, attempts to extend the intellectual hegemony of a

dominant culture by subordinating to it all the events of other cultures that come within the observer's range of vision. The more learned and conscientious a historian is, the more conscious he is of the relativity of his own knowledge, and the more ready he is to treat the culture that he is studying as an end in itself, an autonomous world which follows its own laws and owes no allegiance to the standards and ideals of another civilization. For history deals with civilizations and cultures rather than civilization, with the development of particular societies and not with the progress of humanity.

Consequently if we rely on history alone we can never hope to transcend the sphere of relativity; it is only in religion and metaphysics that we can find truths that claim absolute and eternal validity. But as we have said, non-Christian and pre-Christian philosophy tend to solve the problem of history by a radical denial of its significance.

The world of true Being which is man's spiritual home is the world that knows no change. The world of time and change is the material world from which man must escape if he would be saved. For all the works of men and the rise and fall of kingdoms are but the fruits of ignorance and lust—*mala vitae cupido*—and even the masters of the world must recognize in the end the vanity of their labours like the great Shogun Hideyoshi[5] who wrote on his deathbed:

Alas, as the grass I fade
As the dew I vanish
Even Osaka Castle
Is a dream within a dream.

Yet even the religion that denies the significance of history is itself a part of history and it can only survive in so far as it embodies itself in a social tradition and thus "makes history." The spiritual experience from which a religion receives its initial impetus—like the contemplation of Buddha under the Bo tree

5. [Toyotami Hideyoshi (1536–98), Japanese military leader who helped unify sixteenth-century Japan.—Ed.]

or Mohammed's vision in the cavern on Mt. Hira—may seem
as completely divested of historical and social reference as any
human experience can be. Yet as soon as the teacher comes
down among men and his followers begin to put his teachings
into practice a tradition is formed which comes into contact
with other social traditions and embraces them or is absorbed
by them, until its very nature seems to be changed by this
chemistry of history. Thus we see Buddhism passing from India
to Central Asia and China, and from China to Korea and Japan
and again to Ceylon and Burma and Siam. We see it taking
different forms in different cultures and at the same time changing the cultures themselves, while all the while the religion
itself ignores historical change and remains with its gaze averted
from life, absorbed in the contemplation of Nirvana.

Now at first sight it may seem that this is true of Christianity; that it also has been absorbed against its will in the stream
while its attention has been concentrated on eternal truths and
its hopes fixed on eternal life. It is easy to find examples in
Christianity of world flight and world denial no less extreme
than that of the Indian *sannyasi:* the fathers of the desert, St.
Simeon on his pillar, Thomas à Kempis in his cell and the
countless pious Christians of every age and country who have
regarded this life as an exile in the vale of tears and have ori-
ented their whole existence towards death and immortality. In
fact the current criticism of Christianity is based on this conception and the communist sneer about "pie in the sky when you
die" is merely a crude and malicious statement of what has
always been an essential element of the Christian faith and one
which is nowhere more prominent than in the gospel itself.

Nevertheless this is only one side of the Christian view of
life, for Christianity has always possessed an organic relation to
history which distinguishes it from the great Oriental religions
and philosophies. Christianity can never ignore history because
the Christian revelation is essentially historical and the truths
of faith are inseparably connected with historical events. The
Sacred Scriptures of our religion are not made up of expositions

of metaphysical doctrines like the Vedanta, they form a sacred history, the record of God's dealings with the human race from the creation of man to the creation of the Church. And the whole of this history finds it centre in the life of an historic personality who is not merely a moral teacher or even an inspired hierophant of divine truth, but God made man, the Saviour and restorer of the human race, from whom and in whom humanity acquires a new life and a new principle of unity.

Thus the Christian faith leaves no room for the relativism of a merely historical philosophy. For here at one moment of time and space there occurs an event of absolute value and incomparable significance for all times and all peoples. Amid the diversity and discontinuity of human civilizations and traditions there appears One who is one and the same for all men and for all ages: in whom all the races and traditions of man find their common centre.

Yet on the other hand the Incarnation does not involve any denial of the significance of history such as we find in the Gnostic and Manichaean heresies. It is itself in a sense the fruit of history, since it is the culminating point of one tradition, and the starting point of another. The appeal to tradition is one of the most characteristic features of the gospel. The New Testament opens with "the book of the generation of Jesus Christ the son of David, the son of Abraham," and the first preaching of the apostles starts with an appeal to a tradition that goes back to Ur of the Chaldeans and the earliest origins of the Hebrew people.

Thus, the Christian Church possessed its own history, which was a continuation of the history of the chosen people, and this history had its own autonomous development which was independent of the currents of secular history. We have the age of the apostles and the age of the martyrs and the age of the fathers, each of them built on the same foundations and each contributing its part to the building up of the City of God.

The chief problem, therefore, which we have to study is that of the relations between this sacred tradition and the other countless traditions that make up human history. For Christianity, no less than the other world religions, has entered the stream of historical change and has passed from one race to another, from civilization to barbarism and from barbarism to civilization. Men of different periods with different historical backgrounds and different national or racial traditions all belong to the all-embracing tradition of the Christian Church. We have Hellenistic Christians and Byzantine Christians, Romans and Syrians, Mediaeval Christians and Renaissance Christians, seventeenth-century Spaniards and nineteenth-century Englishmen. Are these differences of culture and race accidental and ephemeral—details that have no relevance to the Christian view of life and the Christian interpretation of History? Or are they also of spiritual significance as elements in the divine plan and forms through which the providential purpose of God in history is manifested?

Now from the early Christian point of view, at least, it would seem that the whole significance of history was entirely comprised in that sacred tradition of which we have spoken. The key to history—the mystery of the ages—was to be found in the tradition of the chosen people and the sacred community, and outside that tradition among the Gentiles and the kingdoms of men there is a realm of endless strife and confusion, a succession of empires founded by war and violence and ending in blood and ruin. The Kingdom of God is not the work of man and does not emerge by a natural law of progress from the course of human history. It makes a violent inruption into history and confounds the work of man, like the stone hewn from the mountain without human agency which crushes the image of the four world empires into dust.

One of the most striking features of the Christian tradition is, in fact, its historical dualism: in the Old Testament the opposition between the chosen people and the Gentiles; in the New, the opposition between the church and the world—in the Augustinian theodicy, the two cities, Jerusalem and Babylon—the community of charity and the community of self-will. Yet this dualism is never an absolute one. Even the Old Testament, in spite of its insistence on the unique privilege of Israel as the exclusive bearer of the divine promise, also recognizes the hand of God in the history of the Gentiles. Even the powers that seem most hostile to the people of God are the instrument by which God works out his purpose. This is shown most remarkably in the Isaianic prophecy with regard to Cyrus, for here a Gentile ruler is addressed by the messianic title as chosen and anointed by God to do his will and to deliver his people. No doubt here and elsewhere the divine action in history always has a direct reference to the fortunes of the people of God. But the converse is also true, for God's dealings with his people are of profound significance for the future of the Gentiles. In the end the Holy City will be the resort of all peoples; the Gentiles will bring their riches into it, and from it there will go forth the law of justice and grace to all the nations of the earth.

And in the New Testament there is a still further recognition of a limited but intrinsic value in the social order and social traditions that lie outside the dispensation of grace. Even the pagan state is God's servant in so far as it is the guardian of order and the administrator of justice. And in the higher sphere of grace, the passing of the old racial restrictions and the opening of the Kingdom to all nations involved at least in principle the consecration of every nation and of every social tradition in so far as they were not corrupted by sin. And so we have the reception into the church of Greek philosophy and scholarship, and of Roman law and leadership, until the whole civilized world found itself Christian. The vital thing was not the conversion of the Empire and the union of church and state, but the gradual penetration of culture by the Christian tradition, until that tradition embraced the whole of the life of Western man in all its historic diversity and left no human activity and no social tradition unconsecrated.

With this coming in of the nations and the establishment of the Kingdom of Christ among the Gentiles the Christian interpretation of prophecy seemed to have been fulfilled. From the time of St. Augustine Christian millenniarism was generally abandoned and the Messianic kingdom was identified with the triumph of the church—"*ecclesia et nunc est regnum Christi regnumque coelorum.*" It seemed to the men of that age witnessing the fall of the Empire and the ruin of civilization that nothing remained to be accomplished except the last things. Consequently the Christian interpretation of history became mainly retrospective, and the present and the future of man's attention were concentrated not on history but on the end of history which seemed close at hand.

But with the passing of ages and the birth of new nations and new forms of culture, new problems presented themselves to the Christian conscience. The Augustinian theology with its intense realization of the inherited burden of evil which weighs down the human race and its conception of divine grace as a supernatural power which renews human nature and changes the course of history, continued to inspire the mediaeval outlook, and the mediaeval interpretation of history is still based on the Augustinian conception of the two cities. But whereas St. Augustine presents this opposition primarily as a conflict between the Christian Church and the heathen world, the Middle Ages saw it above all as a struggle between the forces of good and evil within Christian society. The reform of the church, the restoration of moral order, and the establishment of social justice—these were the vital problems that occupied the mind of mediaeval Christendom from the tenth century onwards; and the whole movement of reform from the time of St. Odo of Cluny to that of St. Bernard and Otto of Freising was consciously based on an interpretation of history which applied the Augustinian concept of the two cities to the contemporary crisis between church and state or rather between the religious and secular forces that were at war within the Christian community. This neo-Augustinian view of history finds its most direct expression in the writings of Odo of Cluny in the tenth century, Bonizo of Sutri in the eleventh and Otto of Freising in the twelfth, but it also inspired some of the ablest partisans of the

Empire such as the author of the treatise *De Unitate Ecclesiae conservanda*. For the mediaeval empire and indeed the mediaeval kingship were not regarded by their supporters as secular institutions in our sense of the word. They were the leaders of the Christian people and the defenders of the Christian faith, and it was to them rather than to the papacy and the priesthood that the government of Christendom as an historical "temporal" order had been committed by God.

This tradition of Christian imperialism was not destroyed by the victory of the papacy over the Empire. In fact it found its most remarkable expression in the fourteenth century in Dante's theory of the providential mission of the Roman Empire as the society through which the human race would realize its potential unity and attain universal peace, and of the particular vocation of the Messianic prince, the mystical *Dux* who would be the saviour of Italy and the reformer of the Church. Here for the first time we have a Christian interpretation of history which looks beyond the sacred Judaeo-Christian tradition and admits the independent value and significance of the secular tradition of culture. There are in fact two independent but parallel dispensations—the dispensation of grace, which is represented by the Church, and the natural dispensation by which humanity attains its rational end by the agency of the Roman people, which was ordained by nature and elected by God for universal empire.

Thus while on the one hand Dante's interpretation of history looks back to the mediaeval tradition of the Holy Roman Empire and the Augustinian ideal of the City of God, on the other hand it looks forward to the humanism of the Renaissance and the modern liberal ideal of universal peace as well as the modern nationalist ideal of the historical mission of a particular people and state. And this idea of a predestined correspondence between the secular tradition of human civilization embodied in the Roman Empire and the religious tradition of supernatural truth embodied in the Catholic Church finds its philosophical basis in the Thomist doctrine of the concordance of nature and grace. If it had been adopted by Thomism as the basis of the interpretation of history, it might well have developed with the growth of historical knowledge into a really catholic philosophy of history in which the different national traditions were shown, on the analogy of that of Rome, as contributing each according to its own mission and its natural aptitudes towards the building up of a Christian civilization. Actually, however, Dante's attachment to the dying cause of Ghibelline imperialism prevented his philosophy from exercising any wide influence on Catholic thought. It remained an impressive but eccentric witness to the universalism of mediaeval thought and the lost spiritual unity of mediaeval culture.

For the close of the Middle Ages was marked by the great religious revolution which destroyed the unity of Western Christendom and divided the peoples of Europe by the strife of sects and the conflict of opposing religious traditions. There was no longer one common Catholic faith and consequently there was no longer a common sacred tradition or a common interpretation of history. It is true that the Reformers inherited far more from the Middle Ages than they themselves realized, and this was particularly the case with regard to the interpretation of history. Their conception of history, no less than that of the Middle Ages, is based on the Bible and St. Augustine, and the Augustinian scheme of world history, based on the opposition and conflict of the two cities, had as great an influence on Luther and Calvin and the seventeenth-century Puritan divines as it had on the Catholic reformers five centuries earlier.

Nevertheless the Catholic interpretation of history is organically related to the Catholic conception of the nature and office of the church, and in so far as Protestantism formed a new conception of the church, it ultimately involved a new interpretation of history. Thus already, long before the emergence of the new schools of Biblical criticism and ecclesiastical history that have so profoundly affected the modern Protestant attitude to the Catholic tradition, a divergence between the Catholic and Protestant interpretations of history is plainly visible.

At first sight the difference between sixteenth-century Catholicism and Protestantism is the difference between the traditional and the revolutionary conceptions of Christianity and of
the church. To the Catholic the church was the Kingdom of
God on earth—*in via*—the supernatural society through which
and in which alone humanity could realize its true end. It was
a visible society with its own law and constitution which possessed divine and indefectible authority. It remained through the
ages one and the same, like a city set on a hill, plain for all
men to see, handing on from generation to generation the same
deposit of faith and the same mandate of authority which it had
received from its divine Founder and which it would retain
whole and intact until the end of time.

The Reformers, on the other hand, while maintaining a similar conception of the church as the community through which
God's purpose towards the human race is realized, refused to
identify this divine society with the actual visible hierarchical
church, as known to history. Against the Catholic view of the
church as the visible City of God, they set the apocalyptic vision
of an apostate church, a harlot drunk with the blood of the
saints, sitting on the seven hills and intoxicating the nations
with her splendour and her evil enchantments. The true church
was not this second Babylon, but the society of the elect, the
hidden saints who followed the teaching of the Bible rather than
of the hierarchy and who were to be found among the so-called
heretics—Hussites, Wycliffites, Waldensians and the rest, rather
than among the servants of the official institutional church.

The result of this revolutionary attitude to the historic church
was a revolutionary, catastrophic, apocalyptic and discontinuous
view of history. As Calvin writes, the history of the church is
a series of resurrections. Again and again the church becomes
corrupt, the Word is no longer preached, life seems extinct, until
God once more sends forth prophets and teachers to bear witness to the truth and to reveal the evangelical doctrine in its
pristine purity. Thus the Reformation may be compared to the
Renaissance since it was an attempt to go back behind the

Middle Ages, to wipe out a thousand years of historical development and to restore the Christian religion to its primitive "classical" form. Yet on the other hand this return to the past
brought the Protestant mind into fresh contact with the Jewish
and apocalyptic sources of the Christian view of history, so that
the Reformation led to an increased emphasis on the Hebraic
prophetic and apocalyptic elements in the Christian tradition as
against the Hellenic, patristic and metaphysical elements that
were so strongly represented alike in patristic orthodoxy and in
mediaeval Catholicism.

Hence we find two tendencies in Protestant thought which
find their extreme expression respectively in Socinianism and
millenniarism. One represents the attempt to strip off all accretions, to separate religion from history and to recover the pure
timeless essence of Christianity. The other represents a crude
and vehement reassertion of the historical time-element in
Christianity and an attempt to strip it of all its non-Jewish,
mystical, philosophical and theological elements. The resultant
type of religion was marked by some of the worst excesses of
fanaticism and irrationality, yet on the other hand it was intensely social in spirit, as we see, for example, in the case of
the Anabaptists, and it made an earnest, if one-sided and over-
simplified, effort to provide a Christian interpretation of history.

But though these two tendencies seem hostile to one another,
they were not in fact mutually exclusive. For example, John
Milton could be at the same time a millenniarist and a Socinian,
and eighteenth-century Unitarians, such as Priestley, who seem
to represent the Socinian type of Protestantism in an almost
pure state, acquired from the opposite tradition a kind of secularized millenniarism which found expression in the doctrine of
progress. The development of this rationalized theology and of
this secularized millenniarism, whether in its revolutionary-
socialistic or revolutionary-liberal forms (but especially the latter), is of central importance for the understanding of modern
culture. It was in fact a new reformation, which attempted to
rationalize and spiritualize religion in an even more complete

and drastic way than the first Reformation had done, but which ended in emptying Christianity of all supernatural elements and interpreting history as the progressive development of an immanent principle.

Thus it is not only the materialistic interpretation of history but the idealistic interpretation as well which is irreconcilable with the traditional Christian view, since it eliminates that sense of divine otherness and transcendence, that sense of divine judgment and divine grace which are the very essence of the Christian attitude to history. This holds true of Protestantism as well as of Catholicism. Nevertheless it must be admitted that the clash is much sharper and more painful in the case of the latter. Partly, no doubt, because the great idealist thinkers, such as Kant, were themselves men of Protestant origin who had preserved a strong Protestant ethos, it has been possible for Protestants to accept the idealist interpretation of history without any serious conflict, and in the same way it was on Protestant rather than on Catholic foundations that the new liberal theology of immanence developed itself.

Catholicism, on the other hand, showed little sympathy to the idealist movement which it tended to regard as an external and non-religious force. Its attitude to history was at once more traditionalist and more realist than that of Protestantism and it did not readily accept the idea of an inevitable law of progress which was accepted by both liberal and Protestant idealists as the background of their thought and the basic principle of their interpretation of history. Consequently there is a sharp contrast between the Catholic and the liberal-idealist philosophies such as hardly exists in the Protestant world. As Croce brings out so clearly in his *History of Europe in the Nineteenth Century*, it is not a conflict between religion and science or religion and philosophy, but between two rival creeds, based on an irreconcilable opposition of principles and resulting in a completely different view of the world. For, as Croce again points out, the idealist conceptions of monism, immanence and self-determination are the negation of the principles of divine transcendence, divine revelation, and divine authority on which the Catholic view of God and man, of creation and history and the end of history is based.

Hence the opposition between liberalism and Catholicism is not due, as the vulgar simplification would have it, to the "reactionary" tendencies of the latter but to the necessity of safeguarding the absolute Christian values, both in the theological and the historical spheres. For if Christianity is the religion of the Incarnation, and if the Christian interpretation of history depends on the continuation and extension of the Incarnation in the life of the church, Catholicism differs from other forms of Christianity in representing this incarnational principle in a fuller, more concrete, and more organic sense. As the Christian faith in Christ is faith in a real historical person, not an abstract ideal, so the Catholic faith in the church is faith in a real historical society, not an invisible communion of saints or a spiritual union of Christians who are divided into a number of religious groups and sects. And this historic society is not merely the custodian of the sacred Scriptures and a teacher of Christian morality. It is the bearer of a living tradition which unites the present and the past, the living and the dead, in one great spiritual community which transcends all the limited communities of race and nation and state. Hence, it is not enough for the Catholic to believe in the Word as contained in the sacred Scriptures, it is not even enough to accept the historic faith as embodied in the creeds and interpreted by Catholic theology, it is necessary for him to be incorporated as a cell in the living organism of the divine society and to enter into communion with the historic reality of the sacred tradition. Thus to the student who considers Catholicism as an intellectual system embodied in theological treatises, Catholicism may seem far more legalist and intellectualist than Protestantism, which emphasizes so strongly the personal and moral-emotional sides of religion, but the sociologist who studies it in its historical and social reality will soon understand the incomparable importance for Catholicism of tradition, which makes the individual a member of a historic society and a spiritual civilization and which influences his life and thought consciously and unconsciously in a thousand different ways.

Now the recognition of this tradition as the organ of the Spirit of God in the world and the living witness to the supernatural action of God on humanity is central to the Catholic understanding and interpretation of history. But so tremendous a claim involves a challenge to the whole secular view of history which is tending to become the faith of the modern world. In spite of the differences and contradictions between the progressive idealism of liberalism and the catastrophic materialism of communism all of them agree in their insistence on the immanence and autonomy of human civilization and on the secular community as the ultimate social reality. Alike to the liberal and to the communist the Catholic tradition stands condemned as "reactionary" not merely for the accidental reason that it has been associated with the political and social order of the past, but because it sets the divine values of divine faith and charity and eternal life above the human values—political liberty, social order, economic prosperity, scientific truth—and orientates human life and history towards a supernatural and super-historical end. And since the modern society is everywhere tending towards ideological uniformity which will leave no room for the private worlds of the old bourgeois culture, the contradiction between secularism and Catholicism is likely to express itself in open conflict and persecution.

No doubt the prospect of such a conflict is highly distasteful to the modern bourgeois mind, even when it is Christian. The liberal optimism which has been so characteristic of Anglo-Saxon religious thought during the last half century led men to believe that the days of persecution were over and that all men of good will would agree to set aside their differences of opinion and unite to combat the evils that were universally condemned—vice and squalor and ignorance. But from the standpoint of the Christian interpretation of history there is no ground for such hopes. Christ came not to bring peace but a sword, and the Kingdom of God comes not by the elimination of conflict but through an increasing opposition and tension between the church and the world. The conflict between the two cities is as old as humanity and must endure to the end of time. And though the church may meet with ages of prosperity, and her enemies may fail and the powers of the world may submit to her sway, these things are no criterion of success. She wins not by majorities but by martyrs and the cross is her victory.

Thus in comparison with the optimism of liberalism the Christian view of life and the Christian interpretation of history are profoundly tragic. The true progress of history is a mystery which is fulfilled in failure and suffering and which will only be revealed at the end of time. The victory that overcomes the world is not success but faith and it is only the eye of faith that understands the true value of history.

Viewing history from this standpoint the Christian will not be confident in success or despondent in failure. "For when you shall hear of wars and rumors of wars be not afraid, for the end is not yet." None knows where Europe is going and there is no law of history by which we can predict the future. Nor is the future in our own hands, for the world is ruled by powers that it does not know, and the men who appear to be the makers of history are in reality its creatures. But the portion of the Church is not like these. She has been the guest and the exile, the mistress and the martyr, of nations and civilizations and has survived them all. And in every age and among every people it is her mission to carry on the work of divine restoration and regeneration, which is the true end of history.

8

The Christian View of History

THE PROBLEM OF the relations of Christianity to History has been very much complicated and, I think, obscured by the influence of nineteenth-century philosophy. Almost all the great idealist philosophers of that century, like Fichte and Schelling and Hegel, constructed elaborate philosophies of history which had a very considerable influence on the historians, especially in Germany, and on the theologians also. All these systems were inspired or coloured by Christian ideas and they were consequently eagerly accepted by Christian theologians for apologetic purposes. And thus there arose an alliance between idealist philosophy and German theology which became characteristic of the Liberal Protestant movement and dominated religious thought both on the Continent and in this country during the later nineteenth century.

Today the situation is entirely changed. Both philosophic idealism and liberal Protestantism have been widely discredited and have been replaced by logical positivism and by the dialectic theology of the Barthians. The result is that the idea of a Christian philosophy of history has also suffered from the reaction against philosophic idealism. It is difficult to distinguish the authentic and original element in the Christian view of history from the philosophic accretions and interpretations of the last century and a half, so that you will find modern representatives of orthodox Christianity like Mr. C. S. Lewis questioning the possibility of a Christian interpretation of history, and declaring that the supposed connection between Christianity and Historicism is largely an illusion.[1]

If we approach the subject from a purely philosophical point of view there is a good deal to justify Mr. Lewis's scepticism. For the classical tradition of Christian philosophy as represented by Thomism has devoted comparatively little attention to the problem of history, while the philosophers who set the highest value on history and insist most strongly on the close relation between Christianity and history, such as Collingwood and Croce and Hegel, are not themselves Christian and may perhaps have tended to interpret Christianity in terms of their own philosophy.

Let us therefore postpone any philosophical discussion and consider the matter on the basis of the original theological data of historic Christianity without any attempt to justify or criticize them on philosophical grounds. There is no great difficulty in doing this, since the classical tradition of Christian philosophy as represented by Thomism has never devoted much attention to the problem of history. Its tradition has been Hellenic and Aristotelian, whereas the Christian interpretation of history is derived from a different source. It is Jewish rather than Greek, and finds its fullest expression in the primary documents of the Christian faith—the writings of the Hebrew prophets and in the New Testament itself.

Thus the Christian view of history is not a secondary element derived by philosophical reflection from the study of history. It lies at the very heart of Christianity and forms an integral part of the Christian faith. Hence there is no Christian "philosophy

1. In his article on "Historicism" in *The Month*, October, 1950.

of history" in the strict sense of the word. There is, instead, a Christian history and a Christian theology of history, and it is not too much to say that without them there would be no such thing as Christianity. For Christianity, together with the religion of Israel out of which it was born, is an historical religion in a sense to which none of the other world religions can lay claim—not even Islam, though this comes nearest to it in this respect.

Hence it is very difficult, perhaps even impossible, to explain the Christian view of history to a non-Christian, since it is necessary to accept the Christian faith in order to understand the Christian view of history, and those who reject the idea of a divine revelation are necessarily obliged to reject the Christian view of history as well. And even those who are prepared to accept in theory the principle of divine revelation—of the manifestation of a religious truth which surpasses human reason—may still find it hard to face the enormous paradoxes of Christianity.

That God should have chosen an obscure Palestinian tribe—not a particularly civilized or attractive tribe either—to be the vehicle of his universal purpose for humanity, is difficult to believe. But that this purpose should have been finally realized in the person of a Galilean peasant executed under Tiberius, and that this event was the turning point in the life of mankind and the key to the meaning of history—all this is so hard for the human mind to accept that even the Jews themselves were scandalized, while to the Greek philosophers and the secular historians it seemed sheer folly.

Nevertheless, these are the foundations of the Christian view of history, and if we cannot accept them it is useless to elaborate idealistic theories and call them a Christian philosophy of history, as has often been done in the past.

For the Christian view of history is not merely a belief in the direction of history by divine providence, it is a belief in the intervention by God in the life of mankind by direct action at certain definite points in time and place. The doctrine of the Incarnation which is the central doctrine of the Christian faith is also the centre of history, and thus it is natural and appropriate that our traditional Christian history is framed in a chronological system which takes the year of the Incarnation as its point of reference and reckons its annals backwards and forwards from this fixed centre.

No doubt it may be said that the idea of divine incarnation is not peculiar to Christianity. But if we look at the typical examples of these non-Christian theories of divine incarnation, such as the orthodox Hindu expression of it in the Bhagavad-Gita, we shall see that it has no such significance for history as the Christian doctrine possesses. It is not only that the divine figure of Khrishna is mythical and unhistorical, it is that no divine incarnation is regarded as unique but as an example of a recurrent process which repeats itself again and again *ad infinitum* in the eternal recurrence of the cosmic cycle.

It was against such ideas as represented by the Gnostic theosophy that St. Irenaeus asserted the uniqueness of the Christian revelation and the necessary relation between the divine unity and the unity of history—"that there is one Father the creator of Man and one Son who fulfils the Father's will and one human race in which the mysteries of God are worked out so that the creature conformed and incorporated with his son is brought to perfection."

For the Christian doctrine of the Incarnation is not simply a theophany—a revelation of God to Man; it is a new creation— the introduction of a new spiritual principle which gradually leavens and transforms human nature into something new. The history of the human race hinges on this unique divine event which gives spiritual unity to the whole historic process. First there is the history of the Old Dispensation which is the story of the providential preparation of mankind for the Incarnation when "the fulness of time," to use St. Paul's expression, had come. Secondly there is the New Dispensation which is the working out of the Incarnation in the life of the Christian Church. And finally there is the realization of the divine purpose in the future: in the final establishment of the Kingdom of God when the harvest of this world is reaped. Thus the Christian conception of history is essentially unitary. It has a beginning, a centre, and an end. This beginning, this centre, and this end transcend history; they are not historical events in the ordinary sense of the word, but acts of divine creation to which the whole process of history is subordinate. For the Christian view of history is a vision of history *sub specie æternitatis,* an interpretation of time in terms of eternity and of human events in the light of divine revelation. And thus Christian history is inevitably apocalyptic, and the apocalypse is the Christian substitute for the secular philosophies of history.

But this involves a revolutionary reversal and transposition of historical values and judgments. For the real meaning of history is not the apparent meaning that historians have studied and philosophers have attempted to explain. The world-transforming events which changed the whole course of human history have occurred as it were under the surface of history unnoticed by the historians and the philosophers. This is the great paradox of the gospel, as St. Paul asserts with such tremendous force. The great mystery of the divine purpose which has been hidden throughout the ages has now been manifested in the sight of heaven and earth by the apostolic ministry. Yet the world has not been able to accept it, because it has been announced by unknown insignificant men in a form which was inacceptable and incomprehensible to the higher culture of the age, alike Jewish and Hellenistic. The Greeks demand philosophical theories, the Jews demand historical proof. But the answer of Christianity is Christ crucified—*verbum crucis*—the story of the Cross: a scandal to the Jews and an absurdity to the Greeks. It is only when this tremendous paradox with its reversal of all hitherto accepted standards of judgment has been accepted that the meaning of human life and human history can be understood. For St. Paul does not of course mean to deny the value of understanding or to affirm that history is without a meaning. What he asserts is the mysterious and transcendent character of the true knowledge—"the hidden wisdom which God ordained before the world to our glory which none of the rulers of this world know."[2] And in the same way he fully accepted the Jewish doctrine of sacred history which would justify the ways of God to man. What he denied was an external justification by the manifest triumph of the Jewish national hope. The ways of God were deeper and more mysterious than that, so that the fulfilment of prophecy towards which the whole history of Israel had tended had been concealed from Israel by the scandal of the Cross. Nevertheless the Christian interpretation of history as we see it in the New Testament and the writings of the Fathers follows the pattern which had already been laid down in the Old Testament and in Jewish tradition.

There is, in the first place, a sacred history in the strict sense, that is to say, the story of God's dealings with his people and the fulfilment of his eternal purpose in and through them. And, in the second place, there is the interpretation of external history in the light of this central purpose. This took the form of a theory of successive world ages and successive world empires, each of which had a part to play in the divine drama. The theory of the world ages, which became incorporated in the Jewish apocalyptic tradition and was ultimately taken over by Christian apocalyptic, was not however Jewish in origin. It was widely diffused throughout the ancient world in Hellenistic times and probably goes back in origin to the tradition of Babylonian cosmology and astral theology. The theory of the world empires, on the other hand, is distinctively Biblical in spirit and belongs to the central message of Hebrew prophecy. For the Divine Judgment which it was the mission of the prophets to declare was not confined to the chosen people. The rulers of the Gentiles were also the instruments of divine judgment, even though they did not understand the purpose that they served. Each of the world empires in turn had its divinely appointed task to perform, and when the task was finished their power came to an end and they gave place to their successors.

2. Col. ii; cf. Eph. iii.

Thus the meaning of history was not to be found in the history of the world empires themselves. They were not ends but means, and the inner significance of history was to be found in the apparently insignificant development of the people of God. Now this prophetic view of history was taken over by the Christian Church and applied on a wider and universal scale. The divine event which had changed the course of history had also broken down the barrier between Jews and the Gentiles, and the two separated parts of humanity had been made one in Christ, the corner-stone of the new world edifice. The Christian attitude to secular history was indeed the same as that of the prophets; and the Roman Empire was regarded as the successor of the old world empires, like Babylon and Persia. But now it was seen that the Gentile world as well as the chosen people were being providentially guided towards a common spiritual end. And this end was no longer conceived as the restoration of Israel and the gathering of all the exiles from among the Gentiles. It was the gathering together of all the spiritually living elements throughout mankind into a new spiritual society. The Roman prophet Hermas in the second century describes the process in the vision of the white tower that was being built among the waters, by tens of thousands of men who were bringing stones dragged from the deep sea or collected from the twelve mountains which symbolize the different nations of the world. Some of these stones were rejected and some were chosen to be used for the building. And when he asks "concerning the times and whether the end is yet," he is answered: "Do you not see that the tower is still in process of building? When the building has been finished, the end comes."

This vision shows how Christianity transfers the meaning of history from the outer world of historic events to the inner world of spiritual change, and how the latter was conceived as the dynamic element in history and as real world-transforming power. But it also shows how the primitive Christian sense of an imminent end led to a foreshortening of the time scale and distracted men's attention from the problem of the future destin-

ies of human civilization. It was not until the time of the conversion of the Empire and the peace of the Church that Christians were able to make a distinction between the end of the
age and the end of the world, and to envisage the prospect of a
Christian age and civilization which was no millennial kingdom
but a field of continual effort and conflict.

This view of history found its classical expression in St. Augustine's work on *The City of God* which interprets the course
of universal history as an unceasing conflict between two dynamic principles embodied in two societies and social orders—
the City of Man and the City of God, Babylon and Jerusalem,
which run their course side by side, intermingling with one
another and sharing the same temporal goods and the same
temporal evils, but separated from one another by an infinite
spiritual gulf. Thus St. Augustine sees history as the meeting
point of time and eternity. History is a unity because the same
divine power which shows itself in the order of nature from the
stars down to the feathers of the bird and the leaves of the tree
also governs the rise and fall of kingdoms and empires. But this
divine order is continually being deflected by the downward
gravitation of human nature to its own selfish ends—a force
which attempts to build its own world in those political structures that are the organized expression of human ambition and
lust for power. This does not, however, mean that St. Augustine
identifies the state as such with the *civitas terrena* and con-
demns it as essentially evil. On the contrary, he shows that its
true end—the maintaining of temporal peace—is a good which
is in agreement with the higher good of the City of God, so
that the state in its true nature is not so much the expression
of self-will and the lust for power as a necessary barrier which
defends human society from being destroyed by these forces of
destruction. It is only when war and not peace is made the end
of the state that it becomes identified with the *civitas terrena*
in the bad sense of the word. But we see only too well that the
predatory state that lives by war and conquest is an historical
reality, and St. Augustine's judgment on secular history is a

predominantly pessimistic one which sees the kingdoms of this world as founded in injustice and extending themselves by war and oppression. The ideal of temporal peace which is inherent in the idea of the state is never strong enough to overcome the dynamic force of human self-will, and therefore the whole course of history *apart from divine grace* is the record of successive attempts to build towers of Babel which are frustrated by the inherent selfishness and greed of human nature.

The exception, however, is all-important. For the blind forces of instinct and human passion are not the only powers that rule the world. God has not abandoned his creation. He communicates to man, by the grace of Christ and the action of the Spirit, the spiritual power of divine love which alone is capable of transforming human nature. As the natural force of self-love draws down the world to multiplicity and disorder and death, the supernatural power of the love of God draws it back to unity and order and life. And it is here that the true unity and significance of history is to be found. For love, in St. Augustine's theory, is the principle of society, and as the centrifugal and destructive power of self-love creates the divided society of the *civitas terrena*, so the unitive and creative power of divine love creates the City of God, the society that unites all men of good will in an eternal fellowship which is progressively realized in the course of the ages.

Thus St. Augustine, more perhaps than any other Christian thinker, emphasizes the social character of the Christian doctrine of salvation. For "whence," he writes, "should the City of God originally begin or progressively develop or ultimately attain its end unless the life of the saints were a social one?"[3] But at the same time he makes the individual soul and not the state or the civilization the real centre of the historic process. Wherever the power of divine love moves the human will there the City of God is being built. Even the Church which is the visible sacramental organ of the City of God is not identical

3. *De Civ. Dei*, xix, V.

with it, since as he writes, in God's foreknowledge there are
many who seem to be outside who are within and many who
seem to be within who are outside.[4] So there are those outside
the communion of the Church "whom the Father, who sees in
secret, crowns in secret."[5] For the two Cities interpenetrate one
another in such a way and to such a degree that "the earthly
kingdom exacts service from the kingdom of heaven and the
kingdom of heaven exacts service from the earthly city."[6]

It is impossible to exaggerate the influence of St. Augustine's
thought on the development of the Christian view of history
and on the whole tradition of Western historiography, which
follows quite a different course from that of Eastern and Byzantine historiography. It is true that the modern reader who ex-
pects to find in St. Augustine a philosophy of history in the
modern sense, and who naturally turns to the historical portions
of his great work, especially Books XV to XVIII, is apt to be
grievously disappointed, like the late Professor Hearnshaw who
wrote that the *De Civitate Dei* contains neither philosophy nor
history but merely theology and fiction. But though St. Augustine was never a Christian historian such as Eusebius, his
work had a far more revolutionary effect on Western thought.
In the first place, he impressed upon Christian historians his
conception of history as a dynamic process in which the divine
purpose is realized. Secondly, he made men realize the way in
which the individual personality is the source and centre of
this dynamic process. And finally, he made the Western Church
conscious of its historical mission and its social and political
responsibilities so that it became during the following centuries
the active principle of Western culture.

The results of St. Augustine's work find full expression three
centuries later in the Anglo-Saxon Church. Unlike St. Augustine, St. Bede was a true historian, but his history is built
on the foundations that St. Augustine had laid, and thus we get

4. *De bapt.*, V, 38.
5. *De Vera Religione*, vi, II.
6. *In Psalmos*, li, 4.

the first history of a Christian people in the full sense of the word—a history which is not primarily concerned with the rise and fall of kingdoms—though these are not omitted; but with the rise of Christ's kingdom in England, the *gesta Dei per Anglos*. Of course Bede's great work can hardly be regarded as typical of mediaevel historiography. It was an exceptional, almost a unique, achievement. But at any rate his historical approach is typical, and, together with his other chronological works, it provided the pattern which was followed by the later historians of the Christian Middle Ages. It consists in the first place of a world chronicle of the Eusebian type which provided the chronological background on which the historian worked. Secondly there were the histories of particular peoples and Churches of which St. Bede's *Ecclesiastical History* is the classical example, and which is represented in later times by works like Adam of Bremen's *History of the Church of Hamburg* or Ordericus Vitalis's *Ecclesiastical History*. And thirdly there are the biographies of saints and bishops and abbots, like Bede's life of St. Cuthbert and the lives of the abbots of Wearmouth.

In this way the recording of contemporary events in the typical mediaeval chronicle is linked up on the one hand with the tradition of world history and on the other with the lives of the great men who were the leaders and heroes of Christian society. But the saint is not merely an historical figure; he has become a citizen of the eternal city, a celestial patron and a protector of man's earthly life. So that in the lives of the saints we see history transcending itself and becoming part of the eternal world of faith.

Thus in mediaeval thought, time and eternity are far more closely bound up with one another than they were in classical antiquity or to the modern mind. The world of history was only a fraction of the real world and it was surrounded on every side by the eternal world like an island in the ocean. This mediaeval vision of a hierarchical universe in which the world of man occupies a small but central place finds classical expression in Dante's *Divina Commedia*. For this shows better than any purely historical or theological work how the world of history was conceived as passing into eternity and bearing eternal fruit.

And if on the one hand this seems to reduce the importance of history and of the present life, on the other hand it enhances their value by giving them an eternal significance. In fact there are few great poets who have been more concerned with history and even with politics than Dante was. What is happening in Florence and in Italy is a matter of profound concern, not only to the souls in Purgatory, but even to the damned in Hell and to the saints in Paradise, and the divine pageant in the Earthly Paradise which is the centre of the whole process is an apocalyptic vision of the judgment and the reformation of the Church and the Empire in the fourteenth century.

Dante's great poem seems to sum up the whole achievement of the Catholic Middle Ages and to represent a perfect literary counterpart to the philosophical synthesis of St. Thomas. But if we turn to his prose works—the *Convivio* and the *De Monarchia*—we see that his views on culture, and consequently on history, differ widely from those of St. Thomas and even more from those of St. Augustine. Here for the first time in Christian thought we find the earthly and temporal city regarded as an autonomous order with its own supreme end, which is not the service of the Church but the realization of all the natural potentialities of human culture. The goal of civilization—*finis universalis civitatis humani generis*—can only be reached by a universal society and this requires the political unification of humanity in a single world state. Now it is clear that Dante's ideal of the universal state is derived from the mediaeval conception of Christendom as a universal society and from the tradition of the Holy Roman Empire as formulated by Ghibelline lawyers and theorists. As Professor Gilson writes, "if the *genus humanum* of Dante is really the first known expression of the modern idea of Humanity, we may say that the conception of Humanity first presented itself to the European consciousness merely as a secularized imitation of the religious notion of a Church."[7]

7. E. Gilson, *Dante the Philosopher*, p. 179.

But Dante's sources were not exclusively Christian. He was influenced most powerfully by the political and ethical ideals of Greek humanism, represented above all by Aristotle's *Ethics* and no less by the romantic idealization of the classical past and his devotion to ancient Rome. For Dante's view of the Empire is entirely opposed to that of St. Augustine. He regards it not as the work of human pride and ambition but as a holy city specially created and ordained by God as the instrument of his divine purpose for the human race. He even goes so far as to maintain in the *Convivio* that the citizens and statesmen of Rome were themselves holy, since they could not have achieved their purpose without a special infusion of divine grace.

In all this Dante looks forward to the Renaissance rather than back to the Middle Ages. But he carries with him so much of the Christian tradition that even his secularism and his humanism have a distinctively Christian character which make them utterly different from those of classical antiquity. And this may also be said of most of the writers and thinkers of the following century, for, as Karl Burdach has shown with so much learning, the whole atmosphere of later mediaeval and early Renaissance culture was infused by a Christian idealism which had its roots in the thirteenth century and especially in the Franciscan movement. Thus the fourteenth century which saw the beginnings of the Italian Renaissance and the development of Western humanism was also the great century of Western mysticism; and this intensification of the interior life with its emphasis on spiritual experience was not altogether unrelated to the growing self-consciousness of Western culture which found expression in the humanist movement. Even in the fifteenth and sixteenth centuries the humanist culture was not entirely divorced from this mystical tradition; both elements co-exist in the philosophy of Nicholas of Cusa, in the culture of the Platonic Academy at Florence and in the art of Botticelli and finally in that of Michelangelo. But in his case we feel that this synthesis was only maintained by an heroic effort, and lesser men were forced to acquiesce in a division of life between two spiritual ideals that became increasingly divergent.

This idealization of classical antiquity which is already present in the thought of Dante developed still further with Petrarch and his contemporaries until it became the characteristic feature of Renaissance culture. It affected every aspect of Western thought, literary, scientific and philosophic. Above all, it changed the Western view of history and inaugurated a new type of historiography. The religious approach to history as the story of God's dealings with mankind and the fulfilment of the divine plan in the life of the Church was abandoned or left to the ecclesiastical historians, and there arose a new secular history modelled on Livy and Tacitus and a new type of historical biography influenced by Plutarch.

Thus the unity of the mediaeval conception of history was lost and in its place there gradually developed a new pattern of history which eventually took the form of a threefold division between the ancient, mediaeval and modern periods, a pattern which in spite of its arbitrary and unscientific character has dominated the teaching of history down to modern times and still affects our attitude to the past.

This new approach to history was one of the main factors in the secularization of European culture, since the idealization of the ancient state and especially of republican Rome influenced men's attitude to the contemporary state. The Italian city-state and the kingdoms of the West of Europe were no longer regarded as organic members of the Christian community, but as ends in themselves which acknowledged no higher sanction than the will to power. During the Middle Ages the state as an autonomous self-sufficient power structure did not exist—even its name was unknown. But from the fifteenth century onwards the history of Europe has been increasingly the history of the development of a limited number of sovereign states as independent power centres and of the ceaseless rivalry and conflict between them. The true nature of this development was disguised by the religious prestige which still surrounded the person of the ruler and which was actually increased during the age of the Reformation by the union of the Church with the state and its subordination to the royal supremacy.

Thus there is an inherent contradiction in the social development of modern culture. Inasmuch as the state was the creation and embodiment of the will to power, it was a Leviathan—a submoral monster which lived by the law of the jungle. But at the same time it was the bearer of the cultural values which had been created by the Christian past, so that to its subjects it still seemed a Christian state and the vice-gerent of God on earth.

And the same contraindication appears in the European view of history. The realists like Machiavelli and Hobbes attempted to interpret history in non-moral terms as a straightforward expression of the will to power which could be studied in a scientific (quasi-biological) spirit. But by so doing they emptied the historical process of the moral values that still retained their subjective validity so that they outraged both the conscience and the conventions of their contemporaries. The idealists, on the other hand, ignored or minimized the sub-moral character of the state and idealized it as the instrument of divine providence or of that impersonal force which was gradually leading mankind onwards towards perfection.

It is easy to see how this belief in progress found acceptance during the period of triumphant national and cultural expansion when Western Europe was acquiring a kind of world hegemony. But it is no less clear that it was not a purely rational construction, but that it was essentially nothing else but a secularized version of the traditional Christian view. It inherited from Christianity its belief in the unity of history and its faith in a spiritual or moral purpose which gives meaning to the whole historical process. At the same time its transposition of these conceptions to a purely rational and secular theory of culture involved their drastic simplification. To the Christian the meaning of history was a mystery which was only revealed in the light of faith. But the apostles of the religion of progress denied the need for divine revelation and believed that man had only to follow the light of reason to discover the meaning of history in the law of progress which governs the life of civilization. But it was difficult even in the eighteenth century to make this facile optimism square with the facts of history. It was necessary to explain that

hitherto the light of reason had been concealed by the dark
forces of superstition and ignorance as embodied in organized
religion. But in that case the enlightenment was nothing less
than a new revelation, and in order that it might triumph it was
necessary that the new believers should organize themselves in
a new church whether it called itself a school of philosophers
or a secret society of *illuminati* or freemasons or a political
party. This was, in fact, what actually happened, and the new
rationalist churches have proved no less intolerant and dogmatic
than the religious sects of the past. The revelation of Rousseau
was followed by a series of successive revelations—idealist, posi-
tivist and socialistic, with their prophets and their churches. Of
these today only the Marxist revelation survives, thanks mainly
to the superior efficiency of its ecclesiastical organization and
apostolate. None of these secular religions has been more insistent on its purely scientific and non-religious character than
Marxism. Yet none of them owes more to the Messianic elements in the Christian and Jewish historical traditions. Its doc-
tine is in fact essentially apocalyptic—a denunciation of judgment against the existing social order and a message of salvation
to the poor and the oppressed who will at last receive their
reward after the social revolution in the classless society, which
is the Marxist equivalent of the millennial kingdom of righ-
teousness.

No doubt the Communist will regard this as a caricature of
the Marxist theory, since the social revolution and the coming
of the classless society is the result of an inevitable economic
and sociological process and its goal is not a spiritual but a
material one. Nevertheless the cruder forms of Jewish and Christian millenniarism were not without a materialistic element
since they envisaged an earthly kingdom in which the saints
would enjoy temporal prosperity, while it is impossible to ignore
the existence of a strong apocalyptic and Utopian element in
the Communist attitude towards the social revolution and the
establishment of a perfect society which will abolish class conflict and social injustice.

There is in fact a dualism between the Marxist myth, which is ethical and apocalyptic, and the Marxist interpretation of history, which is materialist, determinist and ethically relativistic. But it is from the first of these two elements that Communism has derived and still derives its popular appeal and its quasi-religious character which render it such a serious rival to Christianity. Yet it is difficult to reconcile the absolutism of the Marxist myth with the relativism of the Marxist interpretation of history. The Marxist believer stakes everything on the immediate realization of the social revolution and the proximate advent of the classless society. But when these have been realized, the class war which is the dialectical principle of historical change will have been suppressed and history itself comes to an end. In the same way there will no longer be any room for the moral indignation and the revolutionary idealism which have inspired Communism with a kind of religious enthusiasm. Nothing is left but an absolute and abject attitude of social conformism when the revolutionary protest of the minority becomes transformed into the irresistible tyranny of mass opinion which will not tolerate the smallest deviation from ideological orthodoxy. By the dialectic of history the movement of social revolution passes over into its totalitarian opposite, and the law of negation finds its consummation.

Thus, in comparison with the Christian view of history, the Marxist view is essentially a short-term one, the significance of which is concentrated on the economic changes which are affecting modern Western society. This accounts for its immediate effectiveness in the field of political propaganda, but at the same time it detracts from its value on the philosophical level as a theory of universal history. The Marxist doctrine first appeared about a century ago, and could not have arisen at any earlier time. Its field of prediction is limited to the immediate future, for Marx himself seems to have expected the downfall of capitalism to take place in his own lifetime, and the leaders of the Russian revolution took a similar view. In any case the fulfilment of the whole Marxist programme is a matter of years, not of centuries, and Marxism seems to throw no light on the historical developments which will follow the establishment of the classless society.

The Christian view, on the other hand, is co-extensive with time. It covers the whole life of humanity on this planet and it ends only with the end of this world and of man's temporal existence. It is essentially a theory of the interpretation of time and eternity: so that the essential meaning of history is to be found in the growth of the seed of eternity in the womb of time. For man is not merely a creature of the economic process—a producer and a consumer. He is an animal that is conscious of his mortality and consequently aware of eternity. In the same way the end of history is not the development of a new form of economic society, but is the creation of a new humanity, or rather a higher humanity, which goes as far beyond man as man himself goes beyond the animals. Now Christians not only believe in the existence of a divine plan in history, they believe in the existence of a human society which is in some measure aware of this plan and capable of co-operating with it. Thousands of years ago the Hebrew prophet warned his people not to learn the ways of the nations who were dismayed at the signs of the times. For the nations were the servants of their own creatures— the false gods who were the work of delusion and who must perish in the time of visitation. "But the portion of Jacob is not like these, for he that formed all things has made Israel to be the people of his inheritance." The same thing is true today of the political myths and ideologies which modern man creates in order to explain the signs of the time. These are our modern idols which are no less bloodthirsty than the gods of the heathen and which demand an even greater tribute of human sacrifice. But the Church remains the guardian of the secret of history and the organ of the work of human redemption which goes on ceaselessly through the rise and fall of kingdoms and the revolutions of social systems. It is true that the Church has no immediate solution to offer in competition with those of the secular ideologies. On the other hand, the Christian solution is the only one which gives full weight to the unknown and unpredictable element in history; whereas the secular ideologies which attempt to eliminate this element, and which almost invariably take an optimistic view of the immediate future are inevitably disconcerted and disillusioned by the emergence of this unknown factor at the point at which they thought that it had been finally banished.

9

The Recovery of Spiritual Unity

No ONE CAN LOOK at the history of Western civilization during the present century without feeling dismayed at the spectacle of what modern man has done with his immense resources of new knowledge and new wealth and new power. And if we go back to the nineteenth century and read the words of the scientists and the social reformers or the liberal idealists and realize the mood of unbounded hope and enthusiasm in which this movement of world change was launched, the contrast is even more painful. For not only have we failed to realize the ideals of the nineteenth century, we are all more or less conscious of worse dangers to come—greater and more destructive wars, more ruthless forms of despotism, more drastic suppression of human rights. It is no good going on with the dismal catalogue, we know it all only too well. There is no need to listen to the alarmist predictions of writers like George Orwell or Aldous Huxley: it is enough to read the newspapers to convince ourselves that the cause of civilization is no longer secure and that the great movement of Western man to transform the world has somehow gone astray.

Whatever may be the ultimate cause of this crisis, it is certain that it is a spiritual one, since it represents the failure of civilized man to control the forces that he has created. It is due above all to the loss of common purpose in Western culture and the lack of a common intelligence to guide the new forces that are changing human life. Yet this failure is certainly not due to the neglect of education in modern society. No civilization in history has ever devoted so much time and money and organization to education as our own. And it is one of the most tragic features of the situation that our failure has been the failure of the first society to be universally educated, one which had been subjected to a more systematic and completely national education than any society of the past.

In spite of this, there is no doubt that the modern European and American system of universal education suffered from serious defects. In the first place, the achievement of universality was purchased by the substitution of quantitative for qualitative standards. Education was accepted as a good in itself and the main question was how to increase the total output: how to teach more and more people more and more subjects for longer and longer periods. But in proportion as education became universal, it became cheapened. Instead of being regarded as a privilege of the few it became a compulsory routine for everybody. It is difficult for us to imagine the state of mind of a man like Francis Place, labouring to all hours of the night after a hard day's work, out of sheer passion for knowledge.

In the second place, the establishment of a universal system of public education inevitably changed the relations of education to the state.

It is this above all else which has caused the mind of our society to lose its independence, so that there is no power left outside politics to guide modern civilization, when the politicians go astray. For in proportion as education becomes controlled by the state, it becomes nationalized, and in extreme cases the servant of a political party. This last alternative still strikes us here in England as outrageous, but it is not only essential to the totalitarian state; it existed before the rise of totalitarianism and to a great extent created it, and it is present as a tendency in all modern societies, however opposed they are to totalitarianism in its overt form.

For the immense extension of the scale of education and its ramification into a hundred specialisms and technical disciplines has left the state as the only unifying element in the whole system. In the past the traditional system of classical education provided a common intellectual background and a common scale of values which transcended national and political frontiers and formed the European or Western republic of letters of which every scholar was a citizen.

All the old systems of primary and secondary education presupposed the existence of this intellectual community which they served and from which they received guidance and inspiration. The primary school taught children their letters, the grammar school taught them Latin and Greek, so that educated men everywhere possessed a common language and the knowledge of a common literature or two common literatures.

Now from the modern point of view this traditional education was shockingly narrow and pedantic. It was also useless, since it had no direct bearing on the life of the modern world, on the world's work and on the techniques of modern civilization. Therefore the nineteenth-century reformers insisted first that education should be widened to include the whole realm of modern knowledge, and secondly that it should be made practically useful in order to produce skilled technicians and trained specialists or research workers.

These two great reforms have been generally applied, not without success, all over the world during the last fifty or a hundred years. But what has been the result? The domain of universal knowledge is too vast for any mind to embrace, and the specialization of the technician and the research worker has become so minute that it leaves no common intellectual bond between the different branches of knowledge.

A Russian expert in applied research on plant biology, a French specialist in the history of the romance lyric, an English worker on atomic research, an American expert in social psychology—all these do not belong to any sort of spiritual community like the humanist republic of letters. They are just individuals with special jobs, and there is a much stronger bond between *all* the Russians and all the Frenchmen and so on, than between scientists as such or technicians as such. No doubt the discipline of scientific research does produce a common type of intelligence and even a common type of character, but so did the older professional disciplines, so that there is a considerable similarity between staff officers or drill sergeants in the armies of the different great powers. But a similarity of this kind on the level of technique does not necessarily make for a similarity on the level of culture. And the same holds good for the scientific specialist. Indeed under present conditions the two types are rapidly becoming assimilated, so that the scientific expert and the military expert are alike instruments of the unified power organization of the modern state.

Up to a point this is inevitable, granted the complex nature of the modern scientific and technological order. But if it is allowed to develop uncriticized and unchecked, it is fatal to the old ideals of Western culture as a free spiritual community. It leads to the totalitarian state, and perhaps even beyond that to the completely mechanized mass society, to the Brave New Worlds and the nightmares of scientific utopianism in reverse.

How is it possible to preserve the guiding mind of civilization and to salvage the spiritual traditions of Western culture?

The philosopher, the religious leader, the statesman and the educationist all share this responsibility—all have a part to play. But the responsibility of the educationist is perhaps the most immediate and the heaviest of all, because it is in the sphere of education that the immediate decisions must be taken which will determine the outlook of the next generation.

In the past, as we have seen, education attempted to perform this higher function by means of the traditional classical discipline of humane letters—in other words of Latin and Greek. But we must be careful to distinguish between this particular form of higher education and higher education in general; and

not to reduce the central inescapable problem to the old controversy between conservative classicism and radical modernism.
It is quite possible that the traditional form of classical education has become completely antiquated and can no longer provide the universal unifying element which our civilization requires. But the fact that classical education no longer fulfils that
purpose does not mean that civilization can dispense with such
a unifying element altogether or that it can be found on a purely
technological level.

On the contrary we need it more than ever before—and the
more widely we extend the range of education, the more necessary it is to provide some principle of cohesion to counterbal-
ance the centrifugal tendencies of specialization and utilitari-
anism.

Every form of education that mankind has known, from the
savage tribe to the highest forms of culture, has always involved
two elements—the element of technique and the element of
tradition; and hitherto it has always been the second that has
been the more important. In the first place education teaches
children how to do things—how to read and write, and even at
a much more primitive level how to hunt and cook, and plant
and build. But besides all these things, education has always
meant the initiation of the young into the social and spiritual
inheritance of the community: in other words education has
meant the transmission of culture.

Now the old classical education was a rather specialized and
stylized type of this procedure. It took the tradition of humanism as embodying the highest common factor of Western culture
and trained the young to appreciate it by an intensive course of
philological discipline. At first sight it seems highly absurd to
take an English farmer's son or the son of a German shopkeeper
and drill him into writing imitation Ciceronian prose or copies
of Latin verses. Yet for all that, it did set the stamp of a common
classical tradition on a dozen vernacular European literatures
and gave the educated classes of every European country a common sense of the standard classical values.

But it was only able to succeed in this specialized intellectual task because it was an intellectual superstructure that was built on a common spiritual tradition. Classical education was only half the old system of European education—below it and above it there was the religious education that was common to the whole people, and the higher theological education that was peculiar to the clergy, who provided the majority of the teachers in both the other departments of education.

Now the lowest level of this structure, which has been least studied and least regarded, was the most important of them all. It is true that it differed considerably in different parts of Europe, but for religious rather than material reasons. In Protestant Europe it was founded on the Bible and the catechism, whereas in Catholic Europe it was based on the liturgy and on religious art and drama and mime, which made the Church the school of the people. But in either case it provided a system of common beliefs and moral standards, as well as the archetypal patterns of world history and sacred story which formed the background of their spiritual world.

Thus considered as a means for the transmission of culture, classical education, important as it was, formed only one part of the whole system of social education by which the inheritance of culture was transmitted, so that even if it were possible to preserve or to restore classical education it would by itself prove quite ineffective as a solution for our present problem. What we need is not merely to find a substitute for the classical humanistic element in the old system; it is the system as a whole from top to bottom which has disappeared, and if the spiritual continuity of Western culture is to be preserved, we must face the problem as a whole and remember the importance of the common spiritual foundation on which the superstructure of higher classical education was built.

It is the failure to recognize this fact which has been largely responsible for the separation of higher education from its spiritual roots in the life of the people, so that our idea of culture has become a sublimated abstraction, instead of the expression

of a living tradition which animates the whole society and
unites the present and the past.

If we are to make the ordinary man aware of the spiritual
unity out of which all the separate activities of our civilization
have arisen, it is necessary in the first place to look at Western
civilization as a whole and to treat it with the same objective
appreciation and respect which the humanists of the past devoted to the civilization of antiquity.

This does not seem much to ask; yet there have always been
a number of reasons which stood in the way of its fulfilment.

In the first place, there has been the influence of modern
nationalism, which has led every European people to insist on
what distinguished it from the rest, instead of what united it
with them. It is not necessary to seek for examples in the
extremism of German racial nationalists and their crazy theories, proving that everything good in the world comes from men
of Germanic blood. Leaving all these extravagances out of account, we still have the basic fact that modern education in
general teaches men the history of their own country and the
literature of their own tongue, as though these were complete
wholes and not part of a greater unity.

In the second place, there has been the separation between
religion and culture, which arose partly from the bitterness of
the internal divisions of Christendom and partly from a fear
lest the transcendent divine values of Christianity should be
endangered by any identification or association of them with
the relative human values of culture. Both these factors have
been at work, long before our civilization was actually secularized. They had their origins in the Reformation period, and it
was Martin Luther in particular who stated the theological dualism of faith and works in such a drastic form as to leave no
room for any positive conception of a Christian culture, such as
had hitherto been taken for granted.

And in the third place, the vast expansion of Western civilization in modern times has led to a loss of any standard of comparison or any recognition of its limits in time and space. West-

ern civilization has ceased to be one civilization amongst others: it became civilization in the absolute sense.

It is the disappearance or decline of this naïve absolutism and the reappearance of a sense of the relative and limited character of Western civilization as a particular historic culture, which are the characteristic features of the present epoch. And at the same time we have begun to doubt the validity of the nationalistic approach to history and culture, and to realize the evil and folly of the blind sectarian feuds that have broken up the social unity of Christendom during recent centuries.

Thus it would seem as though the main obstacles to the understanding of Western civilization as a historic reality have begun to break down and the time is ripe for a new positive approach to the whole problem.

But there remains one serious obstacle—or rather there has arisen a new obstacle which was not present in the past. The events of the last forty years have inflicted such a blow to the self-confidence of Western civilization and to the belief in progress which was so strong during the nineteenth century, that men tend to go too far in the opposite direction: in fact the modern world is experiencing the same kind of danger which was so fatal to the ancient world—the crisis of which Gilbert Murray writes in his *Four Stages of Greek Religion* as "The Loss of Nerve".

There have been signs of this in Western literature for a long time past, and it has already had a serious effect on Western culture and education. This is the typical tragedy of the intelligentsia as shown in nineteenth-century Russia and often in twentieth-century Germany: the case of a society or a class devoting enormous efforts to higher education and to the formation of an intellectual élite and then finding that the final result of the system is to breed a spirit of pessimism and nihilism and revolt. There was something seriously wrong about an educational system which cancelled itself out in this way, which picked out the ablest minds in a society and subjected them to an intensive process of competitive development which ended

in a revolutionary or cynical reaction against the society that
produced it. But behind these defects of an over-cerebralized and
over-competitive method of education, there is the deeper cause
in the loss of the common spiritual background which unifies
education and social life. For the liberal faith in progress which
inspired the nineteenth century was itself a substitute for the
simpler and more positive religious faith which was the vital
bond of the Western community. If we wish to understand our
past and the inheritance of Western culture, we have to go behind the nineteenth-century development and study the old spiritual community of Western Christendom as an objective historical reality.

The study and understanding of this cultural tradition ought
to be given the same place in modern education as the study of
the Graeco-Roman tradition received in the classical humanist
education of the past. For the culture of Christendom is not
only of vital importance to us genetically as the source of our
own culture; it also has a greater intrinsic value than even the
classical culture possessed. At first sight this may be questioned
by the humanist, but I think that reflection will show that it
is true even from the humanist point of view, for humanism
itself as we know it is not the humanism of the Greeks and
Romans, but a humanism which has been transmuted, if not
created, by the Christian culture of the West. It is not merely
that Erasmus and Vives and Grotius deserve our attention just
as much as Quintilian and Cicero. It is that behind these men
there is a living tradition, reaching back through Petrarch and
John of Salisbury to Alcuin and Bede and Boethius, and it was
this that built the spiritual bridge across the ages by which
classical culture passed into the life of Western man.

The existence of this spiritual community or psychological
continuum is the ultimate basic reality which underlies all the
separate activities of modern Western societies and which alone
makes Western education possible.

The obvious difficulty that has prevented the study of European culture becoming a part of the regular curriculum of stud-

ies is its vastness and its complexity. The great advantage of classical education was the fact that it involved the study of only two languages and two literatures and histories. But European culture has produced about twenty vernacular literatures, and its history is spread out among an even larger number of political communities. At first sight it is an unmanageable proposition and we can understand how educationalists have so often come to acquiesce in a cultural nationalism which at least saved them from being overwhelmed by a multiplicity of strange tongues and unknown literatures. But the true method, it seems to me, is rather to find the constitutive factors of the European community and to make them the basis of our study.

This means reversing the traditional nationalist approach which concentrated the student's attention on the distinctive characteristics of the national cultures and disregarded or passed lightly over the features that they shared in common. It means also that we should have to devote much more attention to the religious development, since it was in religion that Europe found its original basis of unity.

In the past there has been a tendency to treat political history and ecclesiastical history as self-contained subjects and to leave the history of religion to the ecclesiastical historians. But no serious historian can be satisfied with this state of affairs, since it destroyed the intelligible unity of culture and left the history of culture itself suspended uneasily between political and ecclesiastical history with no firm basis in either of them. It is essential to realize that the Christian community in the past was not a pious ideal, but a juridical fact which underlay the social organization of Western culture.

For more than a thousand years the religious sacrament of baptism which initiated a man into the Christian community was also a condition of citizenship in the political community. The obligations of Canon Law or Church Law were binding in a greater or less degree in Common Law, so that even in a Protestant land, like England, the fundamental questions of personal status and property—everything connected with the marriage contract and the right of bequest—fell within the purview of the Courts Christian.

The old English saying or legal maxim that Christianity is the law of the land faithfully reflects the situation which existed in Europe for a thousand years and more, from the time when the barbarian kingdoms first accepted Christianity. For this reception of Christianity was a solemn public act which involved the acceptance of a new way of life and a corporate adhesion to a new international community.

Now the comprehension of the nature of this sociological and psychological change is of much greater educational importance than most of the history that we were taught in our school and university days. This was a matter that we were supposed to learn from other sources. Whether we did so or not depended mainly on personal experience and family tradition.

Even today very little thought is given to the profound revolution in the psychological basis of culture by which the new society of Western Christendom came into existence. Stated in the terms of Freudian psychology, what occurred was the translation of religion from the sphere of the Id to that of the Super-Ego. The pagan religion of the Northern barbarians was a real force in society, but it was not an intellectual force and hardly a moral one in our sense of the word. It was an instinctive cult of natural forces which were blind and amoral, save in so far as war itself creates a certain rudimentary heroic ethos.

Now with the reception of Christianity, the old gods and their rites were rejected as manifestations of the power of evil. Religion was no longer an instinctive homage to the dark underworld of the Id. It became a conscious and continual effort to conform human behaviour to the requirements of an objective moral law and an act of faith in a new life and in sublimated patterns of spiritual perfection.

The sense of guilt was transferred from the corporate responsibility of the blood feud to the sphere of the individual conscience. It became the sense of sin and produced as a correlative, the act of repentance.

Now this spirit of moral effort and this consciousness of personal responsibility have remained characteristic of Western Christian culture—it may even be argued that they are its essential characteristics and that all its external political and material achievements have been to a considerable extent conditioned by them.

Of course it may be said that all civilizations are Super-Ego structures and that it is precisely this which distinguishes civilization from barbarism. But at the same time there are important differences in the part which religion plays in this process.

In some cases, as in Hinduism, the sharp breach with the forces of the Id which was characteristic of the conversion of the West has never taken place, and life is not conceived as a process of moral effort and discipline but as an expression of cosmic libido, as in the Dance of Siva.

On the other hand, in Buddhism we see a very highly developed Super-Ego. But here the Super-Ego is allied with the death-impulse so that the moralization of life is at the same time a regressive process that culminates in Nirvana.

No doubt similar tendencies were present in the Western world and find expression in the intermittent outbreaks of Manichaeism and other forms of religious and metaphysical dualism. But the characteristic feature of Western civilization has always been a spirit of moral activism by which the individual Super-Ego has become a dynamic social force. In other words, the Christian tradition has made the conscience of the individual person an independent power which tends to weaken the omnipotence of social custom and to open the social process to new individual initiatives.

At the present time historians and sociologists are no doubt inclined to minimize the effect of moral and religious idealism or conscious moral effort on the course of social development and to concentrate their attention on material motives; conflicts of material interests and the influence of economic forces. But whatever our ultimate religious and philosophical views may be, it is unjustifiable to rule out one series of historical factors, because we do not agree with the beliefs and ideals that are associated with them.

Take the case of modern Western colonial expansion. The historian and the sociologist have the right to dismiss the explanations of nineteenth-century imperialists with regard to the civilizing mission of the Anglo-Saxon race, and so forth, as an idealistic excuse to disguise the real facts of imperialist exploitation. Equally they have the right to regard the prospector or the trader as more genuine representatives of the colonial movement than the missionary or the educationalist. But they have not the right to deny the existence of the Western missionary movement as a real factor in colonial expansion, nor even to identify the two elements and to regard the missionary as an agent of capitalism with his collar turned back-to-front.

And the same principle must be applied to the history of Western Christendom in general. The historian may well argue that the feudal baron is more typical of mediaeval culture than the monk or the friar; he may equally point out how the Church became a stronghold of feudal privilege. But he cannot deny that Christianity was one of the formative powers in mediaeval culture or that throughout the whole course of Western history there was a spiritual élite which was sincerely devoted to putting their ideals into practice and making the Christian way of life a reality, while at the same time the whole society was generally united in the acceptance of Christian beliefs and in at least a theoretic acceptance of Christian moral standards.

Now when these conditions have obtained over a continuous period of more than a thousand years, it is difficult to deny that they must have had a great cumulative effect on the life of Western man and the forms of Western thought and feeling. Indeed it may be argued that Western culture as a whole is the fruit of this thousand years of continuous spiritual effort, and that there is no aspect of European life which has not been profoundly affected by it.

If this is true, as I believe it to be, it seems to follow that the history that we ought to study—the history that really matters—is the history of this dynamic spiritual process, rather than that of the conflicts and rivalries of the various European states. But is such a study possible? The main obstacle is certainly not lack of material—it is rather the wealth of material which is still lying unused and sometimes unknown. It is not so long ago that Henri Bremond wrote his literary history of religious sentiment in France in the seventeenth century, which even in its ten volumes is still but a fragment of the work that he had planned. But even so, he disclosed a whole new field of study of which even specialists were largely unaware. And this is only one example of the rich mines of unused material for European cultural history which lie, as it were, at our very doors.

No! The real difficulty that stands in the way of these studies is an ideological or spiritual one, which affects the very heart of the problem. If European culture is the external expression of a dynamic spiritual process, how do we ourselves stand towards it? Are we part of that process or of some different process altogether? And is it possible to study the spiritual process of Western culture without taking sides one way or the other?

Now, in the first place, the acceptance of the Christian faith is not an essential condition for the study of Christian culture. It is perfectly possible in theory to appreciate and to study Western culture as a spiritual whole without being a Christian. That was, after all, the position of many of the great liberal humanitarian historians and sociologists of the nineteenth century. But these men never regarded themselves as outside the European tradition even in its spiritual aspect. They were very conscious of the moral dynamism of Christian culture and they accepted its ethos wholeheartedly. In fact they regarded themselves as having gone one better than their Christian predecessors by the attainment of a higher, purer and more sublimated ethical ideal. In short, they regarded themselves as super-Christians. Matthew Arnold is a typical example of this attitude, as we may see in *Literature and Dogma* or the preface to his *Irish Essays.* All this, however, has become a part of ancient history—an episode in an appendix to the process we have to study. The difficulty to-day is of a different nature.

We have to face the emergence of a more fundamental criticism of Christian culture which rejects its moral ideals and its psychological structure no less than its metaphysical theory and its theological beliefs. It involves the reversal of the spiritual revolution which gave birth to Western culture and a return to the psychological situation of the old pagan world, whether it takes the form of a conscious neopagan movement as with the Nazis, or some form of materialism which is equally opposed to the Christian world view. It is a revolt against the moral process of Western culture and the dethronement of the individual conscience from its dominant position at the heart of the cultural process. Consequently it means that the sense of guilt loses its personal character and is reabsorbed in the mass consciousness, reappearing not indeed in the old form of the blood feud, but in the parallel phenomena of racial hatred and class war, whereby the sense of guilt is extraverted and transferred to a guilty race or a guilty class which thus becomes a psychological scapegoat.

Now wherever this revolution has taken place there is no longer any room for the understanding of Christian culture. It simply becomes a question of *explaining away*, so that to the Nazi the achievements of Christian culture are explained in detail as examples of the Nordic genius asserting itself in spite of the obstruction of Mediterranean Christian and Semitic influences, while for the Marxian the history of Christendom must be rewritten in terms of the materialist interpretation of history, thus entirely altering the sense and direction of the movement of history.

The results of the new historiography may be seen in Rosenberg's *Myth of the Twentieth Century* or in the *Short History of the Communist Party of the Soviet Union*, which is perhaps even more significant, owing to its official and anonymous character.[1]

---

1. It was produced by a commission of the Central Committee of the C.P.S.U. but the authorship is usually attributed to Stalin himself.

This psychological breach with the old European Christian tradition is a much more serious thing than any political or economic revolution, for it means not only the dethronement of the moral conscience but also the abdication of the rational consciousness which is inseparably bound up with it. It is indeed doubtful if Western society can survive the change, for it is not a return to the past or to the roots of our social life. It is too radical for that. Instead of going downstairs step by step, neo-paganism jumps out of the top-storey window, and whether one jumps out of the right-hand window or the left makes very little difference by the time one reaches the pavement.

The alternative to this suicidal technique is to accept the existence of Christian culture as an objective historical fact and try to understand it by its own ideas and to judge it by its own standards, as classical scholars have done in the past with regard to the culture of the ancient world. For it is both unscholarly and unphilosophical to look at Byzantine culture through the eyes of the eighteenth-century rationalist, or mediaeval culture through the eyes of a nineteenth-century Protestant, or Christian culture in general through the eyes of a materialist.

Instead of these ways of looking at the past from outside as something alien, let us try to study Western Christian culture from the Christian point of view—to see it as a new way of life which was brought into Europe nearly nineteen hundred years ago, when St. Paul set sail from Troy to Macedonia, and gradually expanded until it became accepted as the universal standard of the European way of life.

This does not mean that we ought to ignore or slur over the gap between Christian ideals and social realities. On the contrary, the existence of this dualism created that state of vital tension which is the condition of European culture. In every age and every Western society this tension expresses itself in different forms, from the simple straight-forward dualism of Christian culture and pagan barbarism which we see in Bede's *Ecclesiastical History* to the intense inner conflict "piercing even to the dividing asunder of soul and spirit" which we see in a Pascal or a Kierkegaard. Where this tension is absent,—where civilization has become "autarchic", self-sufficient and self-satisfied, there the process of Christian culture has been extinguished or terminated. But even to-day we can hardly say that this has happened. Indeed what we have seen during the last century has been something very different—an increase in spiritual tension which has become almost world-wide, although it has lost the positive element of religious faith that was an essential condition of its creative power in Europe in the past.

It is obvious that there is a profound difference between the old dualism of the Christian way of life and unregenerate human nature on the one hand, and the new dualism between the revolutionary ideas of liberalism, nationalism and socialism and the traditional order of society on the other, but there is a certain relation between the two, so that it is possible to maintain that the whole revolutionary tradition is a post-Christian phenomenon which transposes a pre-existent psychological pattern to a different sociological tradition. But even if that were the case, it would make it all the more important to understand how the archetypal pattern had originated.

We know as yet too little about the modern revolutionary social situation to understand it as a whole. But this is not the case with the ages of Christian culture that preceded it. Here the documentary evidence is more extensive than for any comparable period of world history. We know not only the course of its development from the beginning, we know the lives and thoughts of the men who played the leading part in that development from the beginning. We can study the development on every social and intellectual level from the highest to the lowest and in relation to all kinds of environments and social traditions.

It is from this development that the unity of Western culture is derived. For Europe is not a political creation. It is a society of peoples who shared the same faith and the same moral values. The European nations are parts of a wider spiritual society, and it is only by studying the nature of the whole that we can understand the functions of the parts. We have become so accustomed to studying the parts without reference to the whole that we are in danger of forgetting that there is any such thing as a cultural whole, a thing which the old classical humanist educators never entirely lost sight of, even when they seemed most pedantic. But this neglect of the study of our culture has been accidental rather than intentional—it resulted from a complication of different factors, some of which I have already discussed.

The time has come to repair this mistake. If we deliberately perpetuate it, now that we know what is at stake: if we consciously permit the guidance of the modern world to pass from the leaders of culture to the servants of power, then we shall have a heavier responsibility than the politicians for the breakdown of Western civilization.

No doubt there are very great practical difficulties in the way of a study which involves living religious issues as well as historical ones: difficulties as between Christians and non-Christians and still more between the adherents of the different forms of Christianity. But these difficulties are essentially practical, since none of the parties concerned—not even the non-Christians—is opposed in principle to the study of the Christian culture of the past as an objective historical phenomenon: indeed our own past is so deeply rooted in that culture that any refusal to study it means a refusal of history itself. Moreover, the field of work is so wide that there is ample room for all our schools of thought and all our social and religious traditions to follow their own lines of study without jostling one another.

In history as in other branches of knowledge there must inevitably be controversy and difference of opinion on a thousand particular points. But the justification of such conflicts is that they elucidate and do not obscure or obstruct. The essential task is to understand Christian culture as a whole arising from the impact of Christianity on classical culture and Western barbarism, and creating from these dissimilar elements a new spiritual world which forms the background of modern history.

For if we try to ignore or explain away this creative process in order to enhance the importance of our own national achievement or that of some contemporary political ideology, we deprive ourselves of our own cultural inheritance and narrow the intelligibility of history.

Such mistakes are possible—they have taken place in the past, and in so far as they have occurred they mark the great set-backs in the history of civilization. It is one of the greatest tasks of education to prevent this happening and to keep alive the common tradition of culture through the dark ages, or the periods of sudden catastrophe, when mass opinion is under the influence of passion and fear and when the individual has become the slave of economic necessity.

Index

Philippians, 17
Philistinism, Protestant, 11
Philoponus, John, 165
Philosophy, 75, 79; Christian, 96, 213; and education, 113; flourishing of in Western Europe, 140; Greek, 165; and idealism, 166, 213–14; non-Christian, 199; pre-Christian, 199; of severance, 90; and theology, 157
Pietists, 61
Pilgrim's Progress, 13
Pius X, Saint, 29
Place, Francis, 234
Planning: centralized, 186; culture, 182–94; economic, 184, 192, 193; society, 182, 183, 185, 186
Plato, 165
Platonic Academy (Florence), 225
Pliny, 164
Plowman, Piers, 114
Plutarch, 226
Plymouth Brothers, 61
Poetry: flourishing of in Western Europe, 130; Latin, 101, 167; religious, 58, 75, 101, 161
Poland, conversion to Christianity, 141
Politics: absolutism, 67; control of science and education, 91; and culture, 86–87, 94, 112; democracy, 66, 86, 146; and economics, 127, 183, 190; and history, 241; ideology replaces science of nature, 90–91; and materialism, 124; nationalism, 102; and religion, 179
Polynesia, 47
Porphyry, 156
Portuguese maritime discoveries, 143
Positivism, 127, 131, 213, 228
Post-Christian culture, 134
Post-Renaissance Europe, 142–44
Power, 67
Praeparatio Evangelica, 197
Pre-Christian culture, 134
Predestination, 52
Priesthood, 24
Priestley, Joseph, 145, 208
Proselytization, 99

Prosper of Aquitane, 167
Protestantism, 30; America, 61; Bible, exclusivity of culture, 59, 237; and catechism, 237; Catholicism, differentiated, 207–10; Europe, 61; and history, 206; liberal, 213; sects. *See* Sects; secularization of the arts, 52, 55–56, 59. *See also* Reformation; Reform movements
Prudentius, Aurelius Clemens, 162
Prussia, 188
Psychology: Freudian dualism, 77; and rationalism, 76; and religion, 68, 242–43; social, 188
Ptolemaeus, Claudius (Ptolemy), 164–65
Puritanism, 31, 61, 116, 178, 206

Quadrivium, 154
Quakers, 27, 61
Quintilian, 138, 155

Racialism, 109
Ranke, Leopold von, 45
Rationalism: churches, 228; inadequacy, 76; liberal, 70; modern, 193; modern culture, 77–78, 124, 129; and psychology, 76; and scientific knowledge, 144; social, 184
Ravenna, basilica of, 38
Reason, 146
Reformation, 42, 51, 90, 124, 125, 129, 176, 178, 226, 238. *See also* Protestantism; Reform movements
Reformation, Renaissance, compared, 207
Reform movements. *See also* Protestantism; Reformation: defeat of Papacy by, 41; ecclesiastical, 142; Hussites, 41, 207; Northern European, 42; orthodox reformers, 129; Philip IV of France, 41; Reformation, 42; Waldensians, 207; Wycliffites, 41, 207
Reign of Terror, 146
Religion: and art, 141; and culture, 7, 9, 11, 39, 54, 56–57, 59, 62, 95, 97, 118, 126, 129, 145, 171–73, 176, 179, 189, 190, 238; and